studies in jazz

Institute of Jazz Studies
Rutgers—The State University of New Jersey
General Editors: Dan Morgenstern and Edward Berger

Tom Talbert—His Life and Times

Voices from a Vanished World of Jazz

Bruce Talbot

Studies in Jazz, No. 45

The Scarecrow Press, Inc.
Lanham, Maryland, and Oxford
2004

SCARECROW PRESS, INC.

Published in the United States of America
by Scarecrow Press, Inc.
A wholly owned subsidary of
The Rowman & Littlefield Publishing Group, Inc.
4501 Forbes Boulevard, Suite 200, Lanham, Maryland 20706
www.scarecrowpress.com

PO Box 317
Oxford
OX2 9RU, UK

British Library Cataloguing in Publication Information Available

Library of Congress Cataloging-in-Publication Data

Talbot, Bruce.
  Tom Talbert, his life and times : voices from a vanished world of jazz /
Bruce Talbot.
      p. cm.—(Studies in jazz ; no. 45)
  Includes bibliographical references (p.) and index.
  Discography: p.
  ISBN 0–8108-4812-0 (alk. paper)
  1. Talbert, Thomas. 2. Jazz musicians—United States—Biography.
I. Title. II. Series.
  ML422.T26 T25 2004
  781.65′092—dc22
                                                    2003016344

∞ ™ The paper used in this publication meets the minimum
requirements of American National Standard for Information Sciences—
Permanence of
Paper for Printed Library Materials, ANSI/NISO Z39.48-1992.
Manufactured in the United States of America.

CONTENTS

EDITOR'S FOREWORD

My first encounter with Tom Talbert's music came about in 1957, when Atlantic Records issued his wonderful *Bix Duke Fats* LP (happily once again available at this writing, and sounding better than ever on CD). It revealed a very special musical sensibility and a great arranger's talent for choosing, and bringing out the best in, the right interpreters. Although this record received considerable critical acclaim, Tom Talbert did not become a household name and many of us wondered what had become of him. After some stirrings in the 1970s, he resurfaced in 1991 with a fine sampling of his art and craft, and has been in view since then. Of course, Talbert had a life before and between those landmarks, and in this fascinating book, Bruce Talbot provides all the links. In addition to fashioning a fine biographical portrait, he fills in a rich backdrop that indeed brings to life the vanished world of his title.

Some have forgotten and many never knew just how much jazz, especially in its big band incarnation, was part and parcel of American life. On records and radio and in live performances, in ballrooms and theaters as well as (and even more than) in nightclubs and cabarets, swing was the thing. In these pages, by way of interviews with both better-known and obscure musicians who crossed paths with Talbert, in Minneapolis, in the army, in California, and in New York, and of course from the main man himself, Talbot conjures up the days of touring bands and active studio life, of music woven into the fabric of everyday existence.

As the various voices emerge from the page, the reader is reminded once again of the paramount importance of what we call oral history—another way of saying straight from the horse's mouth. Jazz histories, even the best, have only scratched the surface, and there isn't a scholar or fan of the music we call jazz who won't learn something new and revealing from this book, be it new facts, great stories, or pithy insights. Of the latter, Talbert has plenty to offer, not surprisingly if one knows just a bit of his music, to which his dedication has never flagged. Bruce Talbot, who also loves the music from within (he played tenor sax in big bands and produced and compiled many fine recordings) has come up with a book of which he, and our series, can well be proud.

Dan Morgenstern
Director, Institute of Jazz Studies
Rutgers University

ACKNOWLEDGMENTS

To everyone interviewed in this book—thank you for making the task so enjoyable and rewarding

To Tom Talbert and his wife, Betty, for their warm friendship and hospitality

To Bruce Phillips and Niki Averill at Scarecrow Press

To my wife, Sandra Gregory, for unfailing support, good humor, and forbearance at the chaos and clutter in our "far-from-paperless" office

Finally, to the two Dons—both good friends of Tom Talbert and both fine saxophone players—Don Davidson, whom I had the great pleasure of meeting, and Don Richwine, whom I spoke to by phone. Neither is with us any longer. I'm very grateful for their contributions.

INTRODUCTION

Tom is an original arranger and an original composer and he gets wonderful sounds out of the band.

—Danny Bank

He's a wonderful writer and arranger and could really be considered the father of West Coast Jazz. You can talk about Shorty Rogers and all those guys who were around, sure, but Tom was writing West Coast jazz before there was such a thing.

—Ken Borgers

Who is Tom Talbert and why is this book about him? My own delight in and enthusiasm for his music, dating back to first hearing his *Bix Duke Fats* album when it was released in 1957, was the starting point. But more convincing names than mine (see, for example, Bank and Borgers above) and many others throughout the biography reinforced my conviction that Tom's compositions and arrangements, over half a century of jazz, deserve a great deal more recognition than they have thus far received.

At the beginning of this new century, we've seen centennial celebrations of the birth and work of Duke Ellington and Louis Armstrong. It takes nothing away from their achievements to say that there has, at the same time, been a perceptible narrowing of focus when it comes to the way most media consider the first fifty years of jazz in particular, and popular music in general. Major record companies reissue only the biggest hits by the biggest stars, while film and television soundtracks leave the impression that the only band playing during World War II was Glenn Miller's. Even his considerable output has been reduced in the public mind to "In the Mood," "Moonlight Serenade," and "American Patrol," and knowledge and appreciation of the contributions of many other once revered talents are fading fast.

Where big band jazz is concerned, the work of post–World War II writers like Pete Rugolo, Johnny Richards, Ralph Burns, Gerry Mulligan, George Handy, and Frank Comstock is disappearing into a musical "oubliette" as admirers of the bands led by Stan Kenton, Woody Herman, Boyd Raeburn, Les Brown, and Gene Krupa eventually surrender their coats to T. S. Eliot's "Eternal Footman." Of that writing group, only Rugolo is still with us. His contemporary Tom Talbert seems to have slipped through a hole in the net of fame and recognition, in spite of an extraordinary talent for writing music for the jazz orchestra that is totally original, deeply felt, and successful on every artistic level. As far back as the mid-1940s, Tom Talbert's masterful ability to rephrase tunes, create felicitous and unusual instrumental voicings, and interweave soloist and ensemble anticipated what would be called the "cool" or "West Coast" jazz movement, and his earliest recordings (1946) display an astonishing maturity and grasp of big band possibilities in someone only twenty-one years old.

His mid-1950s *Bix Duke Fats* album marries luminous, haunting arrangements to the work of some of the finest jazz soloists of the day. His 1999 CD *To a Lady* reveals neither diminution of his talent nor unwillingness to conceive jazz that is evolving and new. During a career in music that spans sixty years, Tom Talbert has written for and performed with many of the greatest names in jazz and amassed a sizable collection of recorded works. Yet he is largely unknown in the wider jazz world.

Trumpeter Joe Wilder, who knew Talbert and played his music in the 1950s, as well as recently, said in an interview, "He should be better known, and I don't know why he isn't. He's an American composer and arranger and his style is quite different from a lot of the other more popular composers and arrangers and yet he's in the same league with them. I think if younger musicians especially were exposed to his music, they would be amazed at the talent and I'm sure would get a great deal of joy out of it."

As the reader will discover, Tom Talbert has led a fascinating, unconventional life—even for a jazz musician—and has had a complex relationship with fate. Sometimes he's been the beneficiary of extraordinary good luck, while at other times "the lady" has resolutely turned her back to him. Tom has ridden these unpredictable waves with great style, however, and, to quote Joe Wilder again, "He's sort of the epitome of what we used to think about as musicians. We were always proud; there was a certain amount of pride in the way we dressed and certain things like that, and he still does all that and I kind of admire him for it because he's carrying the ball for the rest of us and it isn't a bad ball to carry, actually." That sense of style and a commitment to the highest standards permeates every aspect of Tom Talbert's music making.

When I began research for this book, it was my intention to try to introduce Talbert and his music to what I hoped would be a new and receptive audience. While this remains my primary concern, along the way I heard and collected vivid stories and experiences that made me want to expand the scope of the book in order to shine some light on lesser-known (or now virtually unknown) musicians who were part of Tom's jazz scene. This world—Los Angeles in the 1940s, New York in the 1950s, and Los Angeles again in the past two decades—was magnificently brought to life for me by many great and well-known musicians who need no introduction. They include Bud Shank, Jack Montrose, Danny Bank, Joe Wilder, Eddie Bert, Milt Bernhart, Maria Schneider, Don Shelton, Bob Efford, Joe Soldo, Howard Rumsey, and Bruce Paulson.

Like many of them, Talbert is one of a dwindling number of men and women whose passions and lives were captured by jazz in the 1930s—the kind of musicians who filled the big bands and later recording studios and jazz club stages. Coming out of the Great Depression, the fortunate ones heard Duke Ellington, Louis Armstrong, Benny Goodman, and Count Basie live, many others via radio or records. For youngsters like Tom and his contemporaries, life would never be the same again and all thoughts of alternative careers would be sacrificed on the altar of this seductive form of music. This book is a portrait of his, and their, vanished world.

* * *

I was driving from the airport into the city on my first visit to Minneapolis. The downtown business skyline gradually appears over the horizon—a grouping of skyscrapers and towers representing dominant architectural trends of the last forty years—similar to those of Philadelphia, Baltimore, or Wilmington, Delaware, seen from the windows of Amtrak. I turned and asked Tom Talbert, who was traveling with me, "What was the skyline like when you were a kid growing up here?"

"See that small, older tower among the new ones? That used to be the tallest building in town. It was called the Foshay Tower and it dominated the skyline. Often heralded as 'the first skyscraper west of the Mississippi,' it was a thirty-two-floor obelisk inspired by the Washington Monument, clad in cream-colored limestone, and trimmed with Art Deco and Art Moderne details. Each floor was slightly smaller in area than the one below it. It's now quite hard to see, surrounded as it is by many taller and broader buildings of glass and steel."

I thought that the Foshay Tower was a nice metaphor for Tom Talbert's work. Elegant, confident, original, beautifully constructed, and overshadowed and almost concealed by the grander, the gaudier, and the fashionable, with all that that last term implies. A striking piece of pure Americana, and well worth celebrating.

1

Some Thoughts about Tom Talbert and West Coast Jazz

Among the characteristics of the music that in the 1950s was termed West Coast jazz were a strong relationship between the improvising soloist and the ensemble writing that surrounded him; a desire on the part of the composer/arranger to experiment with instrumental voicings, unusual combinations of instruments, and instruments not common in jazz, such as French horn, English horn, flute, and oboe; a tendency to eschew vibrato; and a very creative use of individual lines in written passages. Talbert's writing in the mid-1940s, as demonstrated on recordings made by his thirteen-piece band at that time, was in many ways a matrix for the West Coast jazz style that became so popular a decade later. The relationship between soloist and ensemble was critical.

Ken Poston, director of the Los Angeles Jazz Institute, describes Tom's approach.

KEN POSTON: I think the way Tom writes for soloist and ensemble is exemplary. Generally, especially when he made his first records, modern jazz was very formalized in the way that things happened, typically with an ensemble passage that was then opened up for solos. But Tom's is like this organized whole. There's an introduction, then there's this horizontal form where not only is he creating all of these beautiful textures and tonalities but his interweaving it with improvisation to me makes it that pure jazz style of writing. That's what I think is one of the hallmarks of Tom's style. It's something that he's able to do that very few have done successfully—Duke Ellington was a master of that. The piece being an organized whole, not a bunch of sections but a piece flowing through from the beginning to the end. That's one of the truly brilliant things that Tom has always done.

Ken Borgers, at one time the program director at jazz station KLON in Long Beach, also makes the West Coast jazz connection in a recent interview.

KEN BORGERS: I didn't become aware of Tom's music until the 1980s, and I was amazed that I'd managed to miss it till then. But I think he's so quiet as a person that a lot of people aren't aware of his music. He's a wonderful writer and arranger and really could be considered the father of West Coast jazz. You can talk about Shorty Rogers and all those guys who were around, but Tom was writing West Coast jazz before there was such a thing . . . he took off from the West Coast to go back east and wrote film music and classical music and then the West Coast thing hit and Tom was overlooked. He'd been writing wonderful soft, impressionistic music before all those guys.

KEN POSTON: When the big West Coast boom happened in the 1950s, Tom had moved to New York. So it's kind of a case of being in the wrong place at the wrong time . . . I really think that if he'd been here on the West Coast in the early 1950s when Gerry Mulligan and Shorty Rogers became established, he would have taken his rightful place alongside them as one of the pioneers. And he would have fit into that whole Pacific jazz, Contemporary jazz movement that started it.

Don Davidson played baritone sax in Tom Talbert's 1940s Los Angeles band and was also the music copyist. Thus he had an intimate view of Tom's writing and the uncompromising nature of the composer.

DON DAVIDSON: It was quite esoteric, really individual. Whatever his influences were initially I think had been caught up in his own reflection and I don't think you could point to a specific influence in regard to his own way of writing. He has a unique and completely different approach to harmony—he doesn't follow any established lines that I'm familiar with. There were times when I found it difficult to agree with him but on repeated hearings you discover that it works— for him. It's what he wants, regardless of how you might view it in your own mind. Unique and individual and certainly not derivative— at least not to the point where I could describe any derivation. He was very innovative not only in his approach to music but in titling some of his things too. I remember one thing that he did, years and years ago entitled "Recollections of the Future."

Los Angeles woodwind player Don Shelton has played with Talbert since the 1980s.

DON SHELTON: I don't know anybody else writing today who writes the way Tom does. He's very much like a painter—he loves different textures and colors and one of his real strengths that I love so much is his work with ballads, where he has time to develop those sounds, by using bass clarinet, flute, and French horn and muted brass—that's where he really shines, I think. There's a cool quality to his music. Everything simmers on the back burner. He really is his own person musically; he doesn't follow a set pattern of writing like the other bandleaders in the Los Angeles area—or New York, or anywhere for that matter. He hears a certain thing and writes it accordingly, and however you look at it, it is its own unique self.

2
=

Early Days

Tom Talbert was born in Crystal Bay, Minnesota, population sixty, on August 4, 1924. Now virtually a suburb of Minneapolis, Crystal Bay was, at that time, a small community with its own town hall, general store, timber yard, and railroad station—all now vanished. It was a favorite summertime destination for hot, exhausted city dwellers. By the time he was of school age, Tom recalls:

> TOM TALBERT: We were poor. My father was just getting back on his feet during the Depression years. He owned and lost the general store, and then started a small coal business. Our cottage had no running water, no indoor toilet, and no central heating, but we always had food. I went to a two-room, eight-grade school, which was the best teaching I ever had.

Judging by family photographs, Tom's childhood memories, and the author's visit to Crystal Bay, it must have been an idyllic existence for a young boy, especially in the warmer months.

> TOM TALBERT: Thankfully, particularly where Minnesota's weather is concerned, we moved into Minneapolis when I was nine. Then we had the missing necessities, including a furnace!

Tom's father seems to have been smart, energetic, and popular in the business community. Once settled in the city, a coal and coke deal with the Ford Motor Company saw the family's Model A Ford car replaced by one of Henry's new V8s. The family fortunes had definitely begun to improve around the time Tom remembers his first contact with any music that could be described as jazz.

> TOM TALBERT: It was the summer of 1938 and we were riding out to the Minneapolis airport in my father's new Lincoln Zephyr. Flying was

a novelty then, and they were offering rides over the city in a Ford Tri-motor airliner. Our car had a radio and I remember hearing a record that turned out to be Ella Fitzgerald singing "A Tisket A Tasket" with the Chick Webb band. That's the first time I recall hearing the sound of a big band and I knew immediately that I wanted to be involved in that music.

It is difficult for us in the year 2003 to be able to imagine a time when so much of what we now know and love about jazz did not yet exist. For Tom and his contemporaries, there was a huge empty canvas waiting to be filled, and only a small number of musical styles competing for attention.

Tom admits that at that time, at age fourteen, he knew little about music and less about bands.

TOM TALBERT: My grandmother played "parlor piano"—anyone alive in the 1920s or 1930s would know what that meant—popular songs and light classics played from sheet music. When I was seven or eight, she showed me how to read music, and I would sing popular songs while she played for family entertainment. My four aunts found my renditions of "Broken Hearts," "Love Lost and Gone," "Isle of Capri," and "Empty Saddles in the Old Corral" quite hilarious. As well as the piano, we had a large wind-up phonograph and the same thick, heavy black discs as everyone else—Caruso and the Three Black Crows, who were funny but, by today's standards, very politically incorrect.

Until hearing Chick Webb in the car, Tom's main radio memory seems to be his grandfather following the fortunes of the Minneapolis Millers Baseball Team.

Guitarist Jim Robb, who began playing in the Minneapolis area around the time that Tom was starting school, has vivid memories of the Twin Cities scene in the 1930s.

JIM ROBB: I spent all my playing career in Minneapolis. I tried going on the road with local bands when I was in high school and during my first year of college, but it was a bad experience. We were on commission. We'd be playing someplace and there'd be nobody there. Then the guy would say, "Play something hot and fast, there's a car coming down the road." At the end of the night they'd say, "Sorry fellers, but there was a free wedding dance down the road . . . but we like your music very much and hope that you'll come back again." We were listening to records by people like Red Nichols and Bix Beiderbecke at that time. Eddie Lang was my idol when I took up guitar. When I went over from banjo to guitar and was faced with the six strings, I just couldn't figure it out by myself. I finally found a fellow who was playing with Lou Breese at the Minnesota Theater. Breese was from Chicago. His real name was Calabrese and he had a couple of guys in his orchestra who played violin and doubled on guitar—Kenny Spears and Rudy Nordlund. They were the only guys around here I could find who played guitar at all! I talked Kenny into giving me some lessons. I was doing quite well until, at the end of the fourth lesson, he fired me. I was just shocked because he'd told me I was doing so well. I finally phoned his mother and said that I was upset that he didn't want to teach me any more. She said, "Jimmy, can you keep a secret?" I said yes. She said, "That's all he knows!" So I got every Eddie Lang record I could and I'd copy them, and I found a couple of violin players who could play the Venuti parts. We started doing things like "Wild Cat" and we started to get jobs on the university campus, even though I was still only in high school.

JIM ROBB

I was born in Calgary, Alberta, Canada, on May 28, 1914. Music ran in my family—classical, not jazz. My father was a fine pianist, as was my mother. My father had two sisters, one of whom studied under Leopold Godowski; the other was more of a natural, self-taught musician. There was a lot of music in the family. I started on the ukulele. In the summer my family used to go from Calgary to Minaki, in the Lake of the Woods area near Winnipeg. One year, when I was about eight, we were staying on an island about ten miles from Minaki. When it was crowded I would sometimes go down and sleep in the boathouse. On this particular night, the wind must have been in the right direction, because I heard this orchestra music coming down the lake. It later turned out to be Frank Wright's Orchestra—the orchestra from the St. Charles Country Club in Winnipeg—and when I heard it I thought, "That's something I want to do." So that's what first attracted me to music. In the late 1920s our family returned to Minneapolis, which is where we were from, and I began playing in a family band, with my mother on piano and my brother on saxophone. We played all the sheet music of the time, tunes like "Brown Eyes Why Are You Blue?" and "Moonlight Bay."

Not long after I started playing the ukulele, I decided I needed to earn some extra money. I went to a variety store—Hub Variety, at Lake and Hennepin, run by a feller named Mort Joseph. It was a variety store—it sold everything from ax handles to brassieres. I walked in and asked Mort for a job, and he said he didn't need anybody. I said let me try it—I'll work for a week after school for nothing. After a week he thought maybe I could help him out so he paid me the princely sum of two dollars a week, and I worked every day after school till dinner and all day Saturday till nine. Then I heard Ferd Oldre, who was playing solo tenor banjo over at the local radio station WCCO, and thought, "Boy I'd like to do that." So I started saving my spare cash toward getting a banjo. In the meantime I got a banjo-ukulele and I strung it with steel strings to make it sound more like a banjo. Ultimately I got enough money together to get a proper banjo and took some lessons, and it wasn't long before I was playing with Grace Wentzel's Banjo Band on Station WRHM. Then I started playing professionally—I played with George Osborne's Orchestra in 1929, and I teamed up with another fellow to do banjo duets in different spots around town.

In the early days we'd learn by listening to records and then we'd go and jam together. My first big break came in 1933 when I was a freshman at Carleton College. Art Goldberg, a Minneapolis bandleader who had a lot of the Country Club work, was coming down to play the Washington Ball. Someone must have told him about me because he decided not to bring a guitar player with him and hired me instead. And in that band was the cornet player Doc Evans. Goldberg liked my playing and before term was up I was going to Minneapolis to play weekends. The music was strictly society. Goldberg did a marvelous Eddie Duchin style and he'd put Dave Frank on lead tenor. And guess who was on second tenor? Doc Evans!

In the fall, Art Goldberg got a job playing at the Galleries Nightclub above the State Theatre. We played every night except Sundays, even though it was the middle of the Depression. I've always had a hard time explaining this anomaly, except to say that no matter how poor people were they still wanted to go out and have a little fun and forget their troubles. Because we always worked, even if it wasn't too rewarding sometimes. Everyone was in the same boat, so to speak, and everyone seemed to enjoy getting dressed up and going out. Also, you could get a pretty nice dinner for seventy-five cents and a shot of cheap booze for fifteen cents. Prohibition wasn't heavily enforced around here. There were all kinds of lake spots where you could drink—there was booze all over the place. The Bronfmans were big-time bootleggers during Prohibition running booze into the United States from Canada. Later they wound up buying the Seagram Company for $6 million in cash.

In 1934 Art Goldberg decided that the future for the music business here was limited and made plans to go to California. He wanted me to take over the band. I was only twenty, but I had some good connections and I made a deal with him. He said that all he wanted for the band was enough gas to drive out to Los Angeles. He had a Model A Ford Roadster and petrol was about nine cents a gallon. I paid him thirty bucks for the library, the claves, the maracas, and the megaphone for the vocalist. As luck would have it I nailed a good job in a week or so, a big wedding at the Minnesota Club and that cleared my investment. From then on it was all profit. I also landed the Automobile Club Country Club, where the band played three nights a week. I got the contract for the summer and with that I was able to hire anyone I wanted. Doc Evans stayed on and later I got bassist Fritz Hughart, father of Jim Hughart who has played with Tom Talbert here and in Los Angeles. Later Norvey Mulligan's band broke up and I was able to hire Vince Bastien on trombone and Kenny Nash on saxophone. Then we took on Tony Bastien and we had Bob Anderson on piano and Lloyd Horton on drums. That was the best band I ever played on around here. We'd been playing in that Eddie Duchin style but when I heard Benny Goodman and Glenn Miller I saw the light and thought, "The Duchin style isn't going to cut it in the future."

Vince Bastien wrote all our arrangements—we were only eight pieces, trumpet, trombone, alto, and tenor, but Tony and Kenny doubled clarinet and flute. Vince was one of those guys who could write an arrangement that "laid well" for everyone and could often sound like a much bigger band. I guess we got into kind of a Bob Crosby style, ultimately. We had a great run but the war intervened. Then in 1946 I decided

that, with a wife and four children, I'd better get into something more solid than music so I went into business and only
started playing again after I retired.

The greatest band I ever heard come through this area was
when the Ben Pollack band came out and got stranded here
during the Depression. They were out at Wildwood Park on
White Bear Lake at a place called the Plantation. And they
stayed there all summer. I remember Nappy LaMare, Gil Bow-
ers, Eddie Miller. I'm not sure if Ray Bauduc was with them
then but Matty Matlock was. I can remember going out there
one night and jamming with Matty, just the two of us—I was
scared to death. They had Charlie Spivak on one trumpet and
Yank Lawson on the other, Jack Teagarden and a guy called
Bubbles Copsey on trombones. Pollack had his girlfriend Doris
Robbins on vocals. This was the first time I ever heard a really
good example of that expanded Dixie sound for big band.

Jim Robb recently put together a CD of recordings from broadcasts
made in 1939 by his band playing at the Minneapolis Athletic Club.
The recordings are revelatory in many ways: they allow us to hear
what a good local band sounded like in middle America at the height
of the swing era; they also indicate the rich musical environment that
Tom Talbert grew up in. Judging by the recordings, Jim Robb's band,
the M.A.C. Gophers, was very good indeed. The soloists, particularly
the Bastien brothers, were excellent and the arrangements, mostly by
Vince Bastien, sound not only totally professional but also highly
original and well beyond what was probably required for a Saturday
night dinner dance at the Minneapolis Athletic Club. Tony Bastien's
fluent clarinet playing could have graced any of the "name bands,"
and his tenor sax work reflects a strong but not plagiaristic Eddie
Miller influence. Brother Vince frequently wrote his own trombone
as the lead voice in the ensembles and solos with a sound that
ranged, on different occasions, from Jack Teagarden to Juan Tizol.
The rhythm section swings beautifully, the bass player being, as
noted by Robb, Fritz Hughart, father of the noted Los Angeles bassist
Jim Hughart who recorded with Tom Talbert in the 1980s, and the
ensemble playing is tight and well blended. Amazingly, Jim Robb
said, "We never rehearsed as such—Vince would bring new arrangements to the gig and the guys would just play them."

Tom Talbert came to music about ten years after Jim Robb.

TOM TALBERT: I was in Jordan Junior High School and I was mainly interested in drawing, reading, and writing stories. I thought I'd like to be a writer or a pilot. I was introduced to the head artist on the *Tribune* newspaper and became very absorbed in technique, using special pens, special paper, ink, and brushes. I became very good at it.

Music must have seeped in gradually. Using the money earned from a paper route and walking downtown and back to save the fare for purchases, Tom started buying records. First he bought society bands like Blue Barron's, earning some derisive comments from his father, who said the phonograph was passé. Becoming more discerning, he homed in on Benny Goodman, Artie Shaw, and Jimmie Lunceford.

Apart from a couple of friends who played trumpet and saxophone, Tom seems to have made most of his musical discoveries on his own at this time. The juke boxes in the places where the kids hung out carried records by bands like Glenn Miller's and Tommy Dorsey's, but Tom feels that the music of the day was part of the background, and interest in bands and performers does not seem to have been as intense among teens it is today.

But he does recall hearing remote broadcasts of bands from all across the country. Nights when he could lie in bed in Minneapolis and hear the Count Basie Band playing live from the Casino Gardens in Culver City, California.

TOM TALBERT: I'd hear that band and the arrangements by people like Jimmy Mundy, Buck Clayton, and Eddie Durham and I'd get so excited I couldn't sleep. Around 1940 the big band business was at its peak and there were marvelous things happening musically and they were hitting me. When I first heard Jimmie Lunceford I remember thinking this is something that's really worth doing.

He walked to school with a slightly older boy who played second alto saxophone in the high school dance band. He told Tom, "You ought to be the arranger—the arranger is the one who sets the style of the band."

He took Tom to meet Chester E. Groth, a local saxophone teacher who owned a music store and studio. Groth was well-known among professional musicians, and saxophone players with name bands would often take a lesson from him when they were appearing at the Minneapolis Orpheum. Groth in turn took Tom to Hugh Brown, who played trumpet and wrote arrangements for a local hotel band. Tom began learning the basics of arranging from Brown at a dollar a lesson.

TOM TALBERT: He wrote out C scales, in major and minor, telling me that what was true in C was true in all keys. He would write out a lead sheet on a popular song and I had to take it home and voice it in three- and four-part harmony.

Along with learning to harmonize popular tunes, Tom also got to hear, at the end of the lesson, recordings of all kinds of music from Bix Beiderbecke's cornet solos to Modeste Mussorgsky's orchestral compositions—all new to his ears. When he felt he had taught Tom all he could, Brown sent him to a pianist named Del Weibel, who had played and toured with bands like Rudy Vallee's. Weibel introduced Tom to more advanced harmonic musical language and entertained him with stories of life on the road.

TOM TALBERT: Del showed me ninth chords and suspensions, and when I got to the thirteenth chord I figured I'd really arrived. I brought along the Charlie Barnet record "Lament for May," and he analyzed the harmonies for me. About this time I started writing proper arrangements and got some guys to come round to the house and play them. I was using a trumpet, three saxes, and bass and drums.

All this time Tom was still financing his lessons and his record buying by delivering papers.

TOM TALBERT: . . . until an embarrassing age . . . at least well up through high school. On Sundays, when my father was home, I managed to borrow his Lincoln, but when it got too embarrassing to be seen throwing papers from a bicycle I quit.

Seeing the Jimmie Lunceford band in action was something of a milestone in his young life too.

TOM TALBERT: Far and away the most memorable thing I can remember is the first time I heard Jimmie Lunceford's band in person. They played in an Eagles Hall—it had a little stage and a bench all around the whole room and an empty space in the middle where I guess they had banquets and whatnot. The audience was predominantly colored people, I guess you'd say "black" nowadays, and there were maybe eight or nine of us who were all aspiring musicians, hanging on to everything. I particularly remember the whole band was on the stage except the baritone player and they looked very snappy. They were very well dressed and of course they were young, in their early twenties, good-looking guys.

They were all just chatting, all sitting in place and Jimmie was standing in front with about a three-foot baton and they were waiting for Earl Carruthers the baritone sax player. This was wintertime, and he came in and I remember he had this monster double-breasted wool or alpaca coat. He came hurrying in from the wings of the stage and there was a great deal of joshing: "Where you been, what's the matter with you, we're supposed to play tonight" that sort of thing. Of course his horn was already set up for him so he got rid of his coat, sat down, blew a little air in his baritone, looked up at Lunceford and with no counting or tapping or anything, Lunceford just raised his arm and dropped it and—wham—straight into an arrangement of "Blue Prelude," which they'd just recorded for Decca records. I'll tell you, that was a real thrill. That wasn't the first of the name bands that I'd seen but it was the most impressive.

At that time, I thought that "Blue Prelude" was the most wonderful tune I'd heard. I actually submitted my own arrangement of it to two of the better bands in the area and they probably quite correctly passed on it!

The Jimmie Lunceford band, particularly in the years between 1935 and 1940, was renowned for its unrivaled rhythmic drive, terrific showmanship, and impeccable performance of challenging arrangements. It never quite caught the public imagination in the manner of Basie, Ellington, Goodman, Shaw, or Miller, but no one who saw it live ever forgot the experience.

DON DAVIDSON: I think many more people fell in love with the Lunceford band than will really admit it.

Stan Kenton trombonist and composer-arranger Harry Betts was smitten.

HARRY BETTS: There was nothing like the Jimmie Lunceford band . . . it was my favorite—Marty Paich's too, and Glenn Miller's, and Billy May's. I first heard the band around 1942. I was fifteen and growing up in Fresno, and I knew the band was going to be in Oakland. It was an all-colored dance, and it was the night before Willie Smith was going to leave to go with Charlie Spivak. There have been two times in my life when the hair on the back of my neck stood up—and that was one of them. The other time was something Maynard Ferguson played when he joined Stan Kenton's band. The kinds of bands that came through Fresno were like Bob Crosby—great bands but they weren't what I was looking for. I hadn't heard what I was looking for until I heard the Lunceford band.

Tom got that hair-raising feeling from the Lunceford band too.

TOM TALBERT: The only other time I got that feeling was many years later, hearing Stravinsky conduct the Los Angeles Philharmonic at the Shrine Auditorium.

Some of the Lunceford style lodged in Tom Talbert's musical mind and came out later. In the meantime, all of the great bands played the Minneapolis/St. Paul area. Artie Shaw, Tommy Dorsey, Lucky Millinder, Charlie Spivak, Woody Herman, and Glenn Miller are just some that Tom heard at the Prom Ballroom in St. Paul and at the Orpheum Theater in Minneapolis. His memories of the Dorsey and Shaw bands are particularly vivid.

TOM TALBERT: Like so many name bands, the leader wasn't there when the job started. At about the end of the first set, Dorsey arrived, coming through the front door, instead of the back, wearing a great big coat. He gets up on the stand, pulls a quart of whiskey out of his pocket, and throws it back to Chuck Peterson in the trumpet section, takes off his coat, picks up his trombone, and goes straight into "Getting Sentimental over You."

One of the best things I heard at the Prom Ballroom was the Artie Shaw band when he had Jack Jenney on trombone and Billy Butterfield on trumpet, and a string section. Shaw was very important to me because I think he played by far the best repertoire of material. The first time I heard so many of my favorite tunes were when they were played by his band. You just wouldn't hear much Rodgers and Hart, Cole Porter, or tunes like "Alone Together" and "I Didn't Know What Time It Was" played by the combos in the local bars. When "All the Things You Are" was on the hit parade it was summer, and at the end of every broadcast I remember the announcer saying, "'All the Things You Are' is from 'Very Warm for May.' This is the Columbia Broadcasting System."

As far as Woody Herman is concerned, I think I must have been influenced by his version of "Blue Prelude," as I remember alto saxist

Tom Morgan of the Glad Olinger band laughingly putting down my arrangement because it wasn't in the mood or tempo of the Lunceford treatment.

There was nightlife and a jazz scene in 1940 Minneapolis and Tom was getting acquainted with it.

TOM TALBERT: I was out at night too. I don't know where my parents thought I was but there were two kids a year or two older than me and I'd go out with them. They were both big guys and I could get into clubs by sort of gliding in, between them. There were quite a few clubs in Minneapolis at that time that had trios and quartets, so I got to hear a lot of people, particularly in an area that bounded what was called 6th Avenue North, primarily a black district with several barbecue places. They would have jam sessions—some times very good, sometimes not so good—but you'd stop in there and there might be something going on.

Alto saxist Lew Anderson, who has his own big band playing regularly in New York City sixty years later, remembers the same jazz scene.

LEW ANDERSON: There was always somebody worthwhile playing in Minneapolis. There was also the Pettiford family—they'd have a little band in one of these after-hours places—with arrangements for four trumpets and rhythm section and nothing else.

Tom Talbert got to know the Pettifords very well.

TOM TALBERT: One thing that meant a lot to me was meeting the Pettiford family, of whom Oscar was of course the best known—he became world famous as one of the all-time great bass players. They were from Oklahoma originally, I believe and they'd come up to Minneapolis. I think there were about thirteen in the family. There were a lot of kids and when they were younger they had a Pettiford band—Oscar told me he had to stand on a box to play the bass. The one I got to know first and best was Alonzo, who was a trumpet player. I first heard him when the Nat Towles band came through. This was a very good territory band, I believe based out of Omaha, and they had this high-note trumpeter featured on an arrangement of "I Surrender Dear." He sang it and he played it and at the end he wound up on a double high A or something and that turned out to be Alonzo.

I got to know him, and I used to stop in at a place called the Old

Southern Barbecue where he played. Daddy Pettiford would be
there—Daddy played drums, Mama played piano. Alonzo would
come over and sit with us but pretty soon Mama would say, "Alonzo,
you git back over here now." He'd go back over there with his trumpet and the three of them would play. He had a brother named Ira who
was a singer and also a good high-note trumpeter, who I think eventually played with Lionel Hampton. It was in some of these after-hours
places that I first heard Ira or Alonzo sing great blues like "I'm Gonna
Move to the Outskirts of Town." In due course Alonzo played in my
band on some of these little jobs that I began to get.

In the course of his nights "on the town" Tom Talbert could have
encountered Leigh Kamman, who eventually became nationally
known, presenting jazz on the radio and in concerts.

LEIGH KAMMAN: I knew Oscar Pettiford, and also his mother and father. The father was a veterinarian and they came here from Oklahoma. The entire family was musical; the mother was a piano teacher
and they had a family band. Out of this band came, most notably, Ira,
who was a trumpet player and later went with Benny Carter, Harry,
who played the saxophone, and Alonzo.

In 1940 Jim Robb and Leigh Kamman were connoisseurs of the
world that was just opening up for Tom Talbert.

JIM ROBB: The best music you could hear live was played by the black
guys up at the Harlem Breakfast Club and the Musicians' Rest and
Bunny's on Excelsior Avenue, which used to be called the Cotton Club.
That's where Lester Young and trumpeter Rook Ganz, bassist Adolphus Alsbrook, a pianist named Popeye, and the Pettifords all used to
play. The black guys played out there because they weren't allowed to
play in downtown Minneapolis. We used to go out there just to listen
to them. There was a pianist named Frankie Hines—he was the best
ever around here I think.

LEIGH KAMMAN: The band at the Cotton Club was under the wing
of Boyd Atkins. They brought him in from Chicago to Minneapolis to
write dinner music and then they played jazz later in the evening. Ira
Pettiford was in that band and also Lester Young. A man named Pete
Karalis employed these musicians.

JIM ROBB: Pete and I went to high school together and later on he
bought the place. By then it was called the El Patio; everyone pronounced it El Paysho. I played there after my band broke up due to

World War II enlistments. The group there was a combo led by a marvelous violinist named Jerry Henrickson. We had our own local Art Van Damme: Larry Malmberg on accordion, Bernie Sundermeyer on bass, Don Anderson on tenor sax and vibes, and myself on guitar. We played everything from jazz to the light classics and it was probably the most fun I ever had playing.

LEIGH KAMMAN: The Pettiford family was remarkable in so many ways. My main experience was with Oscar and we worked together here on concerts, prior to the war. In the summer of 1941, before he joined Charlie Barnet and his later fame in New York, he was part of an informally organized University of Minnesota Jazz Society. They gave concerts inside the Coffman Union Building, and this was at a time when Dmitri Mitropoulos was conductor of the Minneapolis Symphony Orchestra, later the Minnesota Symphony Orchestra.

Ken Green, a good boogie-woogie pianist who later became a trial lawyer, drummer Sid Smith, who later became Eddie Condon's brother-in-law and a television producer, Oscar Pettiford, and a few others put on a concert. Green wrote a song for it that was titled "Beat Me Dmitri, Eight to the Bar."

They invited Maestro Mitropoulos who sat cross-legged in front of the band with the rest of the students and listened while Oscar played bass and sang the song, which was very much in the current popular Freddie Slack boogie-woogie style. They broke up the audience and Mitropoulos was visibly delighted.

He came up afterward and shook Oscar's hand and said something like, "You are marvelous, skilled, of the pluck method and I wish you good things in your career."

This got a lot of publicity via the *Minneapolis Tribune* and also, I think, the *Dispatch* in St. Paul and it even got a few lines in *Time* magazine. It led to an engagement over Easter week with the "Pagliacci of the piano," Joe Reichmann, and his orchestra, playing spots between the movies. They'd play "Beat Me Dmitri" in each set, which finally annoyed the more snooty members at the top level of the university faculty. It gave Oscar quite a showcase, however. Then in 1942 I moved to Duluth to start a radio program called *Symphony in Riffs* on WEBC, an NBC station, first with recordings and then live remotes from a club called the Flame—a beautiful white-tablecloth place on London Road. The club had booked Coleman Hawkins and Oscar came up and brought his bass with him. While we were doing the sound check, Hawk came over and saw it and said to Oscar, "Why don't you play something for us."

Oscar had completely memorized Jimmy Blanton's "Pitter Panther Patter" and executed it beautifully . . . and that night sat in with

Hawkins. After the gig we adjourned to the studios of the radio station and had a jam session that lasted until dawn. They jammed on numbers like "My Blue Heaven" for forty minutes at a time, then got into some early bop, things like "Mop Mop." Oscar and Hawkins became fast friends and that really sealed Oscar's future career. He went back to Minneapolis for a while then in January 1942 jammed with Charlie Barnet at the Clef Club, another of our after-hours places of the time. Barnet hired him immediately and left town with a two-bass band, Oscar Pettiford and Chubby Jackson!

Meanwhile, Tom Talbert was learning how to be a bandleader.

TOM TALBERT: I didn't know Oscar so well then. One of the first times I had anything to do with him, was when I was about eighteen. I had a band and I'd written arrangements for four brass and four saxes. Wonder of wonders, the Marigold Ballroom in Minneapolis hired us for one night but unfortunately the bass player didn't show up. We had a very fine guitarist and a good drummer but no bass player. Luckily, Ira Pettiford was in the band, and he ran to the phone and pretty soon here came Oscar with his bass. It wasn't even in a case, just under his arm, and he came across the dance floor and got up and started playing. I never got to know him very well then because he went with Charlie Barnet soon after. He was gone, and I was getting ready to be pretty much gone too. But later in New York I often saw him and did a lot of writing for him and used him on my *Bix Duke Fats* recording.

Poster for Marigold Ballroom, 1942.

The fact that this was a multiracial band and that Tom regularly hired black players did not attract much attention in Minneapolis in 1942.

TOM TALBERT: Well, it wasn't noteworthy to me. I myself didn't entertain any philosophy or prejudice—or even lack of prejudice because I didn't think about it. Once in a while somebody would say something but I was playing such a low level of jobs that there was never any problem and there weren't that many jobs either. The crowd was usually so small in the places that we played that I can't remember any reaction, one way or the other.

I recall Harry Pettiford played with me one time when I auditioned for a very nice supper club called the Happy Hour. I had Alonzo on trumpet and Harry playing lead alto. Harry was a very good player with a real Benny Carter-ish tone, who had been with Fletcher Henderson. The last I heard he'd gone back to Oklahoma and become a preacher. Another fellow I used was Leon Vaughan, who used to work as a porter on the trains. He was a very good trumpeter; the story was that he'd played with Basie.

Later, when I was on the road with Whit Thoma's band, we had a kid from Texas named Tex Oldham who played pretty good trumpet. When we were in Minneapolis to play at the Prom Ballroom, Tex and I went down to the record shop that all the musicians went to and we ran into Oscar Pettiford. I introduced him to Tex and we talked for a while. After we left Tex said to me, "That's the first time I ever shook hands with a nigra."

The racial situation was a bit more complicated than the youthful Tom Talbert could have known. Kent Hazen, who is a jazz historian and a leading authority on jazz in Minneapolis/St. Paul, sets the scene:

KENT HAZEN: The black community in the Twin Cities area was quite small—probably no more than 10,000 by 1920. As it was a railroad center there were quite a lot of black Pullman porters and so on. According to Tela Burt, a black musician I interviewed when he was 102, music in the community in the days before World War I was mostly polite—waltzes, mazurkas. There wasn't much in the way of black saloon-type music. By the mid-1920s there was an active after-hours scene up on the near north side—barbecue joints and tippling houses—and there are accounts of visits to some of these places and references to a high quality of musicianship.

The white Fatso Palmer band was popular in the Twin Cities area in the late 1920s. Fatso later became a very distinguished lawyer named John Marshall Palmer Jr., but everyone called him Fatso for obvious reasons. He was a trumpet player and had attended Culver Academy with Red Nichols. Red played first trumpet and Fatso second, and that's one of the reasons why there was such a strong Red Nichols influence here in those days. A musician who played in Palmer's band told us that in 1926 the Pullman Porters Brotherhood asked the Palmer band to play their annual dance, which would seem to indicate that there weren't any good black bands around the Twin Cities at the time; but of course we know that there were. Maybe a white band was a novelty for them. Tela Burt booked colored bands—he had about sixty musicians on his books. Sometimes he'd send out a mixed band and get complaints from people who said, "We ordered a colored band and there were two white guys in it!"

Jim Robb recalls the atmosphere in the 1930s.

JIM ROBB: I could have got myself in trouble but I was too dumb and young to know better. When I had my own band I had a very militant attitude about this racial thing. I hired a black pianist—Sid Williams for the Kappa Kappa Gamma benefit at the Nicollet Hotel. I not only hired him; I hired him as a second pianist, got a great big concert grand, and put a spotlight on him. I did that before Benny Goodman hired Lionel Hampton or Teddy Wilson. Sid Williams was mostly a solo pianist—he played a lot like Art Tatum. He had great facility; he was the ultimate gentleman and everyone just loved him. He played well and knew how to move right—with the right people. Mrs. James Ford Bell, whose husband was the head of General Mills, loved his playing so much that she'd have a piano put up on her balcony and have him come out and play her to sleep!

Tenor saxist Irv Williams remembers the situation after World War II.

IRV WILLIAMS: Minneapolis was tough for black musicians in the 1940s and 1950s. I guess I was used to St. Louis where there were a lot of places to play, white places too. Here the union had a couple of guys who took it upon themselves to keep black musicians out of the downtown area. If you were black you'd get casual jobs and you could play out in the county. Quite often you'd be playing in mixed bands, and although there were some cold shoulders among the white musicians who played downtown, most musicians were against the discrimination. I was really the one that broke the ice—I wouldn't take no for an answer. I got an audition at a place called the Anglesey. The owner came up and told me that he really liked the band but he had to go either black or white. Like this guy, a lot of the owners were Jewish so I went to B'nai B'rith and complained. They really raised sand with him and told him and the others that they wouldn't stand for this discrimination. We finally got a place right off Hennepin Avenue at 5th called Vic's. There was another place right around the corner, called Curly's, where they started having Saturday afternoon jam sessions with some of the older black musicians—guys like Rook Ganz (Rook was a marvelous trumpet player), Ira Pettiford, and bassist Adolphus Alsbrook.

Back in 1942, Tom Talbert was about to sell his first arrangements.

TOM TALBERT: The wonderful pianist from Bob Crosby's band, Bob Zurke, had brought a band into Curly's. They only had clarinet, trumpet, and rhythm, but the girl singer wanted some arrangements written, and Chet Groth recommended me. I think I mainly wrote introductions and endings for her. One of the songs was "Georgia on My Mind," and I got paid something—a few dollars, I think.

There were two bands in the area that were more interesting than the hotel bands and I tried to sell them arrangements. Lloyd Labrie finally bought my chart of "Blue Prelude" for about three dollars. He preferred to copy new parts from the score rather than pay for the parts I'd supplied. The other band, Glad Olinger's, was pretty hip, and my stuff wasn't hip enough for them. Their lead alto was Tom Morgan, who put down my arrangement of "Blue Prelude" and many years later introduced me to Claude Thornhill, with whom he was then playing, in New York.

LEIGH KAMMAN: In the late 1930s and early 1940s, we had some really fine, jazz-oriented big bands here in Minneapolis/St. Paul. Glad Olinger for one. His brother Dale played trumpet and was also a fine guitarist who later worked with Ella Fitzgerald. Jack Nowicki wrote a lot of their arrangements and that band was one of our inspirations. They played in the Lunceford–Sy Oliver–Dorsey style and I think almost every member of the band wound up in a name band, eventually. One of them, trumpeter Buzz Goff, I last saw sitting next to Charlie Shavers in the Tommy and Jimmy Dorsey band at the Café Rouge in New York City.

The cream of the local jazz talent included alto saxist Tom Morgan, who played in the Glad Olinger band and later became an executive at Capitol Records. Drummer Eddie Tolck and cornetist Paul "Doc" Evans were with Red Dougherty at a roadhouse called Mitch's in Mendota, just outside of the Twin Cities. They played Chicago-style jazz; trumpeter Rook Ganz played at the Harlem Breakfast Club and the Elks Club.

After the war, Bob Grunenfelder also played with the band at Mitch's. By this time it was led by Harry Blons, who played clarinet and tenor sax and had worked with Red Nichols and Charlie Spivak. I first heard bop played in this area by the Coleman Hawkins group that Oscar Pettiford sat in with in Duluth; it was beginning to evolve locally by 1946.

Leigh was very much aware of the growing schism between "trad" and modern jazz.

LEIGH KAMMAN: I established a series of jazz concerts here with another of Eddie Condon's brothers-in-law—Bob Smith—on Sunday nights at the Radisson Downtown in Minneapolis, then finally at the Calhoun Beach Club. We presented two-part concerts, We Called It Jazz—the first half traditional Chicago- or New Orleans-style jazz and the second half modern jazz. We used local musicians, and later we had some name guests. We charged ninety-nine cents admission and there was a bar that only sold sodas, so families could come. We found such a division in the audience that you could expect, by intermission, a sizable group coming up, partisan about one style or the other, saying, "Why do you do this?" Some of the people were so uncontrollable we had to give them their money back. We'd say, "Tell you what, don't drive yourself to distraction, just don't come back again." It didn't matter whether we started with trad or modern—one wing would always object.

At the time I had a radio program called the *Swing Club* that ran from one to five on Saturday afternoons on one of the local stations. And no matter what I played we'd get angry phone calls and hair-raising nasty letters demanding, "Why are you playing this stuff?" It was a constant struggle to maintain a balance and convince the audience that we were trying to expand their horizons and stimulate them to explore a bit more.

KENT HAZEN: The Twin Cities area was for decades mostly Dixieland/swing oriented and in the early days of modern jazz there wasn't really a venue for it. Percy Hughes's eight-piece band was the closest thing I can think of as a bebop group—they were very much in the Tadd Dameron mode.

3

Territory Bands and Sleeper Buses

In the spring of 1942 Tom Talbert's horizon was expanding and he was confronting the inevitable: he would be leaving high school.

TOM TALBERT: I was fooling around with these little bands, trying to get a few jobs. Just before school closed, my friend Chet Groth entered my life again and said, "How would you like to go on the road with a good territory band? Cliff Kyes is looking for a piano player."

I said, "I don't know, Chet—do you think I'm good enough?"

I don't think he'd ever heard me play but he said, "Oh sure, you'll be fine" and set up a meeting. They hired me, and the day after I got out of high school I went down to Waterloo, Iowa, and joined the Cliff Kyes Orchestra.

Cliff drove me down, and while I was excited I probably didn't have enough sense to be nervous. We were playing in a ballroom at an amusement park in Waterloo called Electric Park, but I didn't play the first night—I just listened. They had a very good pianist I was replacing, called Don East. Future Kenton trombonist John Halliburton was in the band and he and Don left together a couple of nights later. Lew Anderson was playing lead alto and sang some. The band was on the commercial side but it was very successful and very popular in the territory. While I was with them we hardly ever had a night off.

Tom was cutting his musical teeth at a time when it has been estimated that, on an average Saturday night, there were more than 30,000 bands playing across America. From professional to amateur; "name" bands to high school bands; big bands, medium-size bands, bands with saxophone players and trumpet players and trombone players and drummers and bass players and pianists and guitarists. The urge to play was so strong that Tom and his contemporaries sat upright all night in uncomfortable buses or convoys of automobiles. The really fortunate ones slid into the narrow berths in "sleeper" buses to travel hundreds of miles along two-lane highways from one date to the next.

LEW ANDERSON: Cliff Kyes was the first band I played in where I learned something. The very first band I went on out in Nebraska was Lee Barron's. A terrible band—a sort of Richard Himber "bell-tone" band. The guys got five dollars a night and I got fifteen because I was playing lead alto. A semi truck fitted with bunks, or at worst just mattresses, was the mode of transportation. If you had to go to the bathroom you went in a milk bottle and threw it out the window; I always had the bunk that was where the guys threw it out. Kyes's band was a little classier. It was a nine-piece band and he'd taken over a Greyhound bus and converted it with bunks; there was carpeting on the floors and showers and they could even record in the bus, the sound was so good. The saxophones rehearsed every day in the bus—getting the vibratos together—things that I didn't know anything about. I really did learn a lot in that band.

When I joined Cliff, he wouldn't let me play on the first night. I had to go out and sit in the audience and see what the style was. He had three saxes: alto, tenor, and baritone; trumpet; and trombone. One guy, the baritone player, had written the whole book and the three saxes were always playing with the trombone so you almost had a section. Cliff Kyes fronted the band on marimba, trombone, and tap dance. So the first night I'm sitting in the audience and here he is, this quiet, unassuming man, very quietly spoken—someone introduces him and he came out and beat off the tune, leapt in the air and did about a three and a half turn in the air plié, and landed on the downbeat; I thought "holy crimley." Kyes was very good at what he did. Instead of a drum solo he'd do the break as a tap dance.

This was an era when a band's success relied on more than just the music it played. In these pretelevision days customers down at the dance hall expected a visual show, with fun and games. Tom never forgot the Cliff Kyes routines.

TOM TALBERT: Kyes would feature himself on xylophone or marimba, then cap it by jumping right over the instrument and tap dancing all the way from one end of the ballroom to the other then back again to the strains of something like "Nola."

LEW ANDERSON: Kyes's band was also a very neat band—he wouldn't let you out on the street in the daytime without you having a suit on. He was very strict—we all had numbered hangers for our clothes and shoes and if you left them lying around he'd throw them out on the highway even while the bus was moving. One of the musicians was paid extra to drive the bus, and another to tuck us in so we didn't fall out. The jumps weren't that long, a hundred miles or so, and they never left the territory; they didn't go to Illinois or Indiana or anyplace like that. We played Iowa, Minnesota, Wisconsin, Nebraska.

Lew left the Kyes band shortly after Tom joined.

LEW ANDERSON: I don't think I saw Tom again for thirty or forty years till we were playing at the Red Blazer in New York, and he came in and said, "Remember Cliff Kyes?" I remember Tom being on the band . . . I thought of him as a piano player—he sounded okay to me, very okay.

TOM TALBERT: Lew left to go with Ace Brigode and His Virginians. I lasted on the band for about six weeks until they got a chance to hire someone who could really play. By this time Kyes was no longer leading the band; he was in the navy at the Wold-Chamberlain base at Minneapolis, near the airport. After the war Cliff opened the Cliff Kyes Motel in Mankato, just outside Minneapolis. In Kyes's absence, the band was co-led by two of the musicians. One acted as the business manager and one was a sort of music manager. Sid Bass, who played baritone and did most of the arranging, was the business manager and Don, who played trumpet and vibes, took care of the music. These two guys, who couldn't stand each other, also took turns driving the band bus. They had an agreement that meant that one night Sid would drive and not drink, then the next night Don would drive and Sid could drink two night's worth. Then Sid would drive again and Don could drink his fill. One night somewhere out in southern Minnesota, they got into an argument then suddenly it's "Stop the bus," and pretty soon they're down in the ditch, cars going by, pummeling each other, rolling round in the dirt, until they settled their differences, at least for that night.

We played pop tunes of the day and jazz numbers like "I Wish I Could Shimmy Like My Sister Kate" and the novelties like "Nola." Typical young sidemen, we all thought the music we played was pretty square but we were happy to be on salary. A lot of bands only paid four or five dollars a night, and only on the nights they worked. The Cliff Kyes band was very popular and had enough work that we could be paid by the week. I got thirty-two dollars and with the custom-made sleeper bus I didn't have any hotel bills, so that was actually pretty good for 1942. Our bus was much better than those that were just converted semis where the guys would have to sleep five across on mattresses on the floor.

Tom tried writing a couple of arrangements.

TOM TALBERT: "Flying Home" was one, but in my inexperience I made them too complicated. We tried them but they just didn't work.

Don Davidson shared the same background and experiences.

DON DAVIDSON: Tom and I had sort of parallel antecedents—he came from Minneapolis and I grew up in southern Iowa, although my parents had lived in Minneapolis. He was older than me and went on the road with the territory bands two or three years before I did. When I was seventeen, just out of high school, I first went with Don Strickland: Our slogan for his band was "Play mickey with Strickie's Ickies." It was a terrible, god-awful band—three saxes, two trumpets, a trombone, and three rhythm. People were always leaving. Don had a permanent ad in *Down Beat*—"Wanted, Musicians" because the band was so bad that people would just disappear off it. I remember an alto player named Ollie Stoutland—I was driving the band bus on that particular night and we got into Fort Dodge, Iowa. I parked the bus and was going to go to bed and here's Ollie with his suitcase and his horn, all dressed, waiting by the door. He said, "I'm just going home." It was partly the music and partly Strickland.

Don Strickland wound up in Las Vegas as a dealer in the casinos. He dealt 21—he used to deal to the guys in the band bus. He'd pay them thirty-five dollars a week and start a 21 game and win it all back.

LEW ANDERSON: The Kyes band mostly worked all over Iowa and southern Minnesota, with a bit of Wisconsin and South Dakota. Every town of any size had a ballroom, and while it might not have had a band every night of the week, we certainly played every night of the week somewhere.

We played some old-time and novelty dances but most of the dance halls had a particular night for that kind of music—that's when you got the bands like The Six Fat Dutchmen, the dance halls usually brought in name bands on Saturdays.

Tom Talbert's first road trip was over quite quickly.

TOM TALBERT: Once the Kyes band hired a more experienced pianist, I got two weeks' notice. I went back to Minneapolis and got to writing for my own eleven-piece band again, and we actually got some jobs. I had Ira Pettiford and Leon Vaughan on trumpets and we got into the local ballroom and played at the Student Union. I also started writing a book for three saxes and one trumpet. I'd really liked the Ziggy Elman records that had come out with a similar lineup and we got work with it—mostly out-of-town high school proms and so on. Then in the fall I started going to university but I found it was just like going to high school again—it wasn't interesting at all. Just before Easter 1943 I was offered a place in Whit Thoma's band and I said I'd take it if they would also take a friend of mine, Bick Winston, on drums. They agreed and we took the milk train down to their base at Albert Lea, about a hundred miles southwest of Minneapolis. I particularly remember that it was Easter because we had Good Friday off and then we didn't have another night off before I left the band in June. It was not as polished a band as Kyes's, but it was a bit more advanced musically and hence a bit more interesting to us young guys. They played "Taking a Chance on Love," which had chords with fourths in them and other complexities that were over my head at that time, so I had to play softly.

Traveling with Whit's band, he had a regular sit-up type bus and we were supposed to go from hotel to hotel. The jumps were often as much as five hundred miles, and we wouldn't get in till afternoon. At one time, before the weather got warmer, the heater went out on the bus and Whit wouldn't get it fixed. Bick Winston and I organized a strike. We got into this hotel somewhere in South Dakota and we said *we're* not moving until you get it fixed. He did so but from then on he always referred to us as "my two red shirts." Whit did all the driving and, when I look back, one man doing a five-hundred-mile drive after just playing a gig is a pretty scary thought.

Don Davidson has vivid memories as a traveling musician and as a driver.

DON DAVIDSON: It was cold in those sleeper buses, you had bunks, some along the side and some were in the back. Later when I was with Jack Cole's band the bunks were forward—they had like a lounge in the back and the bunks were up front. There were many different ways to configure the space. Leo Pieper had a great trailer with space for the luggage underneath and the living space on top of that, which gave you some insulation from the cold. They had an observation area looking out over the top of the truck cab and they even had a small piano in there. That was really lush accommodation.

Driving the buses was a bit hairy, especially in the wintertime. Strickland's trailer was towed by a Ford, while Jack Cole's had a cab-over-engine Dodge. When I played in Jack's band, Jack had already gone in the army and it was run by a fellow named Rex Perry—Perry Duane Von Ringenthaler from Rice Lake, Wisconsin. Rex had a stiff left hip and couldn't use the clutch so he would always change gears by using the accelerator and listening for the exact time to change. He taught me how to do that and I could still do it, at least up till 1955. You have to hear from the whine of the gears when to slip it out and how far to push the accelerator in order to get it back into the next gear. When I was with the Stan Kenton band I used to bug Lew the driver: "Hey, let me drive this thing." It was a Greyhound and he never would let me do it. Understandably too. He would have been at terrible risk if anything had gone wrong. But once when we were leaving the Blue Note in Chicago, he was helping get stuff off the bandstand and load the bus. While he was doing that, I got the bus cranked up and I was sitting in the driver's seat when he came out. "What are you doing?" I said, "I'm going to drive it." He said, "Oh no you're not." Anyway we got on the Outer Drive; some of the guys were staying on the north side and I was standing in the well of the bus and I kept bugging him. Finally he just pulled over and says, "Ok, you smartass, drive it." So I did. I got in the driver's seat and I greased it through all four forward gears, never touching the clutch, and he's standing there and his jaw kept dropping and he says, "Why didn't you tell me you could do that?" I said "I've been telling you for the last few months."

LEW ANDERSON: Sleeper buses. There's a little town in Nebraska called Grand Island, a hundred miles west of Omaha, and three or four of us from college in Des Moines got on a train and went out there. We'd seen the ad in *Down Beat* magazine and when we got there, I think there were twelve bands booking out of that little town. And they're all off on Monday night and they're all off at the same bars so you know what was starting there.

They didn't have beds in the buses, because we weren't making long, long jumps, but all over the state of Nebraska, from Omaha to Scott's Bluff . . . they'd have cots that could sleep three or four and they dragged some of the women in there sometimes. It was kind of a crude thing but we were so young we didn't know what was going on. I was about nineteen. The bandleaders traveled in their own cars.

Traveling was not only uncomfortable but hazardous. In 1941, in a profile of a band tour, author Maurice Zolotow noted that although the Musicians Union had passed a law limiting the distance between engagements to four hundred miles per day, a number of bands experienced serious accidents, among them Jack Teagarden's, Charlie Barnet's, Tommy Dorsey's, and Sammy Kaye's. In 1940 there were seventy-eight accidents involving musicians on the road, in 1941 over one hundred.[1] The great tenor saxist Chu Berry was killed when the car in which he was traveling crashed on the way from a Cab Calloway gig in Brookfield, Ohio, to Toronto. The driver fell asleep. The same thing happened to trumpeter Clifford Brown on the Pennsylvania Turnpike in the 1950s.

Trumpeter Pee Wee Erwin recalled an incident while traveling with the Isham Jones band in the early 1930s.

PEE WEE ERWIN: Jones had a fleet of four Fords to transport the band, while he traveled in one of those big Lincolns that you see in old Chicago gangster movies. We were on the way to play at the Virginia Military Institute in Plattsburg, having spent the night in Roanoke, when we had a head-on collision. It was one of those things that happen so quickly there's no chance to do anything about it. We were going down the road and another car was approaching us from the other direction. At the moment we got even with it still another car suddenly pulled out from behind it and we met, radiator to radiator. It was a pretty serious accident. Saxophonist John Langsford was driving and violinist Eddie Stone was in the front seat with him. Eddie went flying through the windshield, and it took twelve or fifteen stitches in his forehead to sew up the cuts from the glass. At that he was lucky. I was in the backseat with the other violinist, Nick Hupfer. I remember being thrown against the side of the car—I suppose we were knocked about in every direction—and then I came together with Nick, obviously a much stronger object than I was, because I broke a shoulder from the contact. They shipped us to a hospital in Christiansberg and took X rays of our injuries. For some reason—either the X rays weren't dry in time or we refused to wait—they just bandaged us up and we took off for the job. I didn't know I had a broken shoulder because no one told me. I knew it was injured because it was wrapped up and it hurt, but that was it. Fortunately it was my left shoulder so I was able to play the job one-handed. It wasn't till I was in Boston a week later that I found out my shoulder had been broken.[2]

Forty years later, the road was still to be reckoned with, as tenor saxist Sal Nistico found, traveling with the Woody Herman band.

SAL NISTICO: I made it down to Houston, met the band, got on the bus, and met the driver. He was a German cat from Berlin. He'd studied eight years in mechanical engineering, and if you gave him raw materials and the proper tools he could probably MAKE you a bus. It turned out he needed that knowledge because he was so reckless. I remember on my first night, we were playing the gig and the bus driver was drinking and dancing . . . It was "hit and run," where you drive all day, play the gig, and then drive all night to the next town. The next town was Shreveport. We got back on the bus and everybody kind of crapped out and started to sleep. This bus driver cat had been dancing and drinking all night. I hadn't learned how to sleep on a bus yet and this was my first night. We were doing about eighty when we hit a patch of ice and actually made a complete 360-degree turn and kept going. This cat was a tremendous driver; he had incredible technique, and he needed it. I thought everybody was asleep but they were drinking. There were many bottles that had come out of cases and the guys were just sitting there. Then we came to a bridge. It was so narrow that it had a traffic light at one end. You were supposed to stop because if another bus or large vehicle were coming the other way there was no room to pass. Our driver ignored the red light and said, "We got it dicked" (his favorite saying), which, thank God, was not a "famous last words" statement. We "threaded the needle" between an oncoming bus and the railings. We actually shot out over this gorge, due to the air captured between the two buses. I tell you, everyone was in a crash position. Many of us thought we'd bought the farm. Like we were up all night after that experience. Bus drivers were very odd personalities. There was one cat that Nat Pierce called "the embalmer." He always wore a full uniform and white gloves and was always full of "speed." Another cat was "Marlon Brando," straight out of *The Wild One*, who would have got us killed if Nat hadn't busted him in the mouth. This cat jumped into the well of the bus to retrieve the wastebasket while keeping one hand on the wheel and no hands on the pedals while doing seventy-five miles per hour through North Carolina's back roads. I think many people overlook the danger factor of riding constantly on the bus for years with tired, sometimes juiced drivers doing inhuman distances. There have been some famous wrecks.[3]

Back to the early 1940s and the recollection of Lee Barron driving the Midnight Flyer, the sleeper bus for his band, which Tom Talbert would certainly have passed, on a dark night somewhere in Minnesota, Nebraska, or Wisconsin.

LEE BARRON: Lights of an approaching vehicle. The first I had encountered on the road since leaving Wichita. Interrupted my thoughts. The amber lights above the headlights indicated it was a semi rig and I wondered if it was another sleeper bus heading for a safe haven from the relentless torrents of rain. I had enough experience behind the wheel to know that when the truck came abreast of us, I would have zero visibility until my wipers could clear the cascading water from the windshield. Fortunately all went well. As the truck passed, I saw it was an oil tanker. I shivered slightly, recalling that on these narrow two-lane concrete highways there was only a scant six inches between buses and trucks when they passed each other. That six inches represented the margin between safety and possible death. I remember one morning, we disembarked the Midnight Flyer and turned around to discover a crease marking the entire length of the trailer. Although no one in the band, including the driver, could recall any bumps or jars, we had apparently brushed against an oncoming truck. Naturally, the men who had slept in the bunks on that side of the trailer were more than a bit shaken. The oil tanker disappeared and once again the pitch-blackness of night engulfed the highway and the countryside. The downpour continued. I hadn't received any signals from the musicians in the trailer and I assumed they decided the best way to pass the time was to sleep. The only means of communication between the cab and the trailer was a doorbell-type buzzer, Whenever an occupant in the trailer wanted to contact the driver he simply pressed the button which activated a buzzer and alerted the driver to pull over. There were times, though, when the apparatus didn't work. "What a helluva night" I thought, and hoped I'd get to Omaha without any problems. I thought of turning on the radio but decided not to because I didn't want to wake up the two men in the cab with me. I squirmed a bit, found a more comfortable position, and resumed my reverie.[4]

But the insouciance of youth, coupled with the thrill of playing music, kept such concerns away. And, as Tom recalls, there was also a sense of being part of something far larger.

TOM TALBERT: It's hard to imagine now, the number of bands that there were—every town of any decent size had a ballroom where the traveling or territory bands would play. You wouldn't believe how many bands there were . . . if you were up traveling at night you were constantly meeting them. You'd see another bus go by or you'd stop at a diner and somebody else would pull in at the same place while you were there.

LEW ANDERSON: There were so many bands out, often ten or twelve would be booked by one agent. All these little towns, especially in Minnesota in the summer, had a lot of dance pavilions by lakes so the bands all played the same places, eventually.

TOM TALBERT: This traveling was, of course, part of the glue that held the big band phenomenon together and one of the reasons why big bands are really over. There was a mystique that derived from the shared experiences of a bunch of guys who don't necessarily care for each other—the Ellington band was a good example—touring from Memphis to Minneapolis to Mobile in a cramped, crowded bus. An overall toughness developed that covered all kinds of sensitivities and emotions, from the brassy to the subtle, and it came out in the music and the regard the musicians would hold for each other in the future too.

Life on the road was not much different for musicians who came along after World War II. Ed Boike and Clyde Anderson, who played with Tom in the 1960s, caught the tail end of the life that Tom, Lew, and Don described.

ED BOIKE: I spent the years 1947 to 1949 touring with territory bands playing these rural dance halls. You'd be playing for farmers and small town people. We played dance music for people who didn't know how to dance. The bandleader had a few good arrangements, what they called specials, in his book, to lure decent musicians out from town to play on the band, but there would be a lot of "mickey mouse" music there too. A song called "Skirts" was still a big favorite in the 1950s and had been since 1930.

   We didn't have a whole lot to do with the people in the dance halls; we didn't talk to them much mainly because they didn't talk to us. There were some ballrooms we played where we'd be concerned for one another's safety. Some of the people would get aggravated and ugly. One of my fellow musicians, Roy Johnson, had a .45 pistol that I sometimes used to carry in those kinds of ballrooms.

CLYDE ANDERSON: We never really met the customers—you'd play a four-hour job and get one twenty- or thirty-minute intermission and that was it. Back on the bandstand, then straight onto the bus at the end of the gig. You didn't have a chance to socialize.

For an eighteen-year-old back in the summer of 1943, the ever present backdrop of the wars in Europe and the Pacific was a greater concern than road accidents or an unfriendly clientele. It was a year and a half since the Japanese had attacked Pearl Harbor and Adolf Hitler had declared Germany in a state of war with the United States.

TOM TALBERT: I'd written a few arrangements for Whit Thoma and they came out pretty well . . . the main problem was getting paid for them. He got mad at me when I got drafted. By this time everyone was going off to one or other of the services. I'd had my draft notice and one extension. This was easy if you were on the road but everyone was going off to war and I didn't apply for a second extension. I didn't feel right about it—I decided that when I got the next notice I would go quietly. I told Whit that I was leaving. He said, "You won't go, they don't want musicians." I replied, "You don't understand—I've gone." I left the band in some small town in North Dakota and had to get a bus and a train to get back to Minneapolis. Eventually I got a check for the arrangements, something like nine or twelve dollars.

NOTES

1. Maurice Zolotow, "One Night Tour" (c. 1941); reprinted in Eddie Condon, *Treasury of Jazz* (New York: Dial, 1956).
2. Pee Wee Erwin, *This Horn for Hire* (Metuchen, N.J.: Scarecrow, 1987).
3. Sal Nistico, quoted in William Clancy, *Woody Herman: Chronicles of the Herds* (New York: Schirmer, 1995).
4. Lee Barron, "Odyssey of the Midnight Flyer" (c. 1987); El Roy V. Lee, a.k.a. Lee Barron, privately published.

4

===

World War II

Tom Talbert's experiences in the U.S. Army were very different from anything he could have been expecting.

TOM TALBERT: I was home for a few days, then I had to report to the induction center at Fort Snelling, just outside Minneapolis. They put me in the Special Services Division of the army and sent me to San Luis Obispo in California. I traveled out on the train by myself and I remember two things in particular: we got into Oakland early in the morning and I was scheduled to take the night train out of San Francisco. The Bay Bridge wasn't built then; the train came right into the ferry terminal and I took the ferry across the bay to San Francisco. This was the first time I'd ever seen the ocean. I spent the day in San Francisco and remember that every bar you went past was playing the Mills Brothers' recording of "Paper Doll."

At San Luis Obispo we were supposed to have basic training. The noncoms were all from places like Georgia and Alabama and they gleefully told us, "The Special Service we want is you with a rifle in your hand." We did the usual drilling and marches but it wasn't too arduous. One thing that has stayed with me—we had a second lieutenant named Lyman Jones who had fought with the Lincoln Brigade in Spain during the civil war. I guess for that reason he was doomed to remain a second lieutenant. He and I became friends, which of course you weren't supposed to do—a private socializing with an officer—but I'd pick up some cans of beer and go up to his hut, in the evening sometimes, and we'd sit around and talk. He was from Ithaca, New York, and very literary, and he gave me a set of lyrics he'd written for a show at Ithaca College. I'd long been interested in Spain and I was fascinated by his experiences there. These days I often wonder what happened to him. The song was "As Soon as I Stop Remembering You," and I would record it with singer Joan Barton in Los Angeles after the war, but it never got released.

At this point fate or the unfathomable ways of the U.S. military stepped in.

TOM TALBERT: I was lucky because initially I was all set to go to North Africa. We'd had our shots and our haircuts in readiness, then I guess some early primitive version of a computer decided I should be put in an educational program called ASTP. So they sent me to Compton College here in Los Angeles, which was a gathering place for those who had been selected for what were called college units. I spent several weeks having refresher courses in the kind of advanced mathematics that I'd never learned in the first place. Then, and I've no idea why, perhaps something in my test results in high school put me on a course of training in engineering at De Paul University in Chicago. I was sent there for classes in physics and chemistry and I stayed for six months. We were housed in an old Catholic high school with bunks in what had been classrooms. At the end of our hall there was a door that led through to the other end of the building and quarters where the holy fathers lived.

Among the guys I met there was this one fellow from New York, Charles VanCook—a very smooth, good-looking type of guy. I'd been noticing that every other night after bed check he'd get up and pull on his clothes and stride out the door. I got to be friends with him and pretty soon I'm doing the same thing. We went out through what we called the holy passage—you'd go down the stairs and out through the priests' kitchen. There'd always be one of them making a ham sandwich or getting a glass of milk. They didn't turn us in but they'd say, "Don't be out too late, boys."

Sneaking out at night entailed more risk than the possibility of being caught.

TOM TALBERT: I got pneumonia and wound up in the hospital twice from going out without an overcoat in the winter and doing without sleep.

Bill Wolfe, another New Yorker who later collaborated on songs with Tom, was also sneaking out and had good connections at Garrick's Club, where the great New Orleans trumpeter Henry "Red" Allen and trombonist J. C. Higginbotham were resident. Tom and Bill made regular trips to the club and hung out with Allen and Higginbotham during intermission.

TOM TALBERT: Higginbotham was the nicest guy in the world. Also in the band at that time was Don Stovall—the loudest alto player that ever was. He could drown the trumpet and trombone out. I also got to know the fine jazz accordionist Art Van Damme who had a trio in a little bar on Randolph Street, just about under the el. He had a bassist and a guy playing vibes who was trying to learn alto and would go down a trapdoor behind the bar and spend the break practicing. Art and I became very friendly and I always used to look him up whenever I passed through Chicago. Later I wrote some arrangements for his group.

Tom also heard Roy Eldridge in a club opposite Garrick's, and New Orleans trumpeter Lee Collins, who was playing in an enormous, usually empty bar near De Paul. Tom had no band to write for or play in, but he found another outlet.

TOM TALBERT: At De Paul some of the students had formed a choral group and I wrote an arrangement of "The Very Thought of You" for them.

This might have been the most important and fateful arrangement Tom Talbert ever wrote.

As the war in the Pacific progressed, the need for ever more fighting men closed down the kinds of training units Tom had been attached to. The army took him back to California, put him in the infantry, and did everything to ensure that in the not too distant future he would be wading through the surf of some Pacific atoll into the teeth of enemy gunfire. Tom's main recollection of this period was of an air of unreality.

TOM TALBERT: Until this time I think I was too young to really be concerned. The Pacific war started to heat up and the program at De Paul was closed down. I got concerned then, especially when they put us on a train to Oregon and told us we were to join the 96th Infantry Division. We heard that it was what was known as a "fuckup" division—it had failed its overseas tests a couple of times and they would be starting over again when we showed up. Eventually we wound up back at San Luis Obispo, where we undertook amphibious training. Then we were sent to a staging area at Camp Beale, out in the desert. Once again I think I was too young to be really scared about the future. A lot of the guys were pretty stoic, and there was a feeling that the future was out of our hands. I think of this often because that 96th Division went to Okinawa, after which they required about a 50 percent replacement, and then they went on to Leyte in the Philippines and lost an awful lot of people there too. I try not to make too much of the fact that I escaped to an army band at Monterey, of all places.

That arrangement of "The Very Thought of You" for the choral group in Chicago may well have saved his life. Bud Bowen, one of his fellow soldier-students in Chicago, was now at Fort Ord near Monterey, a large staging post for military personnel and the home of not just one but three military bands. Bud sang Tom's praises and told the special services officer there that Tom was a "great arranger." This led to a phone call encouraging him to make the trip to Fort Ord to meet the officer in charge of band activities. But first he had to get there.

TOM TALBERT: I remember the trip from Camp Beale to Fort Ord very well. I hitched a ride with someone who was flying down to Salinas in a twin-engine Beechcraft and then took a bus to Fort Ord. I can't remember how I got back to Camp Beale afterward though. Captain Anderson, the Special Service officer at Fort Ord, who happened to be from Minneapolis, suggested it might be possible to get me attached to one of the bands as arranger. There were a couple of bands—the 67th, and the 64th which I wound up with. I think there was a third too. Captain Anderson said, "I think you'd be best off with Mr. Walters, the warrant officer with the 64th Army Ground Force band." And boy was he right; Mr. Walters was so good to me. The captain and I got in his jeep and roared off to the barracks, where he introduced me to Walters, telling him that I was a great arranger. He didn't know that. He'd been told by Bud Bowen and Bud didn't know much either. I went back to Camp Beale feeling quite excited and hopeful. A short time later, one morning at rollcall, I heard, "Talbert, fall out and collect your barracks bag."

Fate had smiled on Tom twice. He was no longer likely to die on some South Pacific beachhead and he had a very good band to write for, full-time. There were some excellent musicians at Fort Ord at that time, including trombonist Milt Bernhart and trumpeter Wes Hensel, who were members of the 67th Army Ground Force band.

Milt Bernhart had been on the base a little longer than Tom and his induction into the band was even more dramatic.

MILT BERNHART: Fort Ord really had been a fort—it was big and stood on Monterey Bay. There were two bands there when I was passing through on my way to the South Pacific. I'd already done my basic training in Texas, at Camp Hood. That was rough—I lived through it and some didn't. At the time I was drafted, the war in Europe was at a critical stage, and the army was at this time not going to give me a chance to get in a band or even ask, for that matter. So eventually one day at Fort Ord, I'm standing in the company street, getting ready to ship out and say good-bye to everything. We knew that we were being readied for an invasion of Japan and that wasn't going to be easy. I was prepared for not coming back. While I'm standing there, somebody called my name. I heard it faintly. Sometimes I look back and wonder. Did it happen? Somebody said, "Hey, is your name Bernhart?" We were lined up waiting for the truck. The truck was momentarily due—lots of trucks, there were about ten thousand of us in the company street. But somebody heard somebody call my name. I may not have. So I yelled, "It's me." A buddy I had made, a very young kid, eighteen like me, said "Whadja do, Bernhart?" I said, "I don't know, I didn't do anything that I can account for." Then a sergeant showed up and said, "Follow me." I felt I'm in trouble of some sort. It turned out that two or three days earlier, one of the two bands on the post had medically discharged one of the trombonists and they were looking for a replacement. And it could have been anyone. No one in the band knew of a replacement, and someone took their finger and went down the list of the ten to twenty thousand soldiers on the base and came to my name quickly, probably because it starts with a B. We were getting ready to leave; in another five minutes I would have been gone.

When you signed up for the service, if you had a trade or profession, you listed it. Most eighteen-year-olds didn't, but because I was proud of what I'd been doing I put "Musician: trombone" beside my name. I followed the sergeant and he came to one of the band barracks and took me in and said, "This is the guy you called for. And everybody looked at me and I was nobody, to be sure. No background—I was just out of high school for about six months and I'd been on a couple of bands, but they didn't make me anybody. I still had to prove myself. I had to get a horn, which I didn't have—they dragged out an army issue trombone and I had to play it. Somehow I managed, with a different mouthpiece and a bad horn. Something was with me. People have said, "You were being watched over." I'm tempted to say that sometimes but then I think of those fellows who were standing in the company street with me who weren't watched over. Because most of them didn't come back. They went to Okinawa and we lost more soldiers trying to take Okinawa than in any other battle of the war. I don't think I would have made it back. Maybe I was watched over or was it pure, pure luck. And the latter is what I believe. It's just luck. I was saved, but what about those who weren't. I think about them—I think about the kid who was my buddy. I said good-bye to him and I got a few postcards from him. I managed to keep in touch and somehow he seemed to know that I was going to be there. Then he sent me a post-card, which was all censored and then the cards stopped coming. A day doesn't go by, not one single day, that I don't think about that and be very grateful that I was standing in the right place at the right time. If God put me there, wonderful! I just can't buy that because what about the rest of the guys? Not to mention the Holocaust. Nobody really has a good answer, so I'm all for luck. Most of the things that happen to musicians that we know who made good happen through luck. Take Henry Mancini, who happened to be at Universal Pictures just writing music for things like newsreels, when a movie came up that nobody wanted to work on. It's nothing that was preordained or that he had planned on. But that started him off—it was an Orson Welles picture, *A Touch of Evil.* He was standing in the right place, and that's a lot of it, especially in music and show business.

Thus far Tom had also been in the right place at the right time. The band that he was attached to played retreat each night and made many trips up and down the state to sell war bond drives and generally bolster the war effort.

TOM TALBERT: I arrived on the band in July 1944 and it was the first time it had a full-time arranger. The nucleus of the outfit was a National Guard band from Carlisle, Pennsylvania. The lead alto player, Jimmy Morrow, from Pittsburgh, was a really good jazz clarinetist; there was quite a solid trombonist and the trumpets, who were from the original National Guard band, were led by a guy named Shoup, who played loud and high. The rhythm section was pretty good on the whole, and the drummer was a good drummer. The piano player, Johnny McAteer from Boston, was basically a society-type player; he was very schooled and played well. Overall, it wasn't all that bad. Every so often there would be tensions between some of the younger players in the band who thought that the older original National Guard players didn't swing, and I was often badgering Mr. Walters to get a more dynamic lead trumpet or a better bass player. The band had gone into the army very early in the war and the fact that Mr. Walters had managed to keep them in the U.S. all this time was quite remarkable. On one occasion when I was making a particular nuisance of myself he said, "Sometimes we have to work with the situation we've got—for instance do you think I really like going bowling with the major every Wednesday? But this is what keeps us in the U.S. and enables us to play nice jobs and lets the married guys live off the base, in Carmel with their wives." That was a good lesson to a young "red shirt."

There was a constant demand for new arrangements and Tom could write virtually anything he wanted, eventually casting his net as widely as Debussy's *Afternoon of a Faun* and Saint-Saëns's *The Swan.*

TOM TALBERT: I must have felt a bit of trepidation at first, but once I got into it and started writing, the guys in the band really became my fans. The routine was relaxed, compared to the infantry, although I obviously had to get up at the same time as everyone else, and so on. I was free to write whatever I wanted and there was no "set amount" that I had to complete. That problem never arose anyway because I was writing prolifically. I didn't try to emulate or copy other bands because, quite frankly, I didn't know how to. I didn't have enough knowledge to be able to figure out what other arrangers had done. I didn't want to write the saxes in the Miller style—I liked some of what Ellington did but mostly his ballads. I didn't go for his uptempo things because I didn't like the way Sonny Greer played the drums. We used to play for the Officers Club with a septet and I wrote some charts for that group. "Love Is a Pleasure," originally called "Never Meant for Me," was something I wrote to feature Don Richwine on alto with the septet.

Saxophonist Don Richwine, who became a close friend, remembers Tom.

DON RICHWINE: A fresh young kid, just out of high school and full of life, joining the band and writing music of a sophistication way beyond his years.
   One night I came back to the barracks late and the lights were all out. As I made my way to my bunk I heard a "pssst" from over by the window. There was a full moon and Tom was sitting on his bunk actually writing an arrangement of "Claire de Lune." He sang some of the bars he'd written, softly. I said, "How can you see to write?" He replied, "The moonlight's enough, and anyway, it's giving me inspiration."

Don Richwine agrees that the 64th band provided the young, inexperienced arranger with the perfect laboratory in which to experiment and learn what worked and what didn't and why.
   Unlike the 67th, which Tom feels was more of a military band, the 64th appears to have benefited from the entrepreneurial skills of Mr. Walters, who actively sought and found nonmilitary venues for the band. Undoubtedly the acquisition of Tom as a full-time arranger

was a big help. The band crisscrossed California, playing bond drives and military bases. On one memorable weekend they played the famous Hollywood Canteen—the rest and recreation facility for servicemen that had been set up by the film industry and was staffed by movie stars. Bands that played there benefited from a network broadcast, and on this occasion Tom got a boost to his confidence as an arranger.

TOM TALBERT: I'd just finished an arrangement of "By the River Sainte Marie." It undoubtedly reflected some Lunceford influences, I guess, and Mr. Walters closed the broadcast with it. The crowd went wild, they really loved it, and they applauded so much that Walters played it for them again, twice. I was learning as I was writing for the band. Although sometimes something I wrote didn't turn out exactly as I thought it would, I don't remember anything actually not working. I don't recall Mr. Walters ever saying, "Don't bother to write something like that again." My biggest accolade came after a few months, when he asked me to start writing a fourth trumpet part . . . he wanted to play my music too. I do remember that he asked me to write a chart on "Sentimental Journey," which I did without reference to the Les Brown hit version of the time. I think my version was more Ellington influenced—I remember writing a clarinet and a trombone in with the saxes. I guess we'll never know—the music is probably at the bottom of Monterey Bay by now.

We played a string of navy bases in the San Diego area and while there I heard Artie Shaw's new band—the one with Roy Eldridge, Herbie Steward, Dodo Marmarosa, Barney Kessel, and Lou Fromm. Little did I know that I'd be working with most of them in a couple of years. If someone had predicted it, I wouldn't have believed them.

Captain Walters helped Tom secure a tiny foothold in that world.

TOM TALBERT: The Charlie Barnet band was also working in the area and Captain Walters made sure I met with Charlie. We had a drink and I wound up writing an arrangement of Juan Tizol's "Lost in Meditation" for Barnet. Trombonist Tommy Pedersen (who was on the band) said Charlie really liked it and, years after, when the Barnet band was no more, Tommy was featuring the arrangement with his own outfit.

Milt Bernhart has many memories of this period in their lives.

MILT BERNHART: At Fort Ord, there were two bands. The other band, the one Tom was in, was our rival. They wanted to be better.

We marched every day for the general, and we played the soldiers out, when they got on trucks to go overseas. Every night at six o'clock we played what they call Retreat, and the band would have to march in formation in front of the general and play something like "Colonel Bogey." The likes of piano players like Tom Talbert were given cymbals or a bass drum. The best part of Fort Ord was that it was very windy. I remember one occasion when we were marching into the teeth of a high wind, which was so strong we weren't moving. Our feet were moving but our bodies couldn't and the guy with the big sousaphone was actually moving backward. The general didn't understand the physical reasons and was angry. "What's the matter with that band?" he was shouting. Another time the trombonist next to me lost his slide while we were marching. We had some sort of a long reach on one piece and he went all the way out to the seventh position and his slide kept on going and left him. Behind him were about seven thousand paratroopers in full uniform and boots and they all marched on that slide. When we retrieved it, I'd never seen anything so thin. It was paper thin, and I lived in dread of it happening to me. But we also had fun—we both had swing bands. At Fort Ord, there was a gigantic structure called the Soldiers Building. I believe they called it a club, but it was as big as an airplane hangar and it could hold as many as a thousand dancers on the floor. Three times a week they had dances for the soldiers on the base and whomever they could get for a date. Lady soldiers, WAACS, and others from the local towns of Salinas, Monterey, Carmel. So our band played there for dancing and we were free to play whatever we wanted. We had a lot of Count Basie stocks, which of course we got out when we had the great experience of Jo Jones from the Basie band playing with us. Jo was passing through Fort Ord on his way overseas and he rehearsed with us. The first number we got out was "Down for Double" and the leader, a clarinet player from Detroit, counted it in. As we started playing, we realized that Jo wasn't. We stopped and the leader looked at Jo and said, "Mr. Jones, maybe you didn't hear me beat off the number." And Jo said with a smile a mile wide, "Yeah, I heard it—go ahead." And we started again and still he didn't play. The leader said, "Mr. Jones, what is the problem?" And Jo said, "There isn't a problem. I just wanted to see if you could play without me." And it was as though someone had lit a light just over my head and about half of the others in the band. Wes Hensel learned something too. We all believed until that moment that without a drummer you couldn't have a band. That's how it had been sold to me. Jo said, "Let's see if you can do it without me. Because if you can't there isn't a thing I can do." It was the revelation of my life. So we called off the rehearsal and started having section rehearsals, and, heaven help us, we couldn't play together without somebody keeping time. But before it was over we were doing it. Ever since that time drummers who insist that they're swinging the band leave me a little bit cold. The band is supposed to swing without them. Don Lamond was my idea of a prime swing band drummer. He'd add little accents and details between the band's figures to send them on. And that wasn't happening with other drummers—they usually played the same figures as the brass played. And that became a horror for me. In studio work that's all I heard. I remember on a Billy May record date a very good drummer coming over and copying down every figure on the first trumpet part. He was going to play them on his snare drum, which is insane. I think I talked to him and he got mad at me.

I saw Jo in later years in New York—he'd started hanging around Charlie's Tavern, always in a dark suit, waiting for someone who needed a drummer at short notice. He always remembered me, and I thought he wouldn't. It is a plum of my existence knowing Jo Jones—and he was in the army with us.

Eventually Tom was able to move off the base.

TOM TALBERT: At one point the first trombone took an extended furlough for at least a month and I was able to rent his house in Carmel.

MILT BERNHART: Carmel was a very small artist colony in those days. A lot of well-known painters, writers, musicians lived there. There were no streetlights, by city ordinance; trees grew in the middle of the roads, by city ordinance. There were a couple of very, very good Russian restaurants and they had a USO for soldiers, but soldiers never went there. Just a handful of musicians from the bands. It was a very well kept secret. They always had food wall to wall and nobody but us to eat it.

TOM TALBERT: Looking back, I think this was the most intensive listening period of my life. My mother came out to visit and I had her bring my phonograph and some of my records. Some of the guys in the band used to come by and we'd sit around and drink wine and I'd sharpen up the cactus needle and play them records by people like Billie Holiday and Lester Young and Teddy Wilson. They really hadn't heard much of this kind of jazz, mainly because it was rarely on the radio.

I was also friendly with a guy named Toby who was the provost in charge of the military police, who was nuts about music and always wanted to talk about it. While in the house in Carmel, the MPs were continually knocking on the door and saying, "We just took this fifth of scotch off a sailor; Toby said to bring it up and give it to you." Whenever Toby came by he'd always have a couple of pints that they'd lifted from someone they'd arrested. I also met my first great love in Monterey, once again through the kind offices of Bud Bowen. This was a local girl, Margaret Hartigan, with whom I eventually lived in Los Angeles. She was the society editor of the *Monterey Herald* newspaper and her parents were the caretakers of what is known as the "First Theater"—the first theater ever built in California. Margaret was very well read and guided me to local writers like Robinson Jeffers and John Steinbeck.

At this point fate was still smiling on Tom. Instead of being shipped off to the Pacific, he was living in Carmel with plenty to eat, liquor courtesy of the MPs, a good band to write for, and a beautiful woman. "Fate smiling" are not his words, though. He has always been uneasy about this good fortune and has never forgotten the fate of his friends who were shipped off to Leyte.

But there was, inevitably, a sense that the war was winding down and life, and careers, could be resumed. Tom's writing definitely impressed the guys who played it.

TOM TALBERT: Toward the end of the war, several of the fellows in the band, good friends of mine, were having discussions about "what's Tom going to do?" not what were they going to do. "What band should Tom be writing for?" We had a big radio in the rehearsal room and on the weekends they would have that on and listen to bands from different places. I came back one time and they were all excited. "We heard the band that you should go arrange for." It turned out it was someone named Johnny Richards. There was another remote broadcast the following Saturday afternoon, which I heard and it was indeed a very exciting band. After I got out of the army he was one of the people I did look up.

In the meantime, the military was not quite through with PFC Talbert.

TOM TALBERT: When the war in Europe was over, Fort Ord became a rumor mill. Most worrying was the one that all those who had not been overseas would be sent either to Japan or as occupation troops in Germany. I was concerned because I was only "attached" to the band and could have been whisked away to clean latrines or worse at a moment's notice. My luck was still holding as I got a discharge in June

1945 that said "no suitable assignment." I can never thank Mr. Walters enough. I returned to Fort Snelling in Minneapolis to be discharged.

Just like the hero in one of the movie serials of the day, Tom was suddenly, "with a single bound," almost unaccountably free. Any sense of unreality must have been internalized psychologically in the form of a recurrent nightmare. From then on, throughout his life Tom was visited by a dream: he would answer a knock on his door and find a pair of military policemen with a half-ton truck, saying, "There was a mistake in your discharge, Private, we have orders to take you back to the barracks."

5

==

Interlude: Johnny Richards

Perhaps the only major influence on Tom Talbert, Johnny Richards, was at this time leading a stylistically very modern big band. Richards, born John Cascales, was a highly skilled writer and musical director who had worked with composer Victor Young in Hollywood for years and "really knew what instruments could do." His 1944 band, on the cusp of bop, was more advanced than other bands Tom was hearing at the time. But the influences were probably more in the areas of complexity and attention to detail, rather than writing style, as Tom Talbert's records don't sound much like Johnny Richards's. It's also likely that Richards's approach to running and rehearsing an orchestra rubbed off on Tom too. He feels that most of the influence had been absorbed by 1950 and pianist Claude Williamson, who knew both writers well, told Tom that his pieces swung more than Richards's did.

Baritone saxist Don Davidson, later an important member of the Tom Talbert band, was listening to Johnny Richards too.

DON DAVIDSON: When I was in high school I used to listen to remotes from somewhere out at Hermosa Beach. Late at night in Iowa, we'd get them—and I remember I was very impressed by John's band. His approach to writing was again completely different from what you ordinarily heard on record and on the radio. I think, to a certain degree, Johnny influenced Tom.

CLYDE HANKINS

I was born in 1918 near Amarillo, Texas. My dad was a cowboy and ran a spread of cattle for Week Valentine—I was seven or eight years old. My dad lived on a horse then. There

47

were no fence lines—the range was all open. I was never a country player though, and when I was about fourteen my dad said, "Son, you like the wrong kind of music." He was a cowboy and wanted me to play hoedowns and stuff—but I always liked jazz. My favorite band at that time was the Sons of the Pioneers because they had a guitarist named Karl Farr who played more guitar than most people did then, and I listened to the band for him. I also liked the Bob Wills band and later I knew some of the guys in it.

After a couple of years my mother wanted to go to San Diego so we moved and my father went into carpentry to try to make a living—if he made a buck a day he was lucky. I was making more money at thirteen, playing banjo for old time dances than he was as a carpenter. I was getting three or four bucks a night, and that was good money in 1932. This is how it happened: I walked into this place and there was this little old lady on piano, and a drummer—that's all. She rented the hall, charged thirty-five cents admission, and she packed three hundred people in there. She sold pie and ice cream at intermission too. I walked up and said, "I know all the songs you're playing." She said "At your age?" I said, "I know every one of them." "What do you play?" "Banjo." "Get the banjo." I had it in the car; my dad always took it with us. I sat in and we played "Sweet Jennie Lee (From Sunny Tennessee)" and the minuet, the Paul Jones, the Varsovienne ("Put Your Little Foot Right Out"). After I'd played the whole job, she paid me and hired me and I was with her for two years playing for these old-time dances. I got two to four bucks a night plus pie and ice cream They were lean times and most kids my age had nothing, but thanks to music I always had money.

I wanted to play jazz, so I'd go to the black hotel—the Creole Palace on Market Street in San Diego. I said to the guys, "I'd like to sit in." They were playing "The Sheik of Araby." They said, "Do you know this song?" "I sure do." "Then get your guitar." They said, "If you know the tunes, then come back every Sunday and sit in." And that's where I began to learn jazz guitar. I can't remember their names now, but there were some good, good players. I saw the Chick Webb band that far back, at a skating rink.

Then at the World's Fair in San Diego in 1935 I heard a guy

by the name of Bud Lee play jazz guitar. In those days if you could just "chunk" rhythm you were considered pretty good. I got acquainted with him—I loved the way he played. He did "All the Things You Are." In those days nobody could play that—very few—it's a tough song, changes key about five times. I thought, "Man if I could ever do that." So I got busy and I got into jazz and I stayed there.

There was a big ballroom in San Diego—Ratliff's Ballroom and around 1937 or 1938 they were looking for a guitarist-banjoist-vocalist. The band was led by Bud Lovell, and they had a great tenor player named Dick Ryan. It was a mickey mouse band but people loved us and we played five nights a week. Ratliff was an old style, high-class guy—he'd throw you out on your ear if you caused any trouble. Later I played in a small group with Bill Beaumont, the pianist/vibes player from the Lovell band.

After my stint with the Johnny Richards band I went to New York. It was Joe Vernon, Johnny's drummer, who said to me, "Would you like to go back east? Bob Astor is looking for a guitarist-vocalist and a drummer." The reason he was looking for a drummer was that Shelly Manne was leaving him to go with Les Brown. So we met Astor at the Pittsburgh Hotel in Pittsburgh, Pennsylvania, played the gig that one night, and then joined the band and went from there to Richmond, Virginia. When we got to New York I got to meet my favorite guitarist, Alan Reuss. From New York City we went to Youngstown, Ohio, for two weeks, then Cleveland, Canton, Flint, Michigan, then back to New York, where the band broke up. After Bob Astor I went with Jerry Wald.

I went to hear him at the Roseland Ballroom in Brooklyn—later it burned down. I met the band and they said to Jerry, "Either hire this guy on guitar or we're all going back to LA." They were just kidding of course, but Jerry said, "The new contract allows for a guitar player, so go get your guitar." That afternoon I got fitted for a uniform and we followed Harry James into the Blue Room of the Lincoln Hotel. Wald was a good clarinetist, even if he wasn't a Benny Goodman—we had Buddy Combine on drums, Larry Elgart on alto (a great guy), Ray Sims and Ralph Pfeffner on trombones, and Gordon Boswell on trumpet. Gordon had been in the Richards band with me.

Then I got my "greeting" in the mail from Uncle Sam and went into the navy. When I joined up I took an entrance exam and I did well so they let me choose my school. Amazingly for a guitarist/vocalist I chose diesel engines and they moved me to the destroyer base at San Diego. I was one of the top ten in the class so they said, "How would you like to be an instructor?"

After the war I went into the heavy equipment business. My stepfather really didn't like music and said, "Son, why don't you learn a man's job?" I was married and I didn't want to travel anymore so I told him, "Okay. I'll do whatever you want," and started working in his asphalt plant. I loved it and also carried on playing guitar at weekends. In 1952 I went back to Texas, to Lubbock, selling tractor parts. Right around that time TV came in and they booked me on a cowboy show when they found out I played guitar. They loved the way I played—so I started playing four hours a week on Circle 13—that was the name of the TV station. There was only one station, so if you tuned in you had to watch us. I sang, did little skits, on these one-hour shows around five or six o'clock in the evening. Some were around noon, and they were all live. We had a pianist named Sam Baker who was a good jazz player too. We also did an hour a week playing jazz. Then I started playing with a great trio—organ, drums, and myself on guitars and vocals. Still in Lubbock I started selling organs and guitars then a friend went to Albuquerque and liked it and said to me get over here—there's good business here. In 1970 I got into wholesale out of LA—traveling to every music store in New Mexico, Texas, and Colorado. I still played too. I've been married sixty years and I teach guitar and still gig—I think I play much better today than I did when I played with the big bands.

Clyde Hankins is a guitarist who remembers, and played with, an earlier edition of the Richards band.

CLYDE HANKINS: I was with Johnny Richards from 1941 to 1942. He begged me not to go to New York, but I went and I missed out on the recording session for Decca in 1942. I knew Stan Kenton well, and although I never played in his band I played a lot of dates with some of his musicians, particularly alto saxist Jack Ordean, and many hours at Sherman's Dine & Dance with tenor saxist Red Dorris. I went down to

Sherman's to hear the Johnny Richards band—it was the first band he had, I think, and there were studio players in it, I believe. I got acquainted with the bass player, Jack Cascales, Johnny's brother who introduced me to Johnny. I thought the quality of the band was unreal . . . I went back to hear them, night after night. Finally I said to Jack, "You've got to get me on this band." He said he'd see what he could do. Although Johnny said bring your guitar down to rehearsal, it was my singing that got me the job, not my guitar playing. I was just getting into soloing, but I played good rhythm and later I had a solo feature on "One O'Clock Jump." I was a good singer though—Johnny said I could have been number one if I'd stayed with him.

At the audition I sang "My Prayer (Is to Linger with You)," and Johnny said, "When can you start?" Even then Johnny was playing tough, complicated arrangements. He had a chart on "Intermezzo" and he had me singing songs like "Sand in My Shoes" and "Maria Elena." I was with him for only two weeks before we moved to the Paramount Theater in Los Angeles, and was I nervous! The bandstand was way back and I felt like I had to walk the length of a football field to get to the mike. So I have to sing "Maria Elena," and it's like my feet aren't even touching the floor, I'm so nervous. Johnny comes out to me and takes off my coat and unties my bow tie, and he says, "You either do what you can do or I'm going to undress you, right here on the stage." People thought it was part of the act, but from that time on I wasn't nervous anymore. The next thing's incredible . . . in the floor show there was an act—two black guys called Stump and Stumpy. I was in my dressing room and there was a knock on the door—"Hey man, what you doing?" It was Stump and Stumpy. "We just wanted you to meet a lady friend of ours—Billie Holiday." I'm a young kid, twenty-two, and they brought her in to meet me. We had a great visit for about a half an hour—Johnny Richards came in too. Billie was so nice.

After two weeks at the Paramount we went on a road tour that also featured the Andrews Sisters. We played Oakland, San Francisco, Reno Nevada, Manteca, San Luis Obispo, and all up and down the coast, back to LA and then San Diego.

Charlie Christian came to San Francisco while I was there and my brother said, "I'm going, come with me." But I had a date and wouldn't go. My brother came back and said, "I've just heard the greatest guitarist ever." I never got another chance to hear him and the date wasn't worth it either.

On this road tour, we traveled by car and I rode with Johnny and the vocalist Pat Kaye in Johnny's car. I was young and didn't have much money so we got a motel room that was big enough for the three of us. Johnny was a wonderful guy—he loved me, he really did. I think I got to him through my mother's fried potatoes and onions and chicken fried steak. I had him out to the house and he just took me under his wing. He liked the way I sang. He was just a great down-to-earth guy and he didn't butter up to anybody for gain. He was very independent. He drank a lot—but I never saw him when he couldn't handle it. He'd take a fifth of scotch up to his room and write an arrangement and copy it and have it all done for rehearsal next day and he didn't even need a piano. Then he'd sit at the bar while he rehearsed the band making observations like "Hey, that should be an A-flat over there."

When I was in LA with Johnny's band I used to go out to Bourston's. The house pianist was Jimmy Rowles and a lot of great players used to come out to jam—guys from Woody Herman's band, Al Hendrickson, Ray Linn, trombonist Skip Layton. Skip was the greatest trombone player—he could swing like nobody's business. Skip and I were close buddies; he was on the Richards band when we were in San Diego. If the band wasn't cookin', Johnny would say, "Put your horns down. Skip—come out here." And he'd have Skip play a couple of numbers just with the rhythm section and that would just kill the band and then they'd be cooking.

Bassist Howard Rumsey of The Lighthouse All-Stars fame was very impressed by the Richards band.

HOWARD RUMSEY: There was a soldier just out of the army who was hanging around the band and bringing arrangements—that was Pete Rugolo. It was a great band. Richards was too much—he was something else, I loved that guy. He had Andy Russell playing drums—Andy's name then was Andy Rabajos. And I'm the guy who got him in that band—I heard him playing with another band—Don Ramone . . . a band with all those Latin cats in it. It was a great band too—I found out about that down at the Hollywood Legion Stadium, when I was playing with Vido Musso and they had the jitterbug contest there. The dancers were in the ring and the band was up in the balcony. There was Vido's band and Don Ramone. We were playing transcribed Lunceford charts; then Don Ramone came on and wiped us right out. Oh, they had some great players—they had Joe Howard on trombone and Andy Russell on drums.

Trombonist Lionel Sesma was playing in the later edition of the Johnny Richards band that so impressed Tom Talbert.

LIONEL SESMA: I joined the Johnny Richards orchestra when I was about nineteen, in late 1943, at the recommendation of an alto player who happened to have been playing lead with Johnny at the time. His name was Joe Glorioso. I'd previously worked with Joe in Ken Baker's band—no relation to the singer. This Kenny Baker was a drummer. I must have gone very highly recommended because I didn't even audition. The band opened at a club called the Del Rio down in San Pedro. We were there for several weeks and it was a very exciting time for me because I had never played such interesting charts before. The drummer/vocalist was Andy Russell; Bus (Bob) Graettinger was playing baritone sax; we had a lot of Pete Rugolo arrangements, one of which was called "Rasputin's Laundry." Pat McCarthy was on guitar. I had no close relationship with Johnny, who was very much aloof from the rest of the band both socially and musically. He was far beyond us musically.

He was dead serious about being a successful bandleader—absolutely. He'd been very successful in other areas like screen writing—he'd been Victor Young's ghostwriter. He was sincere in looking to be a success, but in a way I think he was too musical to make it as a bandleader. He could write all these things away from the piano, just sit with the score sheet in front of him and write the parts for all of the instruments . . . away from the piano . . . he'd hear all these things in his head. He was a very capable conductor; he interacted okay with the audience but I couldn't say he was charismatic. He took all the tenor sax solos but he wasn't an instrument-playing bandleader like Tommy Dorsey or Benny Goodman. He didn't center himself in the arrangements and as a tenor man, he was no Tony Pastor. But he loved to play, he wanted to be involved.

Lionel's memories of Johnny Richards are slightly different from Clyde's in one respect:

LIONEL SESMA: On the other hand, in terms of his relations with the other musicians I'd put it at about 2 or 3 on a scale of 1 to 10. Nothing offensive but he just kept a distance. We didn't have our own bus; we traveled by train for the most part. I don't remember Johnny ever being with us on the train so he probably flew.

I don't think he could have been successful sticking to the music we were playing—it was just too much for the public. Kenton had a lot more commercial stuff than Johnny had, and Kenton was very charismatic too, with a stage presence second to none, which Johnny did not have.

Lionel Sesma, whose parents were Mexican, was not highly amused at being called "Pancho" by Richards.

LIONEL SESMA: Johnny liked to pass himself off as coming from a Castilian Spanish ancestry. In fact I found out much later that the "Cascales" side of his family was Mexican, just like mine.

BILLY MORRIS

My father owned a bar in Detroit during the Depression that had a three-piece band playing in it and somehow I got hold of an old cornet. Once I got some sounds out of it, I must have beaten those guys in the trio half to death, playing with them, wrong notes and all. I started playing trumpet properly in high school. In those days I liked Louis and Roy Eldridge and Ray Nance. By the time I was twenty-one I was playing with the Carol Lofner band in Texas, in the Texarkana and Dallas areas. Most of the music consisted of stock arrangements and we traveled around by bus.

In 1942 I decided to go to Los Angeles and went out there with a friend. When we got there I don't think we had more than six dollars between us. We were walking down Hollywood Boulevard and ran into another friend from Detroit who was working at Earl Carroll's Vanities and got us jobs as bus boys there. They put me with a waiter who had the tier next to the pit band, and when one of the trumpet players was drafted I got his job. I did that for two or three weeks. Then I got an offer to go with an all-colored band—Harlan Leonard's Rockets. I'd become friendly with bass player Bob Kesterson who'd played with Stan Kenton, and we both went on the Leonard band. We played down on Central Avenue at the Dunbar Hotel, I think it was the Plantation Club. Playing with the Harlan Leonard band was the greatest experience of my life and I was just twenty-three! One of my most vivid memories was when we went to Phoenix and played in an open pavilion on this Sunday night. There was segregation then, and it was an all-black audience—Wynonie Harris was singing the blues and all the women were crowding round the front of the bandstand and were so moved they were all crying. I felt such emotion that I got tears in my eyes too, and I looked across at my fellow trumpeter James Ross and he just said, "I know."

I had no problem being white in a black band, and James really took care of me. From there I got an offer to go with Freddie Slack. After I left Earl Carroll's, Lyle Griffin of Atomic Records, who also played trombone, had a group at a place called the Waldorf Cellar on Main Street that included bass player Howard Rumsey. I played down there a few times and on one occasion clarinetist Barney Bigard came in. Barney asked me if I'd like to go with Freddie and I did, and stayed with him for about a year during which we made some movies and some recordings, things like that.

One time Barney said he wanted to take me fishing. I said, "But I don't have any fishing gear." He said not to worry, we've got everything. So he drove me over to this little old house and this little old man came out and we got into his car, an old Plymouth or something. We went way out on Santa Monica Boulevard—out where it was mostly swamp and drainage ditches at that time. They got nets out of the trunk and we caught about two big sacks of crawfish. We did this all day long and I'm talking to this little old guy and I notice that Barney would call him "Hey kid," so on and so on. It turned out that it was Kid Ory! We went back to Ory's house that night where his wife had built a big bonfire and had half a big oil drum filled with boiling water ready to cook the crawfish. I think Kid Ory's house was probably in Watts, but I'm not sure now.

I played with Boyd Raeburn on a tour in 1946 that also had Dodo Marmarosa on the band. We were in Wichita and had to get up early to catch a plane. We went to the airport, but there was no plane. It was late, so some of the guys went up on to the roof where resurfacing work had been going on and there were big piles of gravel. It was warm in the sun and some of the guys lay down and went to sleep. We were called when the plane was ready and we're taxiing down the runway before anyone realized that Dodo was still up on the roof asleep.

I left Los Angeles in 1946 and went to Las Vegas and played around the hotels for two years. My wife had a brother here in Albuquerque and we visited him. Things were so nice and relaxed here compared to Vegas that I went back and played out my contract and came here. I've been here ever since. I still played but there wasn't enough work to live on. My brother-in-law who was an ironworker got me into the ironworkers union and I did that for twenty-nine years. In my spare time I had an eighteen-piece band at the Hilton here that played for all the Las Vegas acts that came in—I had that for a year and a half then went back to club jobs.

In some ways I regretted giving up full-time music, but then some of the guys I knew who were still on the road would come to town and I would see that they were still in the same fix—scraping enough money for a hotel room—and some of them were dopers too. So in that respect I'm glad I made the decision. Then again, doing construction work, high up on a steel beam in cold weather I often thought, "What in hell am I doing here, I could be playing in a nice warm comfortable club."

Billy Morris is a fine trumpeter who played with Tom Talbert in the Midwest and in Los Angeles with Tom's big band.

BILLY MORRIS: I went with Johnny Richards in 1944. We played the Casa Manana in Los Angeles for two or three weeks before we set off on our road tour. That's where we got fitted out for uniforms. I remember playing Denver and Wichita.

At that time everyone else was playing dance music but Johnny was branching out into overtures and things like that. Some of the people would just stand there and look. Johnny would double the tempo in places and the people wouldn't know which was left or right. Johnny was a wonderful guy—when I first joined, he was like my father. I had an old horn that was badly out of tune and one Sunday, while we were in Denver, I got so irritated that I threw the horn down on the floor. Johnny got this big music store to open up so he could buy me a trumpet. If he seemed aloof, I believe it was because he was going through a breakup of his relationship with singer Pat Kaye.

Johnny's brother Jack Cascales and I were very good friends. He'd been in the service and was very pugnacious.

LIONEL SESMA: From the Del Rio Club in San Pedro we went to another club on Sunset Boulevard called the Hollywood Casino, which later became the ABC Radio Studios. Following that engagement of about four weeks we were contracted to do a pair of radio shows. One was *The Jack Carson Program* and the other was *The Phil Baker Take It or Leave It Show*. After our thirteen-week contract was over at CBS, Johnny arranged for a tour of the East Coast, specifically New York. Johnny selected the guys who were able to go. He had a full band—this would be late 1943 or early 1944, and our first engagement was Jerry Jones's Rainbow Rendezvous in Salt Lake City for about four weeks then an open air place in Denver, Colorado, called Elitch's Gardens. We were there for a couple of weeks. As I recall, the reaction to us was favorable there—people were dancing.

How things had changed! Elitch's Gardens in Denver was the engagement that was the nadir of Benny Goodman's now legendary 1935 cross-country tour. George T. Simon in *The Big Bands* says that Goodman called his opening night at Elitch's as "just about the most humiliating experience of my life" and that the customers asked for their money back and wouldn't be mollified until the band started playing waltzes.[1] Paradoxically, the Goodman band survived the Denver gig and went on to incredible success. The Richards band fared less well.

LIONEL SESMA: Johnny was very careful and very aware of his avant-garde repertoire out of which he selected the most mainstream, the most danceable. So when we played these kinds of places he tried to stimulate the dancers. But before the end of the Denver engagement he informed the band that all the subsequent engagements from there to New York had been canceled. However, he was still going to New York and he would be happy to have those of us who wanted to, continue, but he'd pay transportation back home for anyone who didn't want to carry on. I was one of those who decided to continue on to New York, knowing full well that there was no engagement for us when we got there, until Johnny's manager was able to find something. We checked into some second-rate hotel called the Forest on 49th street, off Broadway. I went to work, not as a trombonist but as a bus boy at the Edison Hotel and I was feeding most of the band with sandwiches I would bring back. We were rehearsing and Johnny completed the band with New York musicians like bassist Sibby Brock and trumpeter Tony di Nardi—there were about seven or eight. Finally something broke for us in a barn of a ballroom in Norfolk, Virginia. We were there for a week or so. From there we went to the Roosevelt Hotel in D.C.; we were there for several weeks. From there we went to the only job we had in New York City—at the Lincoln Hotel. I think we were there for a couple of weeks. Then we went to Walter's Post Lodge in Larchmont and that was the end of the band's tour as far as a dancing entity was concerned. We were unemployed for about a month and then a theater engagement came up as a backing band for the famous black comedian Rochester. Our first stop was the Rialto Theater in Boston; from there we went to the Oriental in Chicago, and it was there

that the tour ended, I think in late 1945 Johnny sent us home and that
was it.

That Rialto Theater date in Boston was where Tom caught up with
Johnny Richards. After getting out of the army he took the train
from Minneapolis to Boston, where Richards's band had just begun
its engagement, in the hope that there might be some way he could
work with him.

TOM TALBERT: I had brought four or five scores, and he looked
through them and, very observant, asked me why, at one point in one
of the arrangements I had used only three of the four trumpets available to me. I answered, "Well that's all I wanted." He chuckled, "That's
a good answer."
    He went through the arrangements and said he liked them but un-
fortunately, and he used that word, he had just hired someone as an assistant and couldn't afford anyone else.

Don Davidson remembers a similar incident, and a rather more
"direct" Johnny Richards, a few years later.

DON DAVIDSON: I went down with Tom to Hermosa, or Redondo
Beach—Tom wanted Johnny to critique something Tom had written.
Johnny looked at the score and asked him about several things Tom
had done in it and Tom explained. Johnny handed the score back to
him and said. "You silly fuck—you don't have any idea what you're
doing but you do everything right!" That was his critique of the score.

Richards must have seen something special in Tom's writing. A
year or so later in Los Angeles, he sought him out, encouraged him
to form his own band, assisted him with his first record date, and

TOM TALBERT: Made sure I was eating regularly.

In the meantime, in Boston, with his band about to fold, Johnny
Richards gave Tom some contacts in New York, including bandleaders George Paxton and Jerry Jerome.

TOM TALBERT: I took Jerome an arrangement that I'd done of "Where
or When" for the army band but he wasn't interested. It was a bit
placid and I don't think he was even buying charts at the time. I really
wasn't ready for New York. I had no money. I was living in a fleabag
hotel on 44th Street between 6th Avenue and Times Square in a room

that was probably a broom closet in its earlier life. Out of the blue, I got a call from a tenor player named Vern Wellington in Minneapolis who was taking a band up to a resort—Detroit Lakes. It was made up of pretty good young guys from Minneapolis—about six horns and rhythm so I went up there and played with them through August and wrote some arrangements too. My piano playing had improved a lot since I'd debuted with Cliff Kyes. It still wasn't much good though.

At the end of the summer, back in Minneapolis, Tom got a call from bandleader Bob Strong.

TOM TALBERT: He had a really excellent pianist named Wayne Peterson who was from Minneapolis and possibly had recommended me. I joined Strong's band and we started with a few nights at the Greystone Ballroom in Detroit and then moved to the Latin Quarter for a month. They had showgirls—big, straight off the farm, and a comedian—Gene Bayliss, and Beatrice Kaye guesting for two weeks. The band was good—five brass, five saxes, but once again I wasn't really the pianist for the job. We played from nine till three and on Saturdays there would be three floor shows and a live broadcast—there was hardly room for a dance set. I remember Bob Strong had a big hassle with the guitar player and they actually got into a fistfight backstage. I couldn't believe it. Back in Minneapolis, after the Strong gig was finished, I thought about going to university and I signed up and went for about two days. Once again I felt like I was back in high school so I dropped that idea and carried on playing what jobs I could get. I met a character of a bartender who thought he could be a band booker. He already had a girl he thought was a great singer and I put a band together of a trumpet, three saxes, and rhythm. The bartender bought this big Hudson sedan with jump seats and a trailer for the band equipment and we drove all over the area, in the middle of winter. It was pretty tough going—there were terrible storms and we kept getting stuck in the snow and ice. Billy Morris, who had played trumpet with Johnny Richards, came with us for a while.

BILLY MORRIS: We were playing some USO gig at a base somewhere and that's where I think I first saw Tom. He was in uniform. Then the next time I saw him was when I was still with Johnny on the East Coast and Tom turned up again, just out of the army. He wanted to write for Johnny or copy or generally work for him but things were getting tough and bands were breaking up and he went back home to Minneapolis. He then asked me to come out there to play with a band he had. I stayed with his folks who were very nice and as I remember we had this little band that the bartender had set up and we went to Fargo,

North Dakota. We had an eight-passenger Hudson with a trailer behind it. There had been a lot of snow and the plows had been through. We hit a slick spot and the trailer started weaving and we wound up in a snowbank. Here we were, standing out on the road and it was almost fifty below and no cars going by. Finally an oil tanker came along and pulled us out.

TOM TALBERT: Billy stayed with us just long enough to earn the fare to Los Angeles. Just after New Year 1946 I followed him out and my fate was cast.

NOTE

1. George T. Simon, *The Big Bands*, 4th ed. (New York: Schirmer, 1981).

6

Los Angeles in the 1940s

Although New York, and more specifically 52nd Street, was the center of the jazz world at this time, there was also a great deal of music being played in the Los Angeles area, some, but not all of it, on Central Avenue. Howard Rumsey paints an enticing scene.

HOWARD RUMSEY: In 1943 in Hermosa Beach at Zucca's Showcase, a small ballroom with an upstairs part where people could eat and watch, they had Bobby Sherwood's Elks Parade band, with Zoot Sims playing with his brother's suit on. Then it was followed by Benny Carter and Savannah Churchill, then Johnny Richards's band with Andy Russell singing "When the Lights Go On Again All Over the World." The last band was Freddie Slack's Cow Cow Boogie band.

All the major hotels in downtown LA had tea dances and they had bands—twelve to fourteen pieces. Every beach town from San Diego to Santa Barbara had ballrooms (that was before television and it was groovy). They were good jobs and for the guys that had them, it was marvelous. All the bands had uniforms, the same shoes—it was something to be proud of.

I did a lot of club work around LA in the 1940s. I was working at the Babalu with Barney Bigard, downtown underneath the Orpheum Theater, and I think I was making $37.50 a week or maybe $40. We played borderline Dixieland. Standards of the time.

I went down to Gardena to catch a band I wanted to hear so bad. I can't remember the name of the club, but they had a Dixieland band playing with Buddy Cole on piano, Benny Strickler on trumpet, Bob Hogan on trombone, and the clarinetist was a Mexican named Pancho Villa . . . and it sounded great—they were having a ball. All around town there were places like that, different guys playing, and it didn't matter what kind of music they were playing, they were all playing jazz of some kind, and they were musicians. It wasn't like "Oh I don't like that." Every sound you heard was the thing you wanted to hear. I never saw a bass player in my whole life that I haven't learned something from. I watch 'em all. The scene started to fade about 1948.

Tenor saxists Jack Montrose, Johnny Barbera, and Steve White were important members of Tom Talbert's big band between 1947 and 1949.

JACK MONTROSE: I liked the music scene—it was real. I could go to Central Avenue and play. And Central Avenue was for real—if you didn't play good they wiped you out. They sent you on your way—sent you packing. "Cherokee" very fast or "Tea for Two" in a key that hadn't been invented yet. It was all testing—but it was fun . . . and none of the kids who play now have ever been through that. What they learn at North Texas State isn't nearly on that level. I was able to make a living playing—I went all the way through college from playing—all kinds of gigs. I played strip clubs for about ten years. I did a lot of concert gigs—Gene Norman's things on Sunday afternoons. I was very friendly with Wardell Gray. Wardell was Gene Norman's choice, and when Wardell couldn't do it he'd send me. So I subbed a lot for Wardell. I'd play with Latin bands at Latin ballrooms, and with Jerry Gray or Harry James and get paid very well. I think most guys were doing the same kind of thing. Getting paid for the bad work and playing jazz for fun. There were a lot of clubs that had small bands—sax and rhythm—but they didn't pay enough. I don't know anyone who actually made a living playing those places. The closest anyone came to making a living doing that in LA were Shorty Rogers and Shelly Manne—they had the Giants and they began working in the clubs, Zardi's, the Haig. But the clubs didn't pay enough—a club gig had to lead to something else—a movie call or something.

JOHNNY BARBERA: I started out playing classical clarinet. When I enlisted in the navy I took the test and wound up in Washington, D.C., as a musician. That's when I started playing the tenor. I fell in love with it and never went back to playing clarinet. I heard Lester Young in New York—that's the first jazz musician I heard in person and that's what started me off. I came back to LA, still in the navy, and Herb Geller, who I was at school with, got me in this band that also had Lennie Niehaus in it. That was Phil Carreón's band, this would be 1945–1946. Lennie wrote a lot of the arrangements and he was inspired by Dizzy's band which had come out here, and Billy Eckstine's band—and we were playing straight big band jazz. Billy Byers was on the band, Bobby Williams was also on trombone. The drummer was Joe Young—a Japanese, I think. He's one of the head guys at Wurlitzer

Music now. Another drummer was Arnie Haber—a Jewish boy—tremendous. We had a great time; Arnie wasn't a great drummer but he was a showman. Then Carreón got work up north—we had a little band—four horns, Johnny McComb on trumpet, me and Herb Geller on tenors, Lennie Niehaus on alto, and rhythm. That was the greatest little book I ever heard. Lennie wrote it all. Arnie got to meet Wardell Gray and Teddy Edwards and I started to play with them a lot. I played with Slim Gaillard's big band at Billy Berg's and then his small group—we were broadcasting from Billy Berg's at that time. The atmosphere in LA at that time was just unbelievable. The jazz scene was sort of isolated to the people who liked jazz—there was no interference. There wasn't rock 'n' roll, there were piano bars and there was jazz. It was like a fantastic dream that you didn't wake up from—beautiful music—so inspirational for so many years. Charlie Parker runnin' round the streets, Frank Morgan runnin' round the streets. And I was so young. I was so young I didn't realize. All I was trying to do was play. I wasn't concerned about making a living. I was getting by alright, and I was so caught up with the music that the living part didn't come into focus yet. You could go to anyone's house and stay all night, you could go out to the beach, and stay there all night, it was just a beautiful life—a swinging life—beautiful life.

Billy Berg's that was a great club—Allan Eager, everybody used to come there and play. That was great. I got my biggest thing out of there, with Wardell and Teddy—they took me kind of under their wing you know when I started playing down Central Avenue at the Down Beat—Art Farmer was there, Addison, and a lot of great guys—Chuck Thompson. I was kind of apprehensive but I loved it so much I was willing to get my feet wet and I did. And it was great—I'll never forget it. That's the greatest thing in my life.

You could go down Central Avenue at two in the morning—to the Jungle Room—and they'd start playing and play till seven in the morning. You could take a solo—for an hour and half.

STEVE WHITE: I used to go down to Central Avenue—that's how I learned to play I guess. I used to jam with guys like Leo Watson. I spent a lot of time jamming and never got to read very well so I wasn't a favorite choice for the big band work that was going. But I kept practicing and I took up the bassoon. Although I played in Tom's band, I was never really a good enough reader for his music.

Tom says he wasn't aware of this.

STEVE WHITE: I worked a lot of club dates, particularly in the Long Beach area. I was down there for more than ten years. I also played in an Artie Shaw-type band led by a clarinetist, Bob Keene. I was playing in Hermosa Beach with a group called Two Bops and a Beep—two Mexican guys and myself. We were popular wherever we went—Arizona, Mexico—but the piano player became an alcoholic and eventually killed himself.

As Jack Montrose indicated, club jobs did not really pay enough to live on and had to be seen as a bridge to either studio work or a more permanent band. Bud Shank took the big band route.

BUD SHANK: I think I arrived in Los Angeles in August or something like that of 1946 and January, I guess 1947, somewhere round in there. Herbie Harper, who had been working with Charlie Barnet's band, found out that the manager of the band, Kurt Bloom, did not want to play anymore, and there was an opening on fourth tenor saxophone. He wanted to know did I want to audition for the job. And you know what the answer to that would have been. Of course I did. This is what I'd been aiming at. So I went down to Balboa, to the Rendezvous Ballroom where the band was playing, and did my audition. Charlie said okay, you got the job, a hundred dollars a week. Doc Severinson joined the band that same time as did Claude Williamson. Clark Terry and Jimmy Nottingham were already on the band—it was a really good band. And my job, in addition to playing the fourth tenor saxophone book, was to play all Charlie's solos when he was off drinking or playing around or whatever he did while we were working the dances. So I got a lot to play. And it was fun. It was a good bunch of people.

Johnny Barbera, an excellent swinging post-Lester Young tenor saxist, might have gone on to great things if he'd gone with a name band.

JOHNNY BARBERA: It was close to that. I relieved Art Pepper on a band up north—it was Lewis Olds's (Lou Oles?) band. Art went with Kenton then and I was getting ready but the thing that entered the picture was drugs—you remember Joe Albany? Those were mysterious days to me. I was into jazz and there were a lot of mysterious guys, so to speak, and they were using hard junk. It wasn't a happy thing. It seemed like something you had to do to get in with them—into the clique and it got away from the real music. In the end I went to Vegas as a crap dealer, to get away from the drug scene here.

Steve White, the original tenor saxist at the Lighthouse at Hermosa Beach had a gorgeous tone and a style that built on Lester

Young too. He can be heard for a few tantalizing bars on Tom's 1947 recording of "Between Loves."

STEVE WHITE: Harry Babasin opened a bass shop and had a rehearsal room—I was rehearsing with him and some other guys there one time and one of them said, "Come on Steve, have some of this cocaine—it's free . . . it won't cost you nothin'." I said I was not interested in anything that had a habit with it . . . I'd been like that for a long time . . . I'm not interested in having a habit, so I turned it down. They chased me off, they ran me off . . . they said, "We don't want you around here . . . you don't play that good anyway." So I never heard from them again until I heard they were dead. There were a lot of cliques and you were either in or you were out and as I didn't partake in the idiocy that they were all involved in I was out. Later on there was a lot of hate for musicians and they'd sell you some cocaine that was real cheap and they'd put poison in so it would kill you. I had someone come up to me and say "Come on go with us," and when I was in the car they said, "We're going to take you out in the desert and cook you and eat you." They were some of the guys who poisoned the cocaine—just because they enjoyed killing people.

I was at the Lighthouse in 1949—Howard Rumsey got the job but Harry Babasin played with us while Howard was away. But mostly he wasn't interested in that trip from Hollywood to Hermosa Beach. Mostly we had a guy from Tom Talbert's band on bass—Boris Anastisov. We also had Karl Kiffe on drums and Frank Davenport on piano. We tried to get Frank Patchen but he was always building these symphony things for the music industry—he worked for somebody but he finally got tired of being bullied around so he gave that up. When Howard came back, he fired all of us. We used to get drunk once in a while and that doesn't improve your playing at all. I was expected to go down and visit with the people in the audience—jet pilots from a nearby airfield would come in and get us all crazy. They'd keep buying us drinks and I thought it was impolite not to drink them down. They loved a number I used to sing—"Flying in My New Jet Plane," which got to number 14 in the charts. Sometimes people would come in and sit in—Chet Baker came in a lot. I was the only regular horn player at that time.

Postscript: Steve White and Harry Babasin must have repaired their relationship a few years later, as Steve recorded an album—*Jazz Mad*—for the Liberty label in 1955, fronting a quartet that included Babasin as both bass player and record producer. The music is excellent, especially White's playing. One gets the feeling, however, that, as producer, Babasin had his thoughts elsewhere and there is an unfinished, random feel to the album—presumably derived from the "absolute freedom" extolled in the liner notes. In 1946 the thought of leaving the harsh Midwestern winter and the prospect of exciting musical opportunities were not the only reasons Tom Talbert headed west.

TOM TALBERT: I guess the primary motivation for going to Los Angeles was Margaret Hartigan, my first great love, from Monterey, who had moved to Los Angeles. I flew from Minneapolis to Burbank in a Lockheed Constellation. Even in those days the airfare was comparable to paying for a Pullman berth on the train and in those days Burbank was a busy airport—LAX was mostly bean fields. I hooked up again with Margaret and we began living in hotel rooms, while she worked and I waited out my six-month union period. At some point a musician told me about the Harvey Hotel on Santa Monica Boulevard, and we moved there.

BILLY MORRIS: The Harvey Hotel was one of a kind. I got Tom a room there. It was located on Santa Monica near Western and it catered to all the musicians from the bands.

JOHNNY BARBERA: The Harvey Hotel—that was quite a scene—everyone was at the Harvey Hotel.

STEVE WHITE: The Harvey Hotel was great—if you needed a musician you could always find what you wanted down there—alto, trumpet, pianist.

Tom recalls the scent of hemp that wafted through the hallways. While occasional musicians from name bands, like Stan Getz and Mike Bryan, passed through the Harvey, the hotel also attracted people who "hung out" rather than stayed there. Tom remembers pianist Joe Albany and arranger and multi-instrumentalist Gene Roland.

TOM TALBERT: There were a lot of guys, some of them in pretty bad shape. There was a lot of drugs and a lot of near poverty. I remember a couple of the guys who later played on my band—Ernie Hood the very fine guitarist, and Bill Cherones who played sax and clarinet. They'd go out and buy a half gallon can of tomato juice and that would be their meal for the day—or something crazy like a candy bar.

*Moeller's
Accordion Band*

*Lawrence Welk's
Orchestra*

*Harold Menning
Orchestra*

*Doc Lawson
and His Orchestra*

*Harry O'Nan
and His Orchestra*

*Red Sievers
and His Orchestra*

The sleeper buses.

SATURDAY NITE DANCE

Featuring

A New Band!
Don't miss this new
dance sensation

Tommy Talbert's
Orchestra

Swing, sweet and jive specialty numbers

Saturday, November 14   9-12 p.m.

UNION BALLROOM

Sponsored by Union Board of Governors

ADVANCE SALE	
Established Price	$.52
Federal Tax	.08
TOTAL	$.60
AT THE DOOR	
Established Price	$.77
Federal Tax	.08
TOTAL	$.85

Poster for a dance, University of Minnesota, 1942.

"R & R" at the Delmar Inn. 1944–1945. Left to right: PFC Tom Talbert, Sam Hyster, and unknown. (Hyster, trombone; unknown, trumpet. They were with the Vaughn Monroe band at this time.)

First rehearsal. The Tommy Talbert Orchestra, 1946. Left to right: Edith (?), girlfriend of John Cascales; Tom Talbert; Herbie Steward, tenor saxophone; Bill Cherones, alto saxophone; unknown, bass.

March of Dimes broadcast, c. 1947. Left to right: Tony Rizzi, guitar; Elmer Aiello, a.k.a. "Umpsie," baritone saxophone; Howard Rumsey, bass; Dick Stanton, drums; Tom Talbert, piano.

Recording with Dodo Marmarosa at Radio Recorders, November 4, 1946, for "Flight of the Vout Bug." Left to right: Lyle Griffin, Dodo Marmarosa, Tom Talbert.

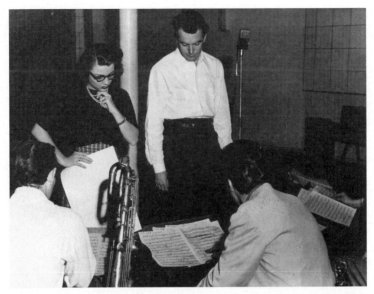

Rehearsal for "On the Air with Joan Barton—Philco Television Time," 1947. Left to right: Don Davidson, baritone saxophone; Joan Barton; Tom Talbert; Johnny Barbera, tenor saxophone.

Rehearsal, Art Whiting's rehearsal studio, 1947–1948. Left to right: Harry Brainerd, trombone; Dick Stanton, drums; John McComb, trumpet.

The Trianon Ballroom, April 1948. Left to right: Bob Stone, bass; Warne Marsh, tenor saxophone; Benny (?), alto saxophone; Roy Harte, drums; El Koeling, alto saxophone; Harry Brainerd, trombone; Bob White, trumpet; Steve White, tenor saxophone; Lou Obergh, trumpet (behind); Gene Norton, trombone; Don Davidson, baritone saxophone.

Program for the Coronet Theater Concert, 1949.

Rehearsal, 1948. Left to right: Dick Stanton, drums; John McComb, trumpet; Steve White, tenor saxophone; Wes Hensel, trumpet.

Johnny Barbera, tenor saxophone.

Bud Shank arrived in Los Angeles around the same time as Tom.

BUD SHANK: I knew that I had a choice to either go to New York or to Los Angeles. I had been to New York several times, riding the bus up there to take lessons from a saxophonist who used to be in Cab Calloway's band, named Walter "Foots" Thomas and a couple of other saxophone teachers. It was a long, long, long bus ride up there but I did it several times. Simply, I just wanted to learn. There was no such thing as a saxophone teacher where I was in North Carolina. That was my first real saxophone coaching. I only took just a few lessons with Thomas but it was really good for me and to this day, I remember things that he told me.

But I decided that I really wanted to see what Los Angeles was about. So I went back to Ohio back to the family farm, and told my father that I wanted to go to Los Angeles and enroll in USC, University of Southern California, which was a damn lie, 'cause I had no intention of doing anything like that. But he says, okay. We'll support you if you go to school. And I said, by the way, will you loan me a hundred bucks so I can buy a flute, which led to another exclamation like, what? You wanna' do what!? But he gave me the hundred dollars. I bought the flute. I had never played one before in my life. Fortunately about that time, I got a call from Ike Carpenter who was living in New York and was on his way driving to California. He says do you want to ride out there with me. I've got two other people in the car and the four of us can share expenses. He had a 1935 Buick. This was 1946. Ah, so it was an eleven-year-old Buick that was hanging by its threads. I met him in Nashville, rode the train down to Nashville, met the guys there and headed for Los Angeles.

We got as far as San Bernardino, California, and all of a sudden we realized nobody had any money. We wired a friend in Los Angeles who in the meantime had arranged a job for Ike and this little band that he had, or was going to have, up in Lake Tahoe. So we went from San Bernardino, as I remember, with the money that he wired us up to Lake Tahoe and worked there for a couple of weeks. And all of us gathered enough funds together to head for Los Angeles 'cause we knew we wouldn't be working in Los Angeles immediately. The union had a six-month waiting period during which you were supposed to not work.

So we all arrived there and I arrived with a tenor saxophone, a clarinet, and a toothbrush. And that's all I had, apart from another change of clothes. And that was the beginning of my career in Los Angeles, no job, no nothing. Before long, I ran into some more musicians who had just arrived the same way. One of them was trombonist, Herbie

Harper, who had just left Charlie Spivak's band, as I remember. And another was another friend of mine from North Carolina. And the fourth person initially was drummer Roy Harte who had found this one-room apartment over on North Orange Drive, right below Sunset right almost across the street from Hollywood High School. Roy Harte was gonna have a commune, and he wanted all of us to join him. So we all agreed, but by the time we were ready to check in, Roy got a job with Lucky Millinder's band and he left town. So we found another guy that had driven out with me from New York—a trumpeter named Bruce King. And he was the fourth guy. All of us were musicians.

The practice routine was, one guy practiced in the main room, one guy in the kitchen, one guy in the bathroom, and the other guy in the backyard. And then that would work for one week and then we would rotate, and everybody would move around to the next session. The sleeping arrangements were the same way. We had two single beds and one foldout couch which was quickly named the rack. You spent one week on the left side of the rack and then the next week on the right side of the rack, the next week on the right single bed and so on. You moved around. And it worked, silly as it may sound. We were all young. I look back on us and say my God, what was all that? How did we do it? But it worked and we lived for quite a long time that way, five months, six months. I'm not sure. A couple of times I sneaked out of town with a band and worked which I was not supposed to do. And by now, my father was well aware that I was not going to USC. So the funds from home stopped very quickly, and I was painting houses and parking cars and doing any kind of odd jobs that I could find to do at that time to help support myself and thankfully the rent was very cheap, probably about four or five dollars a week apiece. But still, I had to arrange a way to find that four or five dollars. My friend Frank Harrell had been in the service, and he had access to the GI Bill funds and he started taking lessons at a place called Mickey Gillette's School of Saxophone on Hollywood Boulevard. He took both flute lessons and saxophone lessons, and then he'd come back to the room and quickly tell me everything the teachers told him. And that's the way I really learned how to play flute and that was my second closest thing to a formal instruction on the saxophone, secondhand from Frank. Later on, I was also able to enroll there after I had become—I guess the word would be solvent.

7

The Tom Talbert Orchestra

Tom Talbert is adamant that, in spite of the quality of the Hot Harvey's jazz musician residents, it was not a venue for mythical Kansas City-style all-night jam sessions. There was a small record company and soundstage next door to the hotel, and it was a useful address and point of contact.

> TOM TALBERT: While playing in Detroit with Bob Strong, I had become friends with drummer Billy Shuart, who had been with the Johnny Richards band.

BILLY SHUART

Billy Shuart played drums and sang with the Tom Talbert Orchestra.

BILLY MORRIS: Back in Detroit where Billy Shuart was also from, we had a little band at a place called the Jefferson Inn. Billy played drums and we had Tommy Howell on piano and an Italian sax player, Frank de Lucia from Rochester, New York. Billy had some rich relatives in Virginia whom he'd never seen. When he got married in Detroit, his dad sent him to visit these relations. They had two Rolls-Royces sitting on blocks and they gave him one. It was a 1928 model and hadn't been run for years, but it started right up. It was designed to be driven by a chauffeur, with a glassed-in back and flower vases on the walls. Billy and his wife drove it out to California and around Pasadena, blew a rod. They hadn't even thought it might need oil.

He got it fixed and when we were staying at the Harvey we used to go to work in it, in our tuxes.

In 1953 I had a club up in Santa Fe and Billy came though and tended bar for a couple of months. He disappeared and I've never heard of him since.

TOM TALBERT: Billy was now in LA and one day called me from the lobby of the Harvey, with the news that Johnny was downstairs and looking for me. I was very flattered that Johnny even remembered me from our meeting in Boston. He no longer had a band and was doing a lot of movie work and recordings for Armed Forces Radio. He took me along to many of these sessions, some of them accompanying singers like Lena Horne.

Johnny insisted that I should have my own band—which I thought was pretty funny given that I had no money, no name, had only just arrived in LA, and knew hardly anyone at all.

His brother Jack was a hustler and had a small record label called Paramount Records. The office was the trunk of his car and the stock consisted of a couple of boxes of records and many more tobacco tins filled with pot. Johnny said, "Jack can be your manager." And that's the first and last manager I ever had or wanted again.

Jack, Johnny, and Paramount were responsible for the notorious *Dizzy Gillespie Plays Jerome Kern with Strings* album, arranged by Johnny and banned for a time by an injunction from the Kern estate. Any artistic value of this musically advanced album was largely negated by the abysmal recording quality achieved in the recording facility next to the Harvey Hotel. Fortunately, when the time came, Tom would be recording at Radio Recorders, the best studio in town at the time, just three weeks after Stan Kenton had been in the same room recording "Rika Jika Jack," "Artistry in Boogie," and "Collaboration." A couple of weeks later Stan recorded his celebrated version of "Lover."

Both Johnny and Jack were insistent that Tom record, and in June 1946 he did. The band was made up of a mixture of musicians who became regular members of Tom's band plus a leavening of star studio players, including the tenor saxist Babe Russin.

TOM TALBERT: About half the band were actually living in the Harvey at the time of the session. When I first started my band in the spring of 1946, everyone said, "Get Herbie Steward on tenor—he's the best." And he was. He made some rehearsals and I remember him on one of the first jobs we played, at the Casino Gardens in Culver City. However, by the time the record date was looming, Herbie was long gone and I was concerned about having a good tenor soloist for the session. I was at an Armed Forces broadcast with Johnny, and Babe Russin was in the band. I said to Johnny, "Gee, I wonder if Babe would think of doing something like my record date?" Johnny said, "If you want Babe, let's go ask him." I guess Babe made one rehearsal and then he did the date and played beautifully.

Russin was the most veteran player on the session, having a pedigree that went back as far as the California Ramblers in 1926, Red Nichols in 1930, Benny Goodman's 1938 Carnegie Hall Concert, and a style in the mid-1940s that embodied all the best attributes of Georgie Auld, Vido Musso, and Ben Webster.

TOM TALBERT: One day in the bar at the Harvey, I met Frank Beach—a great lead trumpet who had been in the first Stan Kenton band. I asked him right away if he'd be interested in doing the record date and he said "Sure" so we had a great trumpet section, Frank, Lou Obergh, and my friend from Minneapolis days, Ronnie Rochat. And we had Lionel Sesma, who had toured with Johnny Richards, on first trombone.

Four sides were cut and an unknown number pressed. It's safe to say that until Talbert reissued them on CD, they had been heard by very few people at all thanks to Jack Cascales's "distribution-lite" system and a sizable yawn from the reviewers at *Metronome* magazine. Often the reception of recordings seemed in inverse ratio to publicity elsewhere in the magazine. In the months leading up to the release of Tom's records he received a number of plugs for his new band in the Hollywood Roundup column of the magazine. He even got an editorial apology after the erroneous statement that "Tom Talbert is the leader of a new band . . . using George Handy arrangements'.[1] In the following issue the columnist said "a red face must admit . . . Tommy Talbert does all his own arrangements."[2] Unfortunately the magazine was obviously not well read by record reviewers Barry Ulanov and George Simon, who opened the review of the four Paramount sides with the crushing line "Tommy Talbert and arranger Ralph Yaw combine to create what they hoped would be impressive sides."[3]

Tom Talbert is quite unequivocal: the writing on these recordings is all his own, and the author can verify that he has seen the scores and they are all in Talbert's unmistakable hand. That the arrangements were bursting with ideas left the critics lamenting, "Too often they get too involved, trying for effect after effect but achieving too little continuity."[4]

Listened to in 2001, measured against the background of all the big band jazz recorded in the past sixty years, the originality and precocity of the then twenty-one-year-old writer is truly astonishing. Talbert displays an endless abundance of new ideas and a real maturity in the use of the instruments. One of his signature trademarks is present too: no matter how involved or experimental the music gets, it always remains accessible and never fails to convey genuine and deep emotion.

TOM TALBERT: After the session was over I was thrilled by the results. Johnny had been in the booth and was very helpful. On the bridge of "Chihuahua" an intended gang vocal by the band didn't work, so Johnny got together with Lionel Sesma and they thought up some dialog for Lionel to speak, while I wrote a backing for the saxes to play.

After almost sixty years Sesma still remembers the session.

LIONEL SESMA: I remember the other trombonist because I had a lot of respect for him—Ollie Wilson. I also worked with him on Boyd Raeburn's band—and I also remember my spoken bridge with the words *tequila, amor y fiesta* on "Down in Chihuahua."

TOM TALBERT: I was walking on air, or I would have been if we'd had any money. As it was, I borrowed a thousand dollars from my father to pay for the session. A few weeks later Jack Cascales turned up with a few boxes of records in the back of his 1936 Ford V8—and that was about the extent of the distribution. Amazingly, over the years, I have found some people who actually own copies of the original 78s.

From the viewpoint of 2003, "Down in Chihuahua" impresses because of Tom's inventive way of dressing up such trite material, the unusual ensemble voicing behind Leighton Johnson's creamy alto lead and Frank Beach's perfect trumpet fills on the first chorus. The trumpet comments sound so good, they could have been written, but Tom says they weren't. Leighton Johnson was one of Talbert's Minneapolis comrades, and another forgotten but good and intriguing soloist is guitarist Ernie Hood—a victim of polio contracted shortly after the session.

Babe Russin is the sound of inspired experience here on "Deep in a Dream" and indeed a star on all of the titles. The arrangement for the ballad indicates ways that Tom would go in the future: classical elements in the intro, hints of the melody to come, unusual atonal voicings, and a composed interlude between the second A section and the bridge. You can hear him using the trombones as substitutes for French horns and his fondness for moving the melody line around different parts of the orchestra.

TOM TALBERT: I did it more then than I would now!

Tom describes himself as a no vibrato man, but he was happy with the style on this session.

TOM TALBERT: That's what they did then.

Perhaps it is his display of youthfulness in resisting the sweetness in "Deep in a Dream," a reasonable act for a twenty-two-year-old determined not to be thought commercial or dance bandish, that gives the piece a spiky, sour sweet flavor.

TOM TALBERT: Johnny Richards used to say that "I didn't let things go on long enough in my arrangements—his term was I always wrung the chicken's neck." And in fact I always felt restless and eager to get on to the next thing.

That's especially apparent on "I've Got You under My Skin," as composer and bandleader Maria Schneider observed fifty years later.

MARIA SCHNEIDER: To me that's just genius writing—the figure that's behind the melody at the beginning and the way he brings it back again at the end, and also the contrast in the piece—it's just so daring. And that's something you don't hear so often. Sometimes it's just walking and very simple and then all of a sudden these bursts, and these incredibly wide skips—things just kind of flying all over the band. I love the sheer energy that he put into the writing and also that the band put into the playing. I think it's very powerful because you can really feel that it's music that's coming out of a time—it's music that's really matching the time—you can feel that there's something very deep and honest about that music being played and written then. It's very powerful and sometimes that's something I miss now—everybody's looking to something else. For him to have had this band then, when he was very young and I guess everyone in the band was quite young too, it must have been really exciting.

As one expert listener exclaimed on hearing the four recordings for the first time, "They really change the history of jazz!"

The fourth song, "Stop Your Knockin'," is even more banal than "Chihuahua" and was not originally slated for the session.

TOM TALBERT: Johnny didn't like the original fourth piece at the rehearsal and gave me "Knockin"—another number by himself and Ralph Yaw. This meant that I had to sit up all night at the piano in the lobby of the Harvey Hotel and write the arrangement, with Ronnie Rochat alongside copying the parts. Of course, we had to record it without prior rehearsal.

The result says a lot for the reading abilities of the musicians. Tom took full advantage, particularly where the trumpets are concerned, writing passages that lost nothing when compared to the contemporaneous work of Neal Hefti and Ralph Burns.

The *Metronome* reviewers liked "Down in Chihuahua" best of the four: "cleverly arranged and has neat, muted trumpeting and some tasty delicate guitaring."[5] Their full scorn was held in reserve for the later Stan Kenton version of the song, which received an appalling review. Thanks to the recordings, Tom's career gained a little visibility, even though his writing had been variously identified as George Handy's or Ralph Yaw's. Writing and recording for the big band was the exciting stuff, but the rent had to be paid with more prosaic kinds of music making.

TOM TALBERT: That summer, Margaret got a job as a shill at a small casino at Lake Tahoe. Her job was to gamble with the house's money to make it look like there was some action going on at the tables. When she got there, she talked them into hiring me to bring in a small dance band. We had Ronnie Rochat on trumpet and Leighton Johnson on alto sax and Dick Stanton on drums. Dick became an important connection for me, but this was the first time I'd met him. I have to assume he was recommended by someone I respected. As we had no bass and I was no stride pianist, it must have been a tough and not entirely enjoyable gig for the horns. We almost didn't make the first night of the job. I was driving up with Dick in Jack Cascales's car. Don't ask me why. The car broke down somewhere near the town of Bishop, California—about two-thirds of the way. We had to make the gig so I chartered a plane, a Beechcraft biplane, and we flew to the only airstrip in Lake Tahoe, which just happened to be outside our casino. It was a tricky landing because the runway sloped down to the lake and that end was about ninety feet lower than the other. The trick was to land uphill, and you hoped that the wind would be in the right direction. We made it down safely, although there were fatalities on other occasions. The casino we were playing in was staffed by some very strange and unusual characters and we played dance music every night to very few people. The war had only been over for a year and things were still pretty quiet. In spite of the dearth of customers we played till 3:00 A.M. and then used to head up to an even smaller casino where we could jam more freely. This place attracted dealers and staff from the other casinos around the lake and was fun until some of the staff from our place were caught cheating at the tables and we were all thrown out. Our boss, a tough guy called "Swede," wasn't very happy about our extramural activities and drove up beside me one morning when I was walking home. He stopped his car and began to complain about our after-hours playing in another joint, and the big-mouth smartass twenty-one-year-old that I'd become said, "Well, if you want an exclusive contract, I'm sure we could work that out." I still can't believe he didn't punch me on the jaw.

In the fall, Tom's relationship with Margaret cooled for a while and Tom moved to a room in Manhattan Beach. Which was a mistake.

TOM TALBERT: It was beautiful, but I didn't have a car. I was getting around on buses and streetcars—which was really difficult, even then.

Howard Rumsey remembers the Tom Talbert of this time and what seemed to be a "semipresence" on the jazz scene.

HOWARD RUMSEY: In the 1940s, when I first met Tom, he was living in Manhattan Beach. I was working every night, but I didn't see him come into the club very often. He didn't hang out on the scene the way other guys did, and no one knows why. He never invited me to his home. My parents had a restaurant out in the valley near Universal Studios and I found out there was a freeway going through there and it became my job to sell the place. In the meantime, I used to invite musicians out there after closing time. Shorty Rogers, Arnold Fishkin, Barney Bigard, Johnny McComb used to be there and Tom would come out on the Red Line car. But he would turn up, he'd be there then he'd disappear—and you never knew when. He was the perfect gentleman—he was quiet, he was so goddam handsome, he was very reserved. He was like a guy who had his hand on the rudder all the time. It was impossible to tell whether he was shy or not because you couldn't get to know him.

Tom certainly recalls the Red Line trolley, and the Rumsey family restaurant.

TOM TALBERT: One of the great things about visiting with Howard was that he'd feed me. I also recollect one night we were sitting there when a garbage truck rolled up behind the restaurant and Howard jumped up shouting, "Oh my god, my stash is in the trash," and raced out to rescue it. One of the reasons why I "disappeared" of course was that I had no car and had to rely on the Red Line schedule to get back home.

Milt Bernhart also recalls the elusive Talbert "semipresence."

MILT BERNHART: If Tom wasn't around, a few people might say, "Where's Tom Talbert?" But if he was gone for long, no one really missed him because he never made himself a presence. He didn't elbow himself into a room and everything stops and "Here's Talbert." Tom could be there and gone and maybe not be missed. In some ways that holds a person back, in terms of "getting somewhere."

This ambiguity about Tom's place on the jazz scene would become more pronounced in future years. In the meantime another recording opportunity came along in November, bringing with it the young piano virtuoso Dodo Marmarosa. After periods with Gene Krupa, Tommy Dorsey, and Artie Shaw, Dodo had recorded with players of the stature of Charlie Parker, Howard McGhee, Lucky Thompson, and Lester Young and was, at this time effectively the house pianist at Atomic Records in Los Angeles.

TOM TALBERT: Lyle Griffin, who owned Atomic Records next door to the Harvey, wanted me to record a big band piece featuring Dodo. I was thrilled as he had been one of my favorite pianists right from the time I heard him with Artie Shaw's band in San Diego. I wrote an original, using the white piano in the lobby of the hotel, and we put a very good band together using some people from my band plus Lucky Thompson on tenor, Al Killian and Ray Linn on trumpets, Ray Sims on trombone, and Lou Fromm on drums. Griffin called it "The Flight of the Vout Bug," inspired by the hip language invented by guitarist/comedian/hipster Slim Gaillard who had been recording, with Dodo, for Griffin's label.

Listened to fifty-five years later, "Vout Bug" is an exciting, spectacular composition with excellent solos by Marmarosa and Thompson and crisp swinging section work from the band. A bit more mainstream than Tom's four arrangements for the Paramount session, it's quite in the mold of the Kenton band of the time, especially with the steady four provided by the rhythm guitar and the pompous brassy introduction.

TOM TALBERT: That intro was satirical, meant to be a joke about film industry producer credits. But no one got the joke.

Least of all the critics: It was greeted with complete indifference by the record reviewers of *Metronome* magazine in March 1947.[6] (In the same issue they were faint in their praise for Duke Ellington's "Happy Go Lucky Local," unimpressed by Dinah Washington's now classic record "Blow Top Blues," and reserved maximum enthusiasm for two quite forgettable sides by Doris Day with the Les Brown Orchestra.)

Although Tom Talbert doubts that Lyle Griffin ever had many copies of "Flight of the Vout Bug" pressed, jazz record collector Jehangir Dalal, who was living in Bombay, India, at the time, was able to order other Atomic recordings featuring Marmarosa and Lucky Thompson from the United States and also from England on the Parlophone label. "I preferred to buy the Parlophone versions because the sound quality of Atomic pressings was terrible," remarked Dalal.

TOM TALBERT: Four pieces were recorded at the session—I did two and another arranger did the others, one of which was "Deep in the Blues" sung by David Allyn, the reverse side of "Vout Bug." I've no idea what happened to my other recording—an original called "Love Eyes." Lyle didn't like it enough to release it, and I think I made the mistake of trying to write something that I thought would be a hit, rather than follow my own instincts. I really wish I'd written something like "Eager Beaver."

Along with the "Vout Bug" recording, Tom was commissioned to write some arrangements for Cab Calloway—mostly pop tunes and one original instrumental. The latter was titled "Look What Your Love Did to Me," but Tom no longer remembers the names of the pop tunes. He continued to rehearse his own band, benefiting from drummer Dick Stanton's very good standing on the local jazz scene.

DICK STANTON

In January 2003 Bob Stanton, a retired insurance executive living in Corona del Mar, recounted the story of his brother's life and tragic death.

BOB STANTON: Dick was born in 1925 and we grew up in South-west Los Angeles—87th and Avalon. Our father was also a drummer and Dick started emulating him—playing the drums with pencils when he was in kindergarten. He stayed with music all of his life. He probably got his first drum set when he was in the band at Edison High School, when he'd have these jam sessions over at the house with guys that included Elmer Koeling on alto sax and Harry Brainerd on trombone. (Both to be members of Tom's band.) There was no problem with the neighbors complaining because we had my grandmother on one side, an alley on the other, and an alley at the back. Dick started playing jobs when he was fifteen. At that time he liked Buddy Rich and Gene Krupa. We had newspaper clippings where he was called "the baby Gene Krupa." He was friends with Art Pepper and trumpeter Frank Beach and he used to go to an after-hours spot on Central Avenue around 130th Street and jam. He used to go to the Lighthouse at Hermosa Beach to sit in too. He left high school when he was seventeen and went up north to Washington state to play with Earl Spencer. He went to the Conservatory of Music in Los Angeles for several years and later played with Skinnay Ennis and with Xavier Cugat in Chicago. Although he stayed with Cugat for two years, he didn't really enjoy it much.

Dick came to the conclusion that there was a limited future in jazz and had just accepted a position as a percussionist with the Utah Symphony Orchestra in Salt Lake City when he was killed. He'd been studying with Forrest Clark of the LA Philharmonic and he realized that the future was either studio or symphonic work, and he felt that the latter was more challenging.

In September 1951, after my father died from cancer, we wanted to take my mother away for a holiday. I had just bought a new Ford, so Dick, my mother, and Dick's young son Glenn and I drove down to Mexico during the rainy season. We had a very exciting, very interesting time—in some places there weren't even roads and we drove along riverbeds—in our new car! In Sinaloa province we got to meet some Mexican guys in a bar in Los Mochis who were selling clothes and trinkets to the Indians in exchange for gold. We hung out with these guys and we all went on to Culiacán and Mazatlán and then Guadalajara. We left them in Guadalajara and, as Dick was beginning to run out of time and still wanted to buy some bongos in Mexico City, we decided to drive all night. Sometime late, while Dick was at the wheel, the car left the road. He was thrown out, I was thrown out, but my mother and Glenn who were in the backseat were okay. I found Dick in the middle of the road, and shortly after a truck arrived. Both my hands were broken and both my legs were sprained. The guys from the truck tried to pick Dick up, and I kept telling them to lay him down flat, not to bend him. They took him to a Red Cross hospital and found us a hotel room. A girl from the hotel stayed with us, and at some point went away and came back and said "Hermano es muerte." They took us to the police station the next day—there was a one-armed chief of police for this little bitty town, and in the corner of the police station they had stacked up everything we'd bought that was in the car—blankets, pottery, they'd even removed the car radio—and the chief of police was trying to find a way to collect money from us. Both my mother and I had traveler's checks but as she had a broken collarbone and couldn't write and my hands were broken so I couldn't write either; neither of us could sign the checks. The mayor of the town came along later that morning and said, "These people have been through enough—I'm going to take them to Mexico City." Eventually, after many hassles with authorities and the U.S. embassy, we finally were able to get on a plane and return to the U.S. Dick's body was embalmed in Mexico and flown back. His funeral took place near Manchester and Raymond, the part of town where he grew up.

Dick and I had a very interesting life growing up—I loved his talent, the way he did things; I loved the recognition he received. In fact I can probably thank him for my achievements, because like him, I tried to excel in everything that I did, so that I could get the same level of recognition that he got. And that probably contributed to the successful career that I had in the insurance business. I can thank Dick for a lot of my success. I was devastated by his death—there are some things you never get over.

JACK MONTROSE: I remember Dick Stanton very well—he was a very good drummer and we played together a lot, not only with Tommy's band but with other bands and at lots of jam sessions. He was well equipped technically and very confident. Had he lived on into the 1950s, he would very likely have made a name for himself on the level of a Shelly Manne or a Stan Levey—he was certainly equipped as a drummer. He was first-class.

There's little doubt that Dick Stanton played a significant role in the evolution of the Talbert band, especially where its personnel was concerned.

TOM TALBERT: The guys in the band were enthusiastic and Stanton knew all the young up-and-coming musicians. Thanks to Dick, we got

Don Davidson on baritone sax and Harry Brainerd on trombone and trumpeter Johnny McComb. Dick Stanton also knew all the places where guys played in the LA area. Although Central Avenue has been likened to 52nd Street in New York, there were in fact clubs and bars all over the city that had trios and quartets. We spent many evenings riding round with some girls and some bottles, visiting clubs where Dick, Johnny, or anyone else with us would sit in.

There was one club in South LA called the Casbah where I first heard Sammy Davis Jr. when he was a member of the Will Mastin Trio. Later we tried to put a band into the Casbah and auditioned unsuccessfully. The band was made up of Shorty Rogers, Art Pepper, Dick Stanton, probably Don Prell on bass, and myself on piano.

DON PRELL: We'd be jamming somewhere every night—there was a place out in the valley, on Ventura I think, called the Showtime, which was really the primo place where you could go—Mingus would be out there and a lot of guys who ended up with Kenton. The other thing that was so neat at that time was I could go home and put the radio on and hear Charlie Parker and Dizzy Gillespie playing live from Billy Berg's Club.

DON DAVIDSON: I got involved with the Tom Talbert Orchestra sometime in 1947. While I was still in Iowa, there was a navy band stationed in our town of Ottumwa and I got to know a trombone player named Harry Brainerd who was in the band. After I got out of the service, I got in touch with Harry and some other old friends, like Elmer Koeling and a marvelous drummer named Dick Stanton. I was involved in a small band—Al Albright's band, four saxes, trombone, and rhythm section, it was a working band—small gigs, Al was playing baritone, I was on tenor, and Elmer Koeling was on lead alto. Through Elmer and Harry, I began playing with Tom's rehearsal band. It was a very awakening experience; he had a completely different approach to things. So many things he did that haven't even been repeated to this day. He did this "Madrid Suite" in three parts, that was all in 5/4, 9/4, 7/4, and nobody had ever attempted anything like that, to my knowledge, until Dave Brubeck came out with "Take 5" and other things with various time signatures. Playing Tom's music was very enjoyable, very different. He had his own approach to things; it was unique.

Davidson said that Tom rarely talked about his music.

DON DAVIDSON: He was too busy writing and we were busy trying to keep ahead of him. He'd be writing in the kitchen on the kitchen table and we'd be in the living room, copying parts as he brought each page of score through. Everything was always in a hurry.

By late 1947, Johnny Barbera and Steve White were the tenor saxists with the band.

JOHNNY BARBERA: I could read better than average. I met Tom around that time. I got to know a couple of guys on the band—trumpeter Johnny McComb, trombonist Billy Byers. They got me on Tommy's band and we rehearsed a lot.

We used to play in Santa Monica at this music studio—A&M Music. We were rehearsing downstairs and Bud Shank, bassist Iggy Shevack, and Jean Louise, the singer, were living upstairs. Bud would be practicing all day and we'd be rehearsing downstairs and we'd get through. We'd go upstairs and people would be smoking weed—they were really fun times.

Tom's music was different from what was going round. It reminded me of Duke, real quick. That kind of writing. It was tremendous.

JACK MONTROSE: Johnny Barbera. In that period, in the mid-1940s amongst the white tenor players, Johnny Barbera was brilliant and very talented and one of the guys I went to and got a lot of help from. In fact I hear guys playing today who aren't playing as well as Johnny was then. I thought a lot of him.

STEVE WHITE: I think Johnny McComb got me into Tom's band. We were all in our twenties. Tom was a great conductor—he was very good for all of us. He'd take the passages that were muddy and freshen them up. But as he never got heard on the radio, he just never got accepted by a wider audience.

Guitarist Ernie Hood was stricken with polio and Tom substituted Tony Rizzi or Barney Kessel for a time.

TOM TALBERT: Eventually I dropped the guitar from the band. Its last appearance may have been the night that Steve White jumped up to go the mike for a solo and tore out all of Barney's jacks on the way. That may also have been the occasion that the guys who were supposed to pick up trombonist Freddie Zito on Western Boulevard were so excited about the gig that they drove right past and left him standing there. Someone had to drive all the way back from this American Legion hall somewhere in South LA to pick him up. Later Freddie Greenwell took Steve White's place on tenor sax.

Freddie was such a wonderful player. I didn't know much about him; I think Dick Stanton got him on the band. He was from Seattle and he played in a Lesterish way but with a bit of vibrato, and a marvelous sound. He later went to New York and, I understand, had a serious drug problem. I heard that he died a few years ago, back in Seattle I think.

Jack Montrose replaced Freddie Greenwell.

JACK MONTROSE: It was a rehearsal band . . . the band rehearsed all the time, and it was good. It was a hell of an experience for a whole bunch of talented jazz players who were around Southern California at that time. Guys were coming in and out of it all the time, and they were some of the most talented people I can remember in my whole life. Art Pepper was there. Tenor saxist Steve White had just the most beautiful sound you ever heard. Claude Williamson, Wes Hensel, Milt Bernhart . . . LA has always been great for that . . . bands just getting together to rehearse . . . just to play some music. Nobody wanted to make any money and nobody cared about making money and we had a lot of disdain for the people who were making money because of what they had to do to make it. Tom's band did some gigs but not very many.

It was a fun band . . . he had a whole bunch of chemically very compatible people. They were all like Bohemian starving artists. He always gave guys room to blow—that was important. There wasn't another band like it around. Every dope fiend in town was on it, but Tom was always straight.

DON PRELL: How did Tom stay so straight? It must have been his upbringing, I think. Also, he wasn't really one of us as far as jazz players were concerned. I never saw him sit in on piano, for instance. He was a composer, while the piano players at the sessions were just straight ahead jazz players—that was it, that's all they did. So that distances you.

Not to mention the fact that Tom Talbert was more interested in writing than anything else.

JACK MONTROSE: Tommy was constantly writing—there'd be new music every week. No one was writing like that at the time. Boyd Raeburn was happening and Stan Kenton, but no one was writing like Tom. I thought he had a lot to offer, especially at that age, the charts he wrote were quite influential at that time. There was scarcely ever any rewriting done or any changes made to his charts. I always had that feeling that he wrote with a lot of certainty about what he was doing. Everyone in Tom's band was a known major jazz player at the top of his game and no one ever turned him down. And there were a lot of bands that couldn't get players—they just weren't acceptable to play with. As a conductor he was very, very cool; he got guys that he liked and so he didn't have to rehearse them a whole lot—he didn't have to go through a lot of contentious meanderings about the whys and wherefores of the music.

The trombone section included Harry Betts, who went on to become an important player with Stan Kenton and later a very successful arranger and musical director for artists like Peggy Lee and Jack Jones.

HARRY BETTS: I remember how impressed I was with Tommy Talbert's music. I was new in town. I'd come out of the service and I was hoping to get into a big band, which I eventually did. I started going to rehearsal bands where you would meet people, and Tommy was one of them. I remember that his music stuck out because it had a different sound to it and I liked it a lot. To me it had a kind of a lacy quality—a transparency to it. It doesn't hit you over the head like Kenton or Buddy Rich or someone but there's a lovely—transparency is the best word I can think of that describes it. I met Tommy and liked him a lot. And then I think I got a job with Jimmy Zito, so I started working right away. I was with Jimmy for a few months; then I got the chance to go with Stan and I was with him for almost five years. Stan and Tommy had one thing in common—they were both gentlemen. As conductors they were soft-spoken but got the job done. Never any yelling or anything like that. They always got good people, so I was sitting there usually with guys who were better than me, which is always a nice feeling.

One thing Stan Kenton and Tom Talbert did not have in common was work for their bands. In 1947 the reputation and demand for Stan's band was phenomenal, while Tom's band was still mostly rehearsing and playing for free.

TOM TALBERT: We played some big benefit concerts for no money, including a March of Dimes broadcast. Then in early summer of 1947 I went on the road playing piano for Anita O'Day. I'd always admired her singing and the chance came up to go on tour with her. I didn't get the gig because of my pianistic virtuosity, and I didn't realize that Carl Hoff, who was Anita's husband and manager, had the hots for Margaret, my girlfriend, and wanted me out of town. The understanding was that I would be doing arrangements of material that would enable Anita to play classier rooms that paid more money than the gin mills she usually appeared in. I thought that would be great and imagined all the wonderful songs we could work on. Unfortunately that didn't work out. When I got to Chicago, Anita, God bless her, had no intention of changing her repertoire at all, so we were still doing songs like "Exactly Like You" and playing in taverns. I was no Jimmy Rowles as pianists go and, to make up for that, through the William Morris office we got a very good bass player and a good drummer. We were playing at a place called Jumptown, which was out by the stockyards. Nowhere near the Loop—about thirty-eight blocks out of the way, and hot! I don't know if they didn't have air conditioning but it was just terrible. I didn't pretend to be anything I wasn't. She wasn't really happy with me and I wasn't happy with the situation but we settled down and did the job. But God, she'd have trouble setting the tempos and frequently stop and start over again. Bob Cooper and June Christy were in the audience one night and when I went over to sit down with them, Bob said, "I could have told you it would be like this." His knowledge of Anita's ways went back to the days when they were both in the Kenton band.

We did have some laughs though—I was having a beer in the bar with the bass player. They had great draft beer, but the bar was so dark you could hardly see a thing. Here comes this black dude wearing dark glasses, who calls out "Hey Tom!"

It was Howard McGhee. The bass player just broke up: "The joint is so dark you can't read the label of the bottle you're drinking from and in walks this guy wearing dark glasses who recognizes you from the other end of the room."

I liked Howard. I'd met him when I was doing some arrangements for a guy who had a little band—I think his name was something like Lew Olds [Lou Oles?]. We did a series of recordings, some with a girl singer and Howard and Russ Freeman on piano. About ten years ago I asked Russ if he knew what had happened to the recordings, and he said, "I never ever heard from the guy after we did the dates." I do recall one tune I did for the dates—"It's Easy to Remember." Howard McGhee never got the credit for being the innovator he was—he was twenty times the player that Miles Davis was.

I worked with Anita for a couple of months then left and went to New York. I went to New York because Johnny Richards was there with Boyd Raeburn. I'd done some writing for Boyd out in Los Angeles—"Prelude to a Kiss" was one arrangement. But I don't think it was quite what Boyd was expecting, or wanting. I used to go to hear the band often in LA. I knew a lot of the guys on the band and it was fun to listen to, although I didn't care too much for George Handy's writing. Things like "March of the Boyds" I thought very pretentious.

Another reason for going to New York was that by this time I really felt I wanted to go to music school. So I went to talk to Johnny about it. He had an apartment at 1 Christopher Street. I had some long talks with him and he took it very seriously. He considered the people I could study with—David Diamond was at NYU, Howard Hanson was at Eastwood, but then he said, "Do you realize that if you go to one of these schools you won't be doing any writing for two years? "And there went my idea of studying. Looking back I regret it, but at the time I felt I'd been out in the world too much by this time and didn't relish the idea of spending two years in schoolrooms. To soften the blow, Johnny said, "You can always come to me if you want to learn something—get in touch anytime."

The word was out that Caesar Petrillo, the boss of the Musicians Union, was about to call another recording ban and consequently there was a lot of recording going on in Los Angeles so I went back.

Tom wrote some arrangements for a singer named Joan Barton.

TOM TALBERT: She was the girlfriend of a big-time Los Angeles car dealer known as "Mad Man Muntz" because of the crazily cheap prices he advertised. He had television connections that got her a show on KTLA at 7:30 on Wednesday nights. It was called *On the Air with Joan Barton* and was sponsored by Philco. Joan appeared, lip-synching songs that she had recorded with my band. We used a septet on some programs and the full band on others. I believe that Joan eventually married Sonny Burke the arranger and record producer.

Tom managed to squeeze an instrumental recording into the end of a Joan Barton session on December 31, 1947, right before Petrillo's second recording ban. "Love Is a Pleasure" was played by a contingent from the rehearsal band and allows us to hear El Koeling's sensitive alto sax playing, a rare solo from tenor saxist Dave Madden, and, rarest of all, a solo from pianist Tom Talbert.

The band continued to rehearse, worked benefits, and occasionally got a paying job. Milt Bernhart played in the trombone section for a time during 1947.

MILT BERNHART: I rehearsed with Tom while I was sitting it out waiting for Stan Kenton to reorganize. In 1947 when I was with Stan Kenton, Stan had a nervous breakdown and the band was broken up in Tuscaloosa, Alabama. Most of the guys came back to Los Angeles and sat around town waiting for Stan to find himself again. Tom's band came in very handy for keeping up my chops and I enjoyed it . . . I considered his music very unlike Kenton's. It was much quieter and I detected the strong influence of Ellington in his writing. I feel that Ellington has been his muse for quite a long time. I remember being impressed by his writing for the army band back at Fort Ord. It was mainly quiet, soulful originals—he didn't like to write arrangements of other people's tunes. He could do it but he was really aiming to be a composer as well as an arranger and that's what he's done, mainly. But I remember there was one arrangement in particular that really impressed me. An arrangement of "The Swan" from Saint-Saëns's *Carnival of the Animals.* I hope it's still in his book. He arranged it as a saxophone solo from beginning to end and it was so beautiful—he improved on the original chords, orchestrated them very quietly and moodily. Poetically. And I remember saying, "Let's do it again."

Don Davidson also remembers that arrangement.

DON DAVIDSON: "The Swan" he wrote specifically for Elmer Koeling, who was on lead alto.

MILT BERNHART: I was greatly impressed by that. It opened my ears to what he was doing. He was also dabbling in what all the arrangers were doing and that was to write in the new idiom, bebop, and it didn't come that easily to Tom. I don't think he was ever, nor did he want to be, a bebopper, a Shorty Rogers—he figured to extend beyond that. I always thought that Tom must have had some training in music. Some background.

Milt Bernhart articulates one of the misconceptions that gradually arose about Tom Talbert—this one being the thought that the quality of his writing and his musical tastes must reflect a well-schooled background.

MILT BERNHART: We began to talk about my collection of symphonic music and I'd go to his apartment and bring some records—I brought Stravinsky and Delius. I think I helped him to discover Delius, which he really followed through on. He didn't copy Delius but there are indications and I was pleased.

Stan Kenton, on the other hand, also aimed to be more than a dance bandleader, to have a concert orchestra and play new music and some old music, but Stan didn't have enough background in what was what in that field. The first time he heard Wagner's music he was a grown-up man and he decided to record some of it the next day. He got so excited, as though it hadn't been there before, and did a lot of things from "The Ring." It was a nice try, but Stan was totally unprepared and was discovering that music as he recorded it. He'd never bothered to get to know it till then. But Tom comes from a different edge of the forest and we found each other very close on that basis with plenty to talk about and to listen to.

Another misconception followed in later years with an assumption by some that, thanks to a private income and/or support from indulgent parents, Talbert didn't have to scuffle for jobs or "pay his dues." But this was never the case. Tom led a precarious existence in Los Angeles spending three years writing for his band and trying to get it noticed. Ken Poston looks back.

KEN POSTON: The band worked occasionally in the LA area, but it wasn't recording for a label, so the only way you could hear the band was to go and hear it live. The people who did hear it and the musicians who participated recall it as a spectacular experience.

MILT BERNHART: I rehearsed with him regularly and he had a lot of good young players—Art Pepper was there I remember; Harry Betts who was later with Kenton and who was aiming to be an arranger too, and Tom was helping him. John McComb, a forgotten but very talented trumpet player from whom Chet Baker learned a lot. Johnny was already an icon when Miles Davis was just getting started in those days.

There are short and tantalizing solos by John McComb on Tom's 1949 recordings.

JOHN McCOMB

In January 2003 John's widow, Beverly McComb, looked back at his short and colorful life.

BEVERLY McCOMB: I was introduced to John by Warne Marsh, whom I was dating at the time. Both guys were playing in a group called the Canteen Kids that included, besides John and Warne, drummer Karl Kiffe and pianist Neil Cunningham. John got his start as a child when his father bought him a trumpet and he just started playing it. He was in the Sheriff's Boys band in Los Angeles, which was a very prestigious band at the time. It used to play at things like the Sunrise Easter Service at the Hollywood Bowl. When he was fifteen, he dropped out of Glendale High School and went on the road with the Ted Fiorito band and then he was with Ozzie Nelson's band for a long, long time. John loved to play Latin trumpet so he got into the Latin scene here in LA playing with the Eddie Cano band. When he was drafted, he got into a navy band and spent his two years in Panama, which is where he really built up his technique.

He liked Tom Talbert's band a lot. He appreciated Tom's creativity, maybe more than some of the other kids in the band did. They were all very young in those days right after the war. John was playing around Central Avenue a lot at that time and with a lot of little pickup bands—I remember him playing at the Club Alabam. We had a great time on the scene then. I remember going down to Billy Berg's with John and hearing Billie Holiday when Herbie Steward was in the band with her. We used to know Zoot and Ray Sims very well. Zoot was a wonderful, uncomplicated guy who just loved to blow. Ray was the same.

Later John went on the road with Woody Herman and a Latin band led by Luis Acarás. This is where things went wrong for John. He'd been doing drugs, in fact got hepatitis from a dirty needle when he was with Woody's band in Canada. Woody's band was notorious for drugs and had been for a long time. After he left Herman, he was down in Texas with Luis's band. It was Cinco de Mayo and a guy came up to the bandstand and handed John a joint, saying, "Come on, it's Cinco de Mayo—it's a celebration day!" No sooner had John taken the joint in his hand than the police came up and busted him. It was a terrifying experience because of all the jails in the U.S., Texas must have the worst. I had just got engaged to John and we had to scrape around and find money to get him out and get an attorney; he was locked up for almost five months. He was very disenchanted after that. He still loved jazz and still played it and never ever got it out of his system. But that did it as far as making a career out of it was concerned. Gerry Mulligan wanted John to come on his first quartet. He asked John before he asked Chet Baker and John turned him down. We talked about it and I wanted him to go with Gerry. I said, "God, this is a terrific opportunity." But he said, "Gerry just 'got off the farm' and I just don't think I can get involved in that scene again." He knew that after his Texas arrest he risked winding up in jail possibly for years. The police were so into harassing musicians at that time and drugs were even more prevalent than they are now. It's a great shame because I think John would have been very good with Gerry's quartet. John had a very good reputation at that time. As a matter of fact John told me that he was just a couple of years ahead of Chet at

Glendale High School, and everybody went around in awe of his playing, including Chet, who idolized him and tried to play like him. When he decided to not go with Gerry, I was surprised and disappointed. I thought it was such a waste. But we don't know what would have happened had he joined. John thought that Chet was good—not great, but he thought he did well with what he had.

He still played casuals and played for fun but he really began to rethink his life. He never went on the road again, and went back to school. He went to City College in Los Angeles and got his Associate in Arts then finished up two years at UCLA where he got his BA in sociology. One of his sociology teachers at UCLA recommended him for an NDEA fellowship at the University of Oregon. This was a grant that enabled him to bypass the master's and go straight to a Ph.D. After three years in Oregon we moved to Berkeley, where I worked at UC Berkeley and John finished his dissertation. We still hung out with jazz musicians and John played once in a while but just for fun. While we were in Berkeley John began to experience some strange pain in his shoulder, which was finally diagnosed as cancer. He was forty-two years old when he died. He had a short but happy life and he loved every minute of the music part of it.

He was very ambivalent about his own playing and told me that he didn't think he really learned how to play the trumpet properly until his time in the navy. He also studied composition and orchestration with Dr. Wesley La Violette in Los Angeles and composed a beautiful string quartet that was recorded privately. He liked Dizzy, Clifford Brown, Louis Armstrong, Howard McGhee. His favorite was actually the Mexican trumpeter Rafael Mendez. He always played in a cool understated way and always felt that "less was better." He listened to and studied classical music so much and I think he was trying to develop his own approach—his own "thing." He was always trying to get into himself when he was playing and he wasn't interested in doing all the high-notes things at all. He loved that lower register and he sounded great on the mellophone too.

DON PRELL: I thought John was a real sweet kind of player—he didn't blast. We had a couple of those kinds of trumpeters on the band who went on to studio work.

JACK MONTROSE: Johnny was a beautiful player—extremely talented—and totally unequipped to live on this earth. Or in this society. It's entirely possible that Gerry Mulligan asked John to go with the quartet—but he probably sounded out several players before he got to

Chet. One wouldn't have come up on a player like Chet all of a sudden; there's a process leading up to it. It would be hard to compare John or anyone to Chet; Chet was so fluent and so immensely talented while John was less consistent and exhibited flashes of brilliance. I loved John's playing but he was very fragile. You could hear him play for years and then one time he could play an eight-bar solo with Tommy's band and it would be astoundingly beautiful.

Don Prell, bassist with the Tom Talbert Orchestra in 1949, was another musician who, like John McComb, got his start and went on the road at an amazingly young age by today's standards.

DON PRELL: I wanted to be a drummer but in junior high school the teacher said, "We've got too many drummers; you're tall so you can play the bass."

I went on the road with Frank Ortega's band when I was fourteen—Herb Geller was also on that band and he was fifteen. We went to Texas. It was during the war and they were short of musicians so I guess you could get away with that then.

I can't remember exactly how I got on to Tom's band. I'd been playing around LA with Johnny Barbera and several of us had also been with Phil Carreón's band. That was a great band—we played a lot of Basie stuff. Herb Geller and John McComb and Billy Byers were in the band. We also had a trombonist named Robert Huerta who used to get up and play "Sweet and Lovely" and that's all he did. The rest of the time he just sat there and smoked dope. I don't think he even played any of the parts. That was in the middle of the Pachuco period—the time of the zoot suit riots. We were playing at a dance hall called the Sons of Herman at 25th and Main Street. I had to hold the door to the stage shut with my foot because people would barge in and use the bandstand to jump off into the middle of the audience and start beating people up. When you parked your car, you had to wait for another member of the band to arrive before you'd get out.

Somehow we all wound up in Tommy's band.

Tenor saxist Warne Marsh was in the reed section when the band was booked into the Trianon Ballroom in April 1948, and 1949 saw a concert at the Coronet Theater on La Cienega Boulevard. The band that night included Herbie Harper on trombone and Bart Caldarell, who subsequently went with Stan Kenton playing tenor and bassoon, on second alto. Among the music played was Tom's "Madrid Suite," which is described in the program thus: "His Madrid Suite is an idiomatic study of a state of being. Madrid '35 concerns the days of happiness. Madrid '37 is a besieged city. Madrid '39 laments itself in days of sadness. The suite typifies his approach to concert jazz and is perhaps his most comprehensive work to date."

It is likely that some of the conversations Tom had with the one-time Lincoln Brigade veteran in the camp at San Luis Obispo impelled him to write this suite. Considered along with the invention and imagination to be found in the examples of Tom's writing from the 1940s that were recorded, it's obvious that the twenty-five-year-old was aiming to be much more than a utility or journeyman arranger and composer.

Not long after the Coronet, the band was playing a concert at a Veterans Hospital. At this time, it could be said that the Talbert luck began to change for the worse.

TOM TALBERT: God, it was hot—but the band was wonderful. We went back to the apartment to celebrate, and there was a guy there who was driving up to San Francisco. I'd been wanting to get up there to see if I could get something going for the band and he offered me a ride. First of all we had to go all the way back to his place at Manhattan Beach. Then once we got there he said, "I'm pretty tired, why don't you drive for an hour, then I'll be okay to take over. We'd had a lot to drink at my apartment, but I started driving anyway. After about fifty-five minutes, somewhere north of Malibu I went to sleep and drove into a telephone pole. I was thrown out of the car through the windshield. I had terribly severe concussion and broken teeth. Fortunately I had my discharge papers in my wallet and the ambulance took me to the Veterans Hospital in Westwood. They had a terrific staff there and, it being just after the war; they'd seen and worked on everything. I was in there for about three weeks. The owner of the car was luckier—he'd been asleep on the backseat and was just bruised when he was thrown on to the floor.

Once Tom recovered, he and his new girlfriend, Anita, decided to take a holiday, with more unexpected and unwanted results.

TOM TALBERT: We went down to Ensenada in Mexico with another couple. We'd only been there a day or so when we got the stupid idea to rent some horses. I don't think I'd ridden before. Foolishly I got the horse galloping and the cinch broke on the saddle and I fell off flat on my back. We were along the beach, miles from Ensenada, and I was badly hurt. My shoulder and arm were smashed up and I was concussed again. Fortunately our companion Jack Melchior, one of my closest friends, had been in the Philippines during World War II and was pretty savvy about what to do, even though he admitted that he was plenty worried. He managed to organize someone with a flatbed truck to take me to a small infirmary run by Catholic nuns. He then organized an ambulance to come down from San Diego to take me back to a hospital there. I was in tremendous pain from the pins inserted in my arm and the brace holding it still. And when I recovered from all of this and got back to the band, this was the point at which I stopped playing piano and we got Claude Williamson instead. I'd admired Claude's playing for a long time—since I'd heard him with the Charlie Barnet band. He seemed to like my writing and was often in the small audience that came to our weekly rehearsals.

By now it was really exactly the band I'd wanted. We had Art Pepper in it, Don Prell was playing bass, Jimmy Pratt was the drummer, and I think it was as viable a band as any of the established ones. I knew, of course, that we needed management. Harry Betts brought over someone who'd been managing Stan Kenton and he listened to some recordings we'd made and said "My God! That's only thirteen players. What does Stan want with forty when you make thirteen sound like that?"

That was about the time that the word went out that Stan was putting his Innovations Orchestra together. At this time both Jimmy Pratt and Art Pepper told me that they'd go on the road with me and the band for any reasonable salary if I could get something organized.

There was little interest on the part of the booking agencies in arranging a tour for a band virtually unknown outside a small circle of Los Angeles fans and totally lacking in any radio or record exposure. Woody Herman, Stan Kenton, Duke Ellington, and Claude Thornhill with Gil Evans writing for him, were recording for major labels and doing a lot of broadcasts. Even Boyd Raeburn was making records and working. Tom's band wasn't, even though it was playing music that impressed those who heard it. It also lacked the pop-oriented dance charts the other bands played, along with their more progressive jazz arrangements, which gained them more work.

Tom decided that the only way the band could progress would be by "going east." To this end he made a set of demo discs in hopes of getting a contract from one of the record companies. Once again the band recorded at Radio Recorders, the studio where Stan Kenton had recorded some of his most celebrated numbers. Tom also shared Kenton personnel at one time or another, including, as mentioned, alto saxist Art Pepper, trombonists Milt Bernhart, Harry Betts, and also John Halliburton, trumpeters Frank Beach and John Anderson.

He also had a rhythm section—Claude Williamson, Don Prell, and Jimmy Pratt—that would tour Europe in 1957 with Bob Cooper and Bud Shank and play in South Africa with Bud in 1958. In November 1949 the band recorded six titles: five standards and an original, two of them vocals by singer/pianist Jean Louise. The local Musician's Union officials delivered a crass and tasteless insult to the music.

TOM TALBERT: One thing I hadn't bargained on—I had always been scrupulous in observing union rules and I informed the local that we were making audition recordings. They sent some creep out who'd probably been sitting idly round in the lobby with nothing to do but play cards. He interjected, over the microphone, on every take, the words "This is an audition record" in order to make sure it couldn't be released. I sent the discs to RCA but they weren't interested. I may have approached a couple of other companies too, but no one wanted to give us a contract. Harry Betts and Art Pepper were about to join Stan Kenton's new band, so I decided to close up shop and head for New York. There just wasn't enough for me to do out here. Bands had been breaking up constantly over the past couple of years and it just seemed impossible to get a new unknown band off the ground.

The recordings are as fine as anything recorded by Tom's contemporaries, but the listener should be warned that removing the union functionary's demo message deleted several bars of music on each piece. What sometimes appears to be an odd, perhaps imaginative transition or rephrase is in fact several inches of missing recording tape. In particular, the excised union message ruins the saxophone passage on the bridge after the vocal on "April in Paris."

Among the highlights of the session, "I Cover the Waterfront" exemplifies Tom's penchant for rewriting melody lines and his developing cool approach.

TOM TALBERT: One of my things is simplifying melodies—I often leave out pickup notes.

The use of interweaving contrapuntal lines and vibrato-less saxes gives the piece a feeling that is very West Coast, right down to the understated trumpet of John McComb and the lyricism of early Art Pepper. A performance such as this is a good example of the two-way street that connected performance and writing at this time, the sounds and styles of the musicians undoubtedly influencing the way Tom and his contemporaries wrote.

Tom had this to say of John McComb:

TOM TALBERT: Johnny was way ahead of Chet Baker. Chet copied him and never had the lyricism of John at his best.

"I Get a Kick Out of You" and "April in Paris" were written to accompany singer Jean Louise.

TOM TALBERT: Jean Louise was so great; she had perfect pitch. You could write any kind of intro you wanted. I think she was married to the piano player Frank Patchen. She played piano as well and was working as a single when I came back to LA in the 1970s.

"Kick" must be one of the brassiest arrangements Tom has written, and uncharacteristic as such. He may have been demonstrating just how much power he could get out of just three trumpets and two trombones. It certainly rivals the effect of the much bigger Kenton brass section.

Jean Louise certainly needed her sense of pitch on "Paris," and it's a mystery how she managed to get in. Tom made the following observation, fifty years later.

TOM TALBERT: If I wrote an arrangement like that, these days we'd be in the studio for weeks. Half beat triplets with the guys playing every other one? As you can hear, I had great confidence in my musicians.

More than the other vocal item, this is a strange mix of the sweet and the tart, with some interesting sounding, if not quite perfectly balanced, woodwind passages in the background. A nagging thought for the future and the question of Tom's ability to survive in the commercial world—these were arrangements for a band in search of a recording contract.

"Is Is Not Is," a boppish Talbert original, has a title that even Tom can no longer explain. Once again, just five brass get a big, hot sound written in a way that . . .

TOM TALBERT: Is so simple.

It's also an opportunity to hear Jimmy Pratt swinging the band. Tom thinks that Jimmy Pratt joined the band when Dick Stanton went off to join Xavier Cugat.

TOM TALBERT: Jimmy was such a groovy player.

And a cross-section of the soloing talents getting into a twelve-bar blues—Jack Montrose, Harry Betts, John McComb, and John Barbera.

The audition records went off to New York, but their failure to thrill A&R managers caused Tom to decide reluctantly that the band had run its course. A record contract was almost a prerequisite for bookings back in 1949, just as exposure on radio was critical for a band's success.

MILT BERNHART: In the old days radio stations went on the air all day with disc jockeys playing records when they didn't have a live band in the studio. Or all night, when they weren't broadcasting a band from a club. It made the names of the bands and the people and the music, and it was free to the radio stations. They didn't have to pay for it; they loved it. So everybody came out fine, but now it's gone and chances are it won't come back.

If it was tough then it's even harder now. For me, the tragedy today is having a band and writing for it and getting anybody to pay attention. You make records, but then what? What happens after that? You've made records. There has to be an outlet; you still have to get the attention of people who might like to go out and buy your record. There are practically no places on the air today where you can hear Tom's music, or anything like it.

And indeed, this would become a major problem for Tom Talbert in the late 1990s.

Looking back to 1949, in the light of the audition records and the offers from Art Pepper and Jimmy Pratt, the question needs to be asked: How committed was Tom to the reality of touring a band, with all the attendant nonmusical problems, from personnel to travel? Could the band have been successful and financially viable?

DON DAVIDSON: I don't know if Tom was all that dedicated about taking the band out on the road. He wanted to work; he wanted to record it and he wanted it exposed to the audience. He wanted it to work primarily around the Los Angeles area, which was not really all that fertile a ground, particularly at that point in time, to launch a new band. There were only a few bands that came out of Southern California; Les Brown started elsewhere and settled in Southern California. The Kenton band is about the only one that I know of that was successful and was launched out there.

JACK MONTROSE: At the time that we made those audition records, those records were so good that I felt certain that someone would pick them up. Everybody felt that this was going to go somewhere and Tom would be recognized for his efforts. There's no question—they were as good in their own way as anything that Kenton, Raeburn, or any of his contemporaries were doing at the time. But there was one thing that Tom didn't do that many of his colleagues and his contemporaries did do, and that was make himself into a master performer as well as a writer. Tom was always a piss-poor piano player and so he had no recognition in that respect—playing didn't help him. It opened no doors for him. And it was that much more difficult for him to establish a personality in front of the audience. Someone like Dizzy Gillespie was one of the world's great bandleaders but he was also one of the world's great trumpet players in 1946–1947.

Johnny Barbera remembered that Tom had a very relaxed demeanor as bandleader.

JOHNNY BARBERA: Tommy would start the band off and he'd be playing piano and then he'd get up and he was very nonchalant about it. Then he'd go back and sit down and throw a few chords in, then get up and end the number. His forte was being a writer—he was never going to be a piano player.

The band wasn't ready to do dance gigs, to do something like the Palladium. His music was subtle and rich. You had to be a listener to appreciate Tommy's music. Everything he did was so serious—and he meant it. I felt that right away. He didn't really have a book that you could take on the road. And also I don't think anyone pursued it to get it work and get on the road and book it. The only band that was at all like Tommy's at that time was Billy Eckstine's. Tommy was leaning toward Duke I felt, and Billy also had a band that was not rambunctious, like other bands. I guess that was because the band had to back him up on vocals. That band reminded me of Tommy's band—Tommy's band reminded me of that kind of band. I thought Tommy's band needed a strong vocalist and I was thinking of Billy—because everything in the background was just so rich.

While Tom was breaking up his band, Stan Kenton was organizing his huge Innovations in Modern Music Orchestra and Art Pepper, Milt Bernhart, and Harry Betts joined it. Pepper and fellow members tenor saxist Bob Cooper and singer June Christy were all fans of Tom's writing and recommended him to Kenton. Stan asked Tom to write some things for him.

TOM TALBERT: Kenton or someone called me and I drove over to his house one night. He asked me to write two pieces—a cello feature and a swing piece, in typical Kenton rhetoric, "that would still be played in fifty years' time." He was having a concert to introduce the Innovations Orchestra. Although the date was pretty close, I wrote the pieces, the parts were copied, and they were rehearsed. The band had some conception problems but they were sorted out and the pieces sounded good. I went to the concert and Stan didn't play either of them. At a big party afterward, Pete Rugolo was all over me, apologizing that they "just hadn't been able to work them in." I got paid for the charts but that's the last I ever saw of them. I was upset for a while, but heard later that that was what happened to a lot of the music that Stan commissioned.

Don Davidson, who was a member of the Stan Kenton band in the mid-1950s, agrees.

DON DAVIDSON: He had written a piece for the Innovations Orchestra to feature cellist Gregory Bemko—like a concerto for cello . . . I went to a rehearsal up in Hollywood where they played it—it sounded great to me . . . I don't recall whether it was ever recorded or whether they ever used it.

    Tom's pieces were rehearsed but never recorded, a fate that befell many arrangements supplied to Kenton by many writers.

Harry Betts was a member of the Innovations Orchestra's trombone section and saw these arrangements and compositions come and go.

HARRY BETTS: I can understand why Tom's arrangements for Stan didn't work out—my guess is that they wouldn't have been obvious enough. Tom has a different approach to music. I only wrote one arrangement for Stan and I think I probably made the same mistake as Tom. I wrote it for Conte Candoli but it ended kind of down, on a down chord. After they rehearsed it Buddy Childers said to me . . . "That's the first time I've ever heard a trumpet feature that didn't end with a loud crashing chord."

Some writers were able, or willing, to adapt their musical vision to accommodate Kenton's. Tom Talbert, having run his own band for several years, was probably unwilling.

Jack Montrose remembers Stan's approach.

JACK MONTROSE: As a bandleader Stan Kenton was a menace because the band reflected his personality so much. When I was in the
band, Bill Holman was my roommate and Bill was writing everything
in the book at that time. Stan would come up to the room and stand
over him and Bill would be sitting on the bed with a score pad trying
to write down these ideas that Stan was throwing at him. Stan was
making sure that they were his ideas, that they reflected him. I used to
say, "How in the world can you do that? I couldn't do that." He said,
"It just comes out the way it does anyway, whether Stan was there or
not." I'm not sure that I believe that. I'm not sure that's true. Stan
didn't like Holman. His writing reflected Count Basie. But the guys in
the band liked him and the fans loved his writing. If Stan had ever
taken up any of the pieces Tom wrote for him, I'm sure that would
have made a big difference to his future and reputation.

One composition of Tom's that did get played by the Kenton band
was "Sabina's Serenade," which started out as an opening and closing piece for the Fort Ord army band to play on bond drive concerts
and broadcasts. Tom subsequently developed it for his own band
and then rewrote it as a feature for the Kenton sax section. Although
Stan never recorded it commercially, there is an aircheck in existence, a CBS broadcast from the Terrace Ballroom, Fort Wayne, Indiana, on May 2, 1952.

The piece is quiet and gentle with a complex structure and some
very effective interwoven lines that look forward to an arrangement
of "Prelude to a Kiss" that Tom would write for his *Bix Duke Fats* album in a few years time. It's obvious that he revels in the possibilities offered by a skilled sax section. Even though there are some ten-
tative moments in the performance, this very ambitious piece gets a
big round of applause at its end. Art Pepper and Bob Cooper told
Tom that it was a great favorite and was played every night on the
road. Given the date of the aircheck, Kenton obviously liked it
enough to keep it in the book after he folded the Innovations Orchestra and formed the New Concepts band. Scored for just the saxophone and rhythm sections, it would also have been a very useful
number to play after intermission, enabling Stan to start a new set
while the trumpets and trombones were tearing themselves away
from the bar. Tom tried another piece on Stan Kenton called "La
Bayadera" while he was living in New York, and Milt Bernhart describes its rehearsal in the next chapter.

NOTES

1. *Metronome,* June 1946.
2. *Metronome,* July 1946.
3. *Metronome,* August 1946.
4. *Metronome,* October 1946.
5. *Metronome,* October 1946.
6. *Metronome,* March 1947.

8

New York City

By 1950 work for musicians seemed to be diminishing in Los Angeles, and most of it was confined to the studios. Tom Talbert had none at all and no prospect of any, so he decided to try his luck in New York again. He arrived there in the spring to begin the task of "getting a little visible." This was yet another fateful decision and it meant that he would not be around Los Angeles to participate in the still unforeseen rise of West Coast jazz a couple of years later. At the time, things looked promising in New York City.

TOM TALBERT: To me, New York was jumping. There was so much work: hotel society-type bands, solo pianists at the big hotels, supper clubs like the Blue Angel, the Hickory House, Café Society, jazz clubs like Basin Street East, the Roost, Birdland, and the Vanguard. There were ballrooms and guys going on ships. NBC, ABC, and CBS had staff orchestras, there were Afro-Cuban bands like Machito, which I later wrote for, and musicians were just beginning to record commercials for TV.

At that time there was just a tremendous pool of good musicians, and while I didn't know many when I got there, it was a friendly business and there was a kind of ripple effect—when you met people you'd meet their friends.

I'd driven to New York with my girlfriend, Anita, and stayed first with my friend from the army, Bill Wolfe, in New Jersey. I ran into Jimmy Pratt in Charlie's Tavern or some such place and we briefly roomed together up near the Apollo Theater. Anita, who had always had some emotional problems, became ill and wound up in Bellevue. My mother was a great nurse with a warm heart, so I temporarily solved that problem by sending Anita to stay with her in Minneapolis. I got myself a small apartment on 19th Street near Gramercy Park

DANNY BANK

Baritone saxist Danny Bank was one of the New Yorkers who became a close friend and musical comrade. His is the quintessential life, background, and experience of the New York musician of the period.

We started in Brooklyn. A whole group of us saxophone players—Al Cohn, Frank Socolow, Al Epstein, and Alan Greenspan who of course is now chairman of the Federal Reserve Board. I played with Alan in a band at the Paramount Theatre; he was a good jazz tenor man—he played good solos. A big name now—a powerful man. I think Brooklyn was a great incubator. There were so many great jazz players from Brooklyn. Al Cohn was from the same block that I was born on, right down the street, and so was Al Epstein. Socolow lived a little further down and the bass player who used to play with Benny Goodman and Jimmy Dorsey, Barney Spieler—also down the street. All of us right close together about two or three blocks from the old Ebbitt's Field.

I'd been out with all the big bands, and about 1950, when I got off the road, I decided I'd better start studying seriously. But within a year and a half I'd been absorbed into the record business. And into the pit business—Broadway. I was always busy and I didn't have time to study. I used to have to rent studios that were available after midnight in order to practice.

I was on so many albums with people like Patty Page and Johnny Ray, I was on his record of "Cry." A guy came over to me in Japan and said, "I've been waiting to meet you for thirty years." I said, "Why?" He said, "I need your autograph on some of these albums—you made nine thousand albums."

I did every kind of work—all kinds—nightclubs, ballrooms, Spanish bands like Machito. Records. I worked with the Boston Pops, the Philharmonic, the Goldman band, and the various leaders like Percy Faith; I played on sessions for Ella Fitzgerald, Sarah Vaughan, Billie Holiday, Frank Sinatra. I worked with Axel Stordahl, and then of course all the theaters.

I played on Kate Smith's TV show every day. Art Rollini was in the band. His talent was for doubling. He could play all the woodwinds. He could take out an oboe, an English horn, bassoon, flute . . . in those days there were some world famous doublers—I'll never forget them—but I'll forget their names!

I had a nickname—everyone called me Ubiquitous. People would show up and there I'd be. Subbing in the pits and doing two or three record dates every day. One day in the morning I'd be doing the Goldman band or Ravelli's band from Michigan, or the Boston Pops come down for a recording. The LP came in strong, and this was the center of the world as far as that was concerned. And then in the afternoon it might be a jazz date, it might be Ella—or Cannonball Adderley, Dizzy, Charlie Parker. One day I did five record dates. We started out early in the morning backing one of those groups like the Four Lads or the Four Temptations—that kind of stuff. We were booked for three sessions, a morning, an afternoon, and an evening. The evening was supposed to be seven to ten and when it got to ten and they hadn't finished, they wouldn't pay overtime. But they said, "Look, take fifteen minutes off and we'll give you another date, we'll go from ten to one." That's the fourth date. And I'm sitting there with Phil Bodner and we get to one o' clock and again they don't want to go overtime and they feel that they could "do better." So "Whaddya think, fellers? Let's take another fifteen minutes and go from 1:30 to 4:30 in the morning." Well, I'm drinking a lot of coffee and working hard and sure enough it gets to 4:30 and they try it again. So I looked at Phil and I said, "Phil, forget it." And they said, "Okay with you guys?" And I yelled into the mike, "Noooo," and I reached for my case and I put my horn away. And they were angry at me; they didn't hire me after that. But we did five dates in one day—fifteen hours of recording. I'll never forget that. And that was all the time. I think one week I did twenty-one dates—or nineteen dates . . . but those days will never return. In those days it was all live!

Contractors—that's another evil of the business. If they hire you a lot then they expect that you will be there when they call you. That you owe them. And I was so busy that I couldn't do that. If a man a called me up for work and if the spot was open in my diary, then I'm there. Other guys would take the job and then if another job came in that paid a little more then they'd take that job and send a substitute.

But social life? If you had a social life, then you had no time to practice.

BOBBY TRICARICO

Tenor saxist Bobby Tricarico, who became a valued member of Tom's film and television orchestra in Los Angeles in the 1970s, was also already fully occupied in the 1950s New York scene.

There were so many things going on in New York. I was doing the *Tonight Show* and that used to be a panic. I'd take all my horns to NBC then I'd take those I needed for a session at Columbia Records 30th Street studio, get in the car, and go down there and try to find a parking place. Then run back to Columbia and make a session, then get back in time for the *Tonight Show* rehearsal at 3:15. NBC allowed guys to do other work, but some of the other contractors wouldn't. At that time guys were too busy to do a Broadway show. Now that's all they are doing.

At night I was working on 52nd street. I was at the Three Deuces, I was at the Keyboard, but it was a turning point, it was a time when they were losing the jazz groups. New owners would come into the clubs and they would turn them into strip joints. There was still some jazz around, Bird was still playing, Diz, Johnny Dankworth would come over from England . . . that's about the time that I met Tom, on 52nd Street. New York and the big hangout for musicians was Jim and Andy's.

TOM TALBERT: As far as "getting known" was concerned, there were some wonderful watering holes like Jim and Andy's, and Hurley's and Charlie's Tavern, where the guys hung out and for the price of a couple of beers you could see dozens of musicians on any night of the week. I'd run into someone I'd known on the West Coast, meet who he was with and so the circle would expand.

Danny Bank has fond memories of Charlie's Tavern.

DANNY BANK: Oh, it was great—Charlie was such a gentleman. He was an Englishman—a drummer. I forget what his name was (a Jewish name I think), but he bought the title with the bar. He was so kind; he'd cash our checks and he had a good chef and it was home for many, many years. It was a long open bar with a dining room in the back, a couple of phone booths and it was right across the street from the Columbia studios. You met a lot of people there. Bird, all the guys from Basie's band, Duke Ellington's band. And the women—the women were all either photographers in the nightclubs or hatcheck girls or prostitutes who were finished with their business. And the bar was open till 4:00 a.m. So that was your social life.

Among Danny's memories of Charlie Parker was his solution to playing with out-of-tune pianos.

DANNY BANK: I used to drive Bird home from Charlie's Tavern late at night—he used to live on the Lower East Side and I asked him some interesting questions too . . . I'd say, Charlie, you're playing in every club in town, every recording studio in town—do you have any trouble tuning up? You know, one piano's flat, another's sharp. He said, "No I don't have a tuning problem." He said, "I just push in." He said, "If you're sharp you can pull out. If you're flat you're unemployed."

And that's what I teach my students: you pull the mouthpiece out till you can't pull out any further, then you push it in and play a half tone lower.

Danny thinks that he first met Tom Talbert in Charlie's Tavern.

DANNY BANK: I'd finished a morning recording date and come in for breakfast and maybe a Bloody Mary. Until we started talking in the bar, I knew nothing about him. Tom was very friendly—he was from Minnesota, I believe, where I think his father had some hunting grounds where they hunted birds. His father would send a duck to Tom every once in a while, with a note to watch out for the shot and he'd invite me over to his apartment on Perry Street and we used to cook them. That's where I learned that a bird that's killed on the wing tastes different from one in the farmyard.

TOM TALBERT: My father had a relation who was a captain on Capitol Airlines, which was later taken over by Northwest. Dad would make up a package with duck, pheasant, antelope or even moose, and the relation would fly it into LaGuardia and I'd pick it up from him. The antelope came in the shape of chops from Wyoming. Grilled in my brick fireplace, with many drinks and Ravel or Debussy playing in the background, it impressed many dates. The moose came ground. Moose burgers were probably about the best solution there.

DANNY BANK: Tom and I would listen to records and we'd criticize them. Tom was listening to everything . . . he liked Gil Evans . . . some people compared him to Gil but he didn't copy him . . . What Tom does is a very original thing.
About the same time I met John Williams, also a very good piano player—a terrific guy. Tom and John Williams and I—we used to drink at the bar together.

TOM TALBERT: There were some good dinners, good companionship—I had loads of good friends in those days.

Along with the gourmet care packages, Tom's reputation as a writer followed him across the continent.

TOM TALBERT: Trumpeter Lou Obergh, who had been in my band, came into town with Tony Pastor, and I went down to see them playing at the Paramount. Lou introduced me to Pastor: "Boy, you should get this guy to write for your band, Tony." I just happened to have a couple of the demo acetates with me, and when Pastor heard them he thought they were great. Of course he didn't realize that his band wasn't going to sound the same. He had some transcription recording dates coming up and I did about ten arrangements for him. Then Tom "Tip" Morgan, the alto sax player from my Minneapolis days who was now playing with Claude Thornhill, introduced me to Claude. I met with him, and he was a throwback to the old-style bandleader. He left the band before the end of the last set. We went to another place where we sat at the bar and talked. The long and short of it was that I wrote more than ten arrangements for him. He wanted to get some new standards and showtunes in the book; and even though he already had arrangements of some of them, he wanted fresh ones. I particularly remember "Autumn in New York" because his manager said it was his favorite arrangement in his whole library. He was playing mostly for dancing at that time and he was a pleasure to meet and know.
It was very difficult, though, as I didn't have a piano. I used to rent a studio for a couple of hours but it wasn't really satisfactory and I was aware that I wasn't turning in my best work. I felt badly about that and I felt that Tony and Claude didn't get the best arrangements I could have written.
I was talking to alto saxist Hal McKusick, who had been with Thornhill's band. I said I just wish I could find somewhere comfortable with a piano, where I could write. Hal said that Gil Evans, when he was with Thornhill, always used the piano in the lobby of whichever hotel they were staying at. For obvious reasons that didn't help me, but I soon found myself in exactly the conditions I'd been seeking.

I'd become friendly with a photographer named George Meluso, who shared a studio with another guy named Dick Bruguiere. Dick had a private income and was a high-society type from upstate New York. He had a Cord car and his main interest was chasing nineteen-year-old models. I used to go up to their studio on 59th and 3rd Avenue quite a lot, and one day Dick said to George, "You know we ought to introduce Tom to Betty Brabeck—she loves jazz." So she came down one day and she was a tremendously good-looking girl, a real Greta Garbo look-alike.

Although it wasn't a big love affair, she and I spent a lot of time together over the next few years. After I got to know her, she introduced me to her friend Irene, who was being kept by a rich industrialist in a house down in Bucks County. It was a Revolutionary-wars period stone house with a swimming pool. We started going down there and we had a great time—but more important, there was a beautiful grand piano in the living room. The guy who was keeping Irene was Lowell Birrell—he was the chairman and president of Doeskin Tissues and he later was involved in a buyout of the Bon Ami Company. There were a whole series of Enron-type financial scandals, on a much smaller scale of course, and Lowell had to disappear to Brazil suddenly. When he finally came back, I think he did some time in jail. Before all this happened, he'd come to town and take Betty and me to dinner, usually to his favorite restaurant, the Chambord, where he'd usually fall asleep halfway through dinner. Eventually Irene got pregnant by Lowell and decided to have the child, so he sent her to Cuba for the birth, setting her up very grandly at Veradero Beach. He then said to me, "Would you like to stay at the house while Irene is away?"

So I moved down there and kept the apartment on 19th Street as well. George used to come down for weekends with some of his friends and Betty used to always bring down some great-looking girls and we had terrific weekend parties.

There were no musicians at these events, however. Just as Howard Rumsey had noted Tom's ambiguous presence on the jazz scene in Los Angeles, Tom had come to New York to seek success in music and quickly made himself part of a nonmusical social circle, enjoying himself perhaps a little too much for his professional good.

TOM TALBERT: In a way I had more friends out of the music business than in it. I had to wait six months for my union card, but I didn't sit around in some basement with Gil Evans, discussing the blues scale. I spent almost the whole winter of 1950–1951 down at the house. That's when I met a poet named Earl Mohn in a bar in New Hope. Earl was the editor of the local paper, the *New Hope Gazette,* an alcoholic, but a wonderful guy and we became great friends. Every so often he'd give me some work writing book reviews and through him I met the writer Budd Schulberg.

At this time Schulberg was noted for his scathing portrait of the movie industry in *What Makes Sammy Run?* and was shortly to achieve great fame with his screenplay for the Marlon Brando film *On the Waterfront.*

Along with writing book reviews and hanging out on the literary scene, Tom made a last attempt at writing for Stan Kenton, and Milt Bernhart was the less than enthusiastic intermediary.

MILT BERNHART: I tended not to recommend people to the leaders of bands I played in, neither arrangers nor players. I just figured that from what I knew about leaders, although Stan was not typical, if you made a suggestion and it didn't pan out, then you're a fool, and I didn't want to be responsible for having someone on the band who didn't live up to expectations or my sales pitch. I just stayed away from that sort of thing. Also, I didn't get too chummy with leaders, on purpose. When I was about fifteen and the Charlie Barnet band was playing at the Oriental Theatre in Chicago, I asked piano player Marty Napoleon, "What sort of a guy is Charlie Barnet?" The first question I could think of. He replied, "I haven't the slightest idea." I was shocked. He went on to say, "When the band is through playing, I go that way and Charlie goes that way, and we don't see each other until the next job. Then I'm under his control, but not otherwise, cause it isn't a healthy situation, kid."

That's a lesson that stuck with me and I always tended to hang away from the leaders that I worked for—even Stan, who was very likable. I just felt that that was best. So recommending Tom to him didn't come up. Then one day when I was on a tour of the East with Kenton, the phone rang in my hotel in Philadelphia. And it was Tom, who said, "I'm living in the area and I wondered if there's a chance I could bring an arrangement over." He knew we were playing at the Click Restaurant in downtown Philadelphia for a week, and I said to him, "Where are you living? I didn't realize you'd come east." He said, "I'm living in Bucks County, in Budd Schulberg's house."

I'd just been reading Schulberg's *What Makes Sammy Run?* and I was impressed. This was something about Tom that I hadn't known about. How had he got to know Budd Schulberg? I never did find out, but anyway I told him, "There's a rehearsal tomorrow night, but I'll call you back because I have to make sure that it's okay with Stan." Stan said, "Sure." The rehearsal began after the job, at about 2:00 a.m. the following night. Tom turned up about midnight and he wasn't in the best condition. He'd been having a few drinks and that was something about him I hadn't seen before. I did not expect this. The Tom Talbert I had known up to now was not the person who was lurching around, bumping into chairs and tables. Maybe this was a rare occasion, I don't know, I wasn't sure. But really and truthfully I began to entertain thoughts of calling it off that night—maybe this wasn't the time, but somehow I couldn't do that. Tom was with me, standing with me but getting ready to pass out.

The rehearsal started and we played one number. Then Stan said, "Milt, is your friend here?" I introduced him and by that time Tom had calmed down a little bit, and he hadn't gone to the bar, thank God. He had sat there listening to the other number and whispered to me, "Who wrote that piece of junk?" He then passed out his arrangement; I can't remember what it was, and he was passing it out to the equivalent of the Nuremberg jury. The people on that Stan Kenton band were pretty hard to impress—you had the likes of Maynard Ferguson, Ray Wetzel, Buddy Childers, Chico Alvarez, Art Pepper, Bud Shank, Bob Cooper, nice people but few of them knew him. Pepper recognized him; I don't know if he knew Cooper. We started playing the piece and it wasn't exactly a Kenton type of arrangement, which shouldn't have mattered. Eventually Stan had lots of things that didn't fit into the style known as Kenton music. A couple of years later when he started to use arrangers like Bill Holman and Lennie Niehaus and Bill Russo, the style changed drastically. But that night it was still Stan Kenton's progressive jazz and it didn't go so well for Tom. Stan smiled and said very warmly, "It's very nice, Tom but it just isn't something that we'll probably be playing. Maybe we should try it another time, or something else of yours. At this particular time I'm really full up with arrangements and I thank you." And he gave him all the nice clichés.

From Stan they were sincere, but Tom was not happy and showing it. He grumbled something like "Well, do what you want." A great line. He was pretty angry; something must have happened elsewhere and we've all had those experiences. But I felt kind of bad, and actually with another band the piece would have worked fine. It would have been great for Claude Thornhill—it was that kind of thing. It was underwritten, which is an art and something that's not easy to do. It's mainly Tom's style—we hear what the piece is about, the melody isn't covered up, nice harmonies—but it didn't work that night. We walked off the bandstand and out of the room toward the main entrance, which was down two flights of stairs. You looked down and it was like the big staircase in *Gone with the Wind*. I walked Tom to the stairs and then I began to worry and said, "Tom, let me take you down." But he shook me off and said, "What are you talking about, I'll see you later." And with that he took one step forward and missed it and fell down the entire two floors. Not fast, a drum would have been great for cues—boom-de-boom-de-boom-de-boom—and I thought I was going to find him dead at the bottom.

I started to rush down but he got to his feet, smiling. He was okay. Which brings to mind the old tale that people who have been drinking never break any bones when they fall because they're too relaxed. He wasn't hurt and he may have taken a lesson from this incident because he seems to have broken away from all those devils that come to most of us in our business. I say "business" because if you're in the music business and you want to make money, you've got to do what other people want and for a creative person that's a tall order. Inevitably, relying on other means to bolster your sense of security can and does happen. Just about every book about a painter, artist, writer, composer has a large section devoted to their self-destructive period. It happens to just about everybody and I can't think of very many musicians who didn't go through this. For many, specially composers, you're living a life that, when you're writing, is very lonely. No one is there to help you. Tom came out of it, though. After I left Kenton and started to concentrate on studio work in Los Angeles, I got a letter from him and he was still in New York and he was doing some recording. He was getting plenty of work and becoming well acquainted with the New York musicians—marvelous players like alto saxist Joe Soldo, trumpeter Joe Wilder, trombonist Eddie Bert, baritone saxist Danny Bank.

Fifty years later, Tom's recollections of the evening do not include the slapstick elements mentioned by Milt. Tom had, as noted earlier, already met Kenton and written two commissioned arrangements that were rehearsed but did not get into the band's book. Whatever the circumstances of Tom's exit from the Click Club, he was physically intact.

TOM TALBERT: No scars or broken bones . . . and I had no problem driving back to Bucks County too. Eventually my six-month wait for my union card was over and I decided I really had to get to work. Back in New York, a friend was moving out of his apartment on Perry Street and I took it over, and that became my permanent home in New York City. I was also able to get an upright piano.

Tom also met Irv Brabeck, Betty's ex-husband who was an agent at MCA. Irv not only hoped Tom would marry Betty and get him off the alimony hook, he also took a liking to his work and found him some arranging assignments. One of the first, in March 1951, was to be British pianist Marian McPartland's first recording in the U.S. under her own name. She had recorded in Chicago with her husband, Jimmy, on their own label, Unison. But now she was about to open at the Embers in Manhattan and Brabeck, intending to take advantage of what was her first appearance leading a trio in New York, set up a recording date for her.

MARIAN McPARTLAND: I went into the Embers on the heels of Joe Bushkin, who had been very successful there. I was alternating with Eddie Heywood, and frankly neither of us did great business. The owner, Ralph Watkins, beefed up my appearance by bringing Roy Eldridge and Coleman Hawkins to play on my sets. They were so great and so nice to me . . . I was walking on air.

Tom was impressed.

TOM TALBERT: Marian was very interesting, and I liked her immediately. She wanted to do more than just a trio recording. She wanted to record with harp and cello, so that was agreed on and I wrote the arrangements. I was able to have Don Lamond on drums and Marian and I were both delighted by the result.

The four titles, 78 rpm discs, "It's Delovely," "Flamingo," "Four Brothers," and "Liebestraum," were recorded for the Federal label, which was an offshoot of King Records. Marian McPartland plays with tremendous verve and drive, and the writing for piano and harp is, apart from some rather obvious arpeggios, well conceived, sometimes sounding as though Tom Talbert is about to invent the George Shearing Quintet. The cello is very effective in some places—occasionally a bit of an afterthought in others—but the date swings and, typical of Talbert's work, has a real freshness and individuality to it.

Metronome magazine heaped praise on the recordings in August 1951: "Jimmy's brilliant spouse takes a firm hold of her place in jazz history with these sides. Her wisdom in joining her piano with harp, cello, bass and drums is demonstrated; her ability to sustain several choruses and give them intriguing continuity is proved; her expert technique and lovely touch are brightly presented. Enough? There's more. Effective writing for this instrumentation is provided by

Tommy Talbert, without pretension but with taste. Bernard Greenhouse, an unusually talented cellist in the classical idiom, makes his simple phrases into warm and colorful decorations. Reinhard Elster arpeggiates the harp with authority. And Bob Carter on bass and Don Lamond on drums keep a fine beat going. Top this with piquant piano ideas and the rest of Marian's considerable equipment and you have the most refreshing of all the many attempts to give Shearing competition and raise his musical level."[1]

A review like this, a year after his arrival in Manhattan, must have been immensely encouraging to Tom Talbert. A date followed for singer Gene Williams, and the band included Danny Bank and another jazz great who would become a close friend in the future—trombonist Kai Winding.

TOM TALBERT: I think I first met Kai on that date. Gene Williams was a singer who was handled by MCA—they pretended that he had a band. A guy named Hubie Wheeler, who had written for Claude Thornhill, was his regular arranger and, for the record date, he and I wrote two arrangements each. When I found out Kai would be on the band, I included trombone solos.

Tom wrote a totally professional pop music score for the hit of the time, *Pretty-Eyed Baby,* that was quite unlike anything else he recorded, and demonstrated that he was musically well equipped to follow the path taken by commercial arrangers of the day such as Billy May, George Siravo, Hugo Winterhalter, Nelson Riddle, or Buddy Bregman. When I asked him why he didn't do anything more in this field, Tom's reply was, "No one asked me." It's probably fair to say that, given his uncompromising musical values and the style and nature of his writing up until the date for Gene Williams, his heart was not in this kind of work. He could do it but he wasn't really driven to be a serious commercial writer.

The other arrangement that he wrote for the date, on a lugubrious and thankfully now forgotten waltz titled "Now I Lay Me Down to Dream," must have reinforced his feelings about being a writer for hire. Kai Winding's fruity trombone solo adds a definite exclamation point.

TOM TALBERT: Kai Winding came up with a couple of dates that I remember doing with a great deal of pleasure, one with Warne Marsh in April 1951 and another for Savoy records about a year later. We had

Billy Taylor on piano and Jack Lesberg on bass on the first one and Lou Stein on piano, Tiny Kahn on drums, and Eddie Safranski on the latter, where we recorded "Speak Low," "The Boy Next Door," "The Carioca," and "I Could Write a Book."

More jazz dates would follow but Tom must also have been stimulated, and distracted, by the sheer quantity and variety of music being performed in New York in the mid and early 1950s. Along with the exciting developments on the jazz scene, there were also healthy and vibrant activities in the "legit" world, especially where chamber music was concerned. These sparked Tom Talbert's imagination, led him into a new area of writing, and gave him an opportunity to spread his musical wings even further.

DON DAVIDSON: When I was back in New York City in 1952, he was heavily involved in writing for small contemporary classical chamber groups. I heard some of his things and they were very interesting

TOM TALBERT: I found writing chamber music really fascinating and by eating a little leaner and writing a little longer, I started on some chamber pieces. Kai Winding and I used to hang out in a great little bar that Monte Kay ran on West 54th east of 8th Avenue. I think it was called the Down Beat. The pianist Billy Taylor and Oscar Pettiford used to play in there a lot and another guy who used to come in there all the time turned out to be a cellist—George Koutzen who played with the NBC Symphony under Toscanini. As soon as he found out that I was an arranger, he said, "Write something for the cello."

GEORGE KOUTZEN

My father was a violinist from the Ukraine, very much in the Fritz Kreisler style. When he came to the U.S., he began playing in a hotel orchestra, straight off the boat! Stokowski heard him and immediately hired him for the Philadelphia Orchestra. Later we moved to New York, when my father joined the NBC Symphony under Toscanini. I was first cello with the Kansas City Symphony when I was seventeen. Then after the war I joined the NBC too. That orchestra lasted seventeen years and my father played the first nine and I was there for the remaining eight. When I was in high school I became a big band freak. I loved bands like Benny Goodman and Glenn Miller but I only played the records when my father wasn't home. Once I played him a Glenn Miller record and I said to him, "Isn't this beautiful?" He said, "No, the harmonies are too close," which is what I thought was so beautiful. On the other hand, one time when my father was out I was playing the Jimmie Lunceford recording of "Blues in the Night." I guess I was playing it a bit loud because my mother heard it and she said, "Oh—I like that!"

When the NBC Symphony folded after Toscanini died, I stayed on at NBC in the orchestra for the *Steve Allen Show* going from being conducted by Arturo Toscanini to Skitch Henderson. In addition to Tom Talbert and Kai Winding, I also played with Marian McPartland, although not on the recordings Tom arranged, and Charles Mingus. My most exciting jazz experience was appearing at Carnegie Hall when Norman Granz presented three concerts featuring Charlie Parker with strings, as part of Jazz at the Philharmonic. Music politics kept me off the Parker with Strings record date but I did the concerts, sitting in front of Buddy Rich who kept muttering all through the performance "What are all these fucking string players doing here?" While I was playing the midnight concert, I reflected that I'd also been at Carnegie Hall earlier in the day playing the Berlioz Requiem under Leon Barzin.

GEORGE KOUTZEN: I met Tommy in a nightclub called The Three Deuces where Oscar Pettiford was playing. Oscar was a great guy and a wonderful musician. I was interested in him because, apart from being a terrific bass player, he played the cello—and tuned it like a bass. The club was just a few doors from where I lived, and on one occasion I came in with my cello and Oscar asked me to sit in and we played duets. Tommy came over and told me he was writing some stuff for five woodwinds and cello and he asked me if I would like to play on them.

TOM TALBERT: Kai and I had been trying to think of a different sound for a combo and I suggested we try something with woodwind quartet, cello, and trombone. The cello could play the bass part but also play a cello part. I wrote some arrangements like this and Monte Kay used to let us rehearse them in the bar of the Down Beat during the afternoon when it was closed. Don Lamond would bring his snare drum and brushes over and sit in, if he wasn't working and that added a lot to the sound. I also knew a good singer from California, Midge Parker. She was ideal, a great voice, good looking and thrilled with the idea of singing with that type of group.

Then I got the idea that I'd like to try a "serious" or "classical" piece, so I wrote "Four Atmospheric Pieces for Sextet." It was the same instrumentation and that was the start—once again I just walked in and started writing blindly—writing what I heard in my head. That was played on a number of composers' forums. The flute player, Jerry Sanfino, played alto sax on some pieces, including a feature that became part two of "Shadows on Forgotten Streets."

Tom's habit of "speaking his mind," as typified in the incident with Swede back in Lake Tahoe, contributed to a bizarre encounter with the NYPD near Monte Kaye's club.

TOM TALBERT: Oscar Pettiford, Max Roach, and I were drinking at the bar one night. Sometime around midnight we decided to go and eat, and we left and got into Oscar's black Lincoln Continental coupe. I was in the back and probably not very visible. Oscar drove round onto Seventh Avenue and stopped outside the Winter Garden while we discussed where to go. Suddenly there is a loud pounding on the roof of the car and one of New York's finest is all worked up and yelling at us to "get out and put our hands on the car." He is shouting, "What are you doing parked here? Who are you? Where have you been?" I looked over my right shoulder and saw my friend Oscar, arms up leaning on the roof and I dropped my arms, turned to the cop, and said, "What are you doing?"

The cop answered, "Oh a wise guy, huh?" I said something like, "No, not at all, but what are we doing wrong? We're just three friends deciding where to go to get something to eat." After some more dumb talk back and forth, the cop announces that he's going to "take me in." He's so incensed that he's forgotten the two black guys who were probably his original targets, and grabbing me by the back of my collar leads me off toward Broadway. By the time we got halfway to Eighth Avenue, I decided I'd better do something. I told the cop I wanted to call my good friend Max Lerner, a liberal columnist on the liberal *New York Post*, and I threw in Murray Kempton's name for good measure. (Neither of them had ever heard of me, of course.) Lerner's name did the trick. The cop stopped. "You know Lerner?"

"We're good pals, he'll love this story."

Something made him pause, and while he didn't kick the proverbial dirt, he suddenly allowed that I didn't seem too dangerous, and let me go. By this time Oscar and Max were long gone and I took the subway home, glad not to be in the klink.

The next evening Kai Winding called. He often worried about me saying too much to the wrong guy. He said Oscar had told him that I'd fought the whole of the Civil War in those blocks between Seventh and Eighth. It was worth it though. At least none of us were charged with sitting in a car.

In the more civilized area of Manhattan life, Tom became involved with an organization called the Composers Group of New York City.

TOM TALBERT: A very nice elderly lady, shaped rather like a pigeon, ran it and she kind of herded everybody into periodic concerts where different members would have their pieces played. I was performed quite a bit and I was very fortunate in that the woodwind and brass players were interested enough in the music that they would come and rehearse and play for nothing. I'm eternally grateful to them, and their interest in turn encouraged me to continue writing. A little later my ambitions extended to a string section and I found out that string players had a better organization and they wanted a little something to be paid for rehearsal.

GEORGE KOUTZEN: I don't know what the string players thought of his writing but I know that the woodwind players—people like Joe Soldo—thought that it was terrific. The fact that he was able to get people together to play for nothing is in itself a compliment. Then he wrote a cello rhapsody for me.

TOM TALBERT: I'd been going to a bar at Madison and 69th named the Mayflower. Shades of the Hot Harvey in LA, it was known by the regulars as "Ma'flower" and was noted for its call girls. The maître d', a very nice fellow named Guy Ferrari, took an interest in my music and decided I should have a concert at Carnegie Hall. The Carnegie Recital Hall, to be exact, which is now the Kurt Weill Theater. The scale was so low in those days that the total cost amounted to something like $1,600 and Guy put up the money. We had five woodwinds, a trumpet, two French horns, a trombone, a small string section, and percussion. I wrote a piece for flute and strings called "Summer Evenings" that featured Joe Soldo, and a set of three art songs. I had never done anything like this before, so I had to find out what the range of soprano and mezzo-soprano was, and then I picked three poems by a poet I liked. This was Ernest Dowson who wrote the famous poem that "Days of Wine and Roses" comes from. I chose "They Are Not Long," "To a Lost Love," and "Autumnal," and I set them to music using flute, English horn, clarinet, and cello. After the concert, they got played on a few programs . . . and I then wrote a suite called "Shadows on Forgotten Streets" and a four-minute piece featuring guitarist Johnny Smith called "The Wharf." I also wrote the "Cello Rhapsody" for George.

The concert took place on April 23, 1953. The *New York Times* concluded, "Mr. Talbert's music is an odd mixture of many influences including those of jazz, Debussy and Stravinsky. But the composer combines then in a manner that is his own. The music was cordially received by the audience."[2]

"T.M.S." in the *Herald Tribune* was much more enthusiastic: "Mr. Talbert is not a theoretical composer, fortunately, since he writes from the instrument out: his scoring is always clear and his colors warm and imaginative. He adds a strong motor impulse, stemming from jazz, to his lively sounds and his melodies are lyrical in a way that resembles our best popular tunes. In the cello rhapsody, beautifully played by Mr. Koutzen . . . the phrases and sonorities were genuinely musical, definitely contemporary in aspect, and the most natural adjustment between jazz and 'serious' music that this reviewer has heard to date."[3]

Down Beat said, "Talbert's writing showed fine workmanship, entitling him to serious consideration among contemporary composers."[4]

Almost fifty years later, George Koutzen commented on the rhapsody.

GEORGE KOUTZEN: I love it—it's my cup of tea . . . I think it's one of his great works

In the author's opinion, one of Tom Talbert's finest chamber pieces was *Suite for Three Flutes* included in a later concert at the Carnegie Recital Hall. The *New York Times* reviewer said, "The most interesting work heard by this listener was Thomas Talbert's Suite for Three Flutes. One might expect to grow quickly bored by the sound of three flutes. Instead the sonorities were varied and fascinating. The musical style was spontaneous and unassuming.

Neo-classical perhaps, perhaps, if one had to give it a label, but above all fresh."[5]

Fifty years later Tom talked about it.

TOM TALBERT: I don't remember what prompted it—it wasn't a commission—I just decided to write something for three flutes.

When I asked him how he went about writing the suite and inquired about the origin of the material, the frustrating answer was,

TOM TALBERT: I just started writing. I just thought it up as I went along.

A recording from a broadcast of the piece reveals the composer's fascination with voicings and textures, particularly in the lower registers of the instruments and an unabashed impressionistic element.

GEORGE KOUTZEN: He wrote a piece called "October Sketches" for my chamber group the Knickerbocker Chamber Players.

"October Sketches," which Tom thinks "really was the best chamber piece I ever wrote," was premiered at the Metropolitan Museum of Art on February 13, 1955. George Koutzen liked it too.

GEORGE KOUTZEN: It was unusual for people from the jazz world to write this kind of music at that time. Later a lot of people did it, but at that time he was one of the first. He did a good job and the reviews of the concert were excellent. I've never liked to categorize music. I think there's either good music or bad music.

The *Herald Tribune* critic was a little more measured in his opinion this time: "Thomas Talbert's '[October] Sketches' contained a full quota of genuinely imaginative sounds and rhythms, attractively juxtaposed but they wandered about without clear direction during the second half of their twenty minute span.[6]

TOM TALBERT: I found it comparatively easy to get a work premiered, but more difficult to get it played again. I enlarged "The Wharf" to a big orchestra, and we had one rehearsal, where it sounded great. Then the conductor died just before the performance, and it was canceled. At that time there weren't the grants and there wasn't the availability of financing that there is now. As the encouragement ebbed, so did my "serious" writing.

At the same time as I was writing chamber music I was alternating my thought processes with a number of jazz recordings. After using guitarist Johnny Smith on my concert piece "The Wharf," I wanted to work with him again and I arranged a date for him and tenor saxist Paul Quinichette that turned out very well. I also did four sides with Don Elliott that had Kai Winding, Jimmy Lyons on piano, and Phil Urso on tenor. Don played trumpet and mellophone . . . that was very nice too.

I wrote much of the book for a group that Kai took into Birdland in the summer of 1953.

This group was playing opposite Charlie Parker and had Brew Moore and Phil Urso on tenors, Cecil Payne on baritone, and a rhythm section of Walter Bishop, Percy Heath, and Philly Joe Jones.

In a *Metronome* review, George Simon wrote, "Kai Winding has one of the greatest small groups playing the small clubs these nights. ("Why shouldn't it be great?" asked one of the hipper members on opening night. "After all, we had FOUR rehearsals.") But it's great nevertheless. Sporting a book of good arrangements, many by Tommy Talbert, this low-voiced aggregation not only blows interesting stuff harmonically, but it also does what not enough of the small modern outfits do—it swings! . . . as a matter of fact, the four-way section gets a great sound, an unusually good blend for a quartet of its variety and tonal depth, and despite its lack of tonal height, does manage to reach some exciting summits."[7]

Sadly, this group did not record. Tom also wrote for a band that Oscar Pettiford took into Snooky's, a club on West 45th Street, renowned, according to Ira Gitler, as the place where Dizzy Gillespie's trumpet got famously bent.

This group also featured Kai Winding, along with Lee Konitz, Kenny Dorham, Jerome Richardson on tenor, Horace Silver, and Philly Joe again. Later in the year Pettiford recorded, but not with this band or these arrangements.

TOM TALBERT: Later when Kai formed his four-trombone group he wanted me to do a lot of the writing. I wrote about a half dozen arrangements but they had a big hassle at rehearsal with Carl Fontana leading some of the members of the group who thought my stuff was too difficult and too much work. Fontana claimed that "Jack Teagarden always said that if you can't play something dead drunk then it's too complicated." Kai did record my arrangement of my own tune "Every Girl Is My Valentine," but I also had an arrangement on

"There's a Small Hotel" that I really liked and I wish they'd used. It had some broken rhythm and took a bit of rehearsing, a bit of work, but they didn't want to do that.

Like many of his contemporaries, Tom Talbert was eking a marginal living from varying amounts of freelance work in what was still the jazz capital of the world. In the opinion of Jack Montrose, albeit based on the Los Angeles late 1940s period, Tom was well equipped musically to succeed in the commercial world. But how did he survive financially? Jack was one of those who wondered about Tom's source of income.

JACK MONTROSE: He was a very, very good commercial writer, that's what he was, and he wrote some very, very nice arrangements. At the same time it seemed that he didn't need to seek commercial acceptance because he seemed to have a source of income from some place else . . . i.e., not from music.

George Koutzen knew more about Tom's situation.

GEORGE KOUTZEN: Tommy wasn't well known, nor did he have a lot of money in those days. He had a little place down in Greenwich Village and seems to have survived, writing arrangements for people like Claude Thornhill. He refused to let his parents help him financially, and I know he was scraping by in New York. He never asked them for help—he's a very proud person. But he's not a pusher—not an operator.

TOM TALBERT: New York City in the 1950s was a good place to live. None of my friends made a lot of money but we lived quite decently. We enjoyed most everything—we didn't have tailored shoes or such but we lived well and enjoyed life. I think it's just that costs were in proportion to what people could make then.

I wrote about ten or twelve arrangements for Buddy Rich's band. Buddy wanted things in the style of Benny Goodman's "Don't Be That Way," and I remember arranging "Perfidia" and also selling him a blues chart that I'd done for the army band. He was getting ready to go on the road. He was a mean son of a bitch—he used to be particularly hard on the guys in his band who really needed the job. Kai Winding had warned me about the problem of getting paid by Buddy. I was writing an arrangement a night and I'd go to the rehearsal the next day and as soon as it was over I'd go to the manager's office and get a check. I always had an excuse like "I have to pay my rent," "I have to go to the dentist, so I need the money now." Then I'd go straight to his bank and try to get the check certified. I got all my money and I think I'm the only arranger who worked for him who did. Later on he stranded that band somewhere down in Mississippi or Alabama and took off for Europe. When he came back, the union arranged for him to settle with the guys in the band for ten cents on the dollar.

Around that time I caused wall-to-wall mirth in Charlie's Tavern when I admitted that I'd submitted some charts to Sammy Kaye for his TV show.

Patty McGovern, the singer on Tom's first LP, became a close friend.

PATTY McGOVERN: People say Tom was shy and withdrawn, but I never found that. In fact I thought he was pretty forthright—and very funny. He lived downtown in an unassuming apartment—nothing to write home about. He didn't have any money in New York, I know that. But at the same time it seemed as though he didn't have to work, and I wondered about his father and the barge business. My recollection is that he wasn't pushing all that hard to get work and he was having a very good time along the way. Maybe too good.

Beyond paying the rent and getting his music played, Tom seems to have had no driving ambition at this time. Perhaps scarred by the demise of his Los Angeles band, he showed no desire to regroup in New York and seems to have been content to concentrate on writing for other people.

TOM TALBERT: I never got the sense that there was a place, or that anyone was looking, for a new band. I'd got very involved in writing chamber music and I was also writing arrangements but not necessarily to order.

Danny Bank was one of the musicians who was heavily involved in Tom's classical ventures.

DANNY BANK: He told me about his woodwind writing and I was invited to some rehearsals. He would show us some interesting music and bring us to a composer's workshop where we would play it for people, and sometimes on a radio broadcast. There was always a particular atmosphere when you were on the radio. You got a special buzz when you were young and you saw the red light go on—that meant 4 million people were listening. It was really crazy! A friend of mine

took a downbeat from Tom one night and his music fell off the stand.
Just as the downbeat came down, the music unfolded like an accordion
and it was the funniest thing I ever saw, and of course there was no
splicing or editing in those days.

Woodwind player Joe Soldo played on some of the classical dates
and began an association with Tom Talbert that would last a half a
century.

JOE SOLDO: Tom was an innovator. When I think back, and it's almost
fifty years, he wrote things long before other guys tried to do the same
kind of writing. At that time I always thought of Tom as a classically
orientated writer. When you play with a jazz band there's not too
many "rubs" there. By "rubs" I mean an A against a B, and F against
an F-sharp, it's usually pure. Tom's music had all these rubs in it.
When you listened to it you would jump up the first time but when
you heard it the second and third time you knew it was right.

Ken Poston feels that Tom Talbert had a special ability to blend
two seemingly exclusive genres of music.

KEN POSTON: There weren't too many writers other than Tom and a
few others who were coming out of that combined background. He really represents this whole new breed of composers who came along at
that time who were just as influenced by Bartok and Stravinsky as they
were by Basie and Ellington. Tom was one of the most successful of
those who were able to utilize those classical influences without it being an either/or or back and forth kind of thing. It wasn't like a little
section of classical writing followed by some jazz blowing, it was a real
synthesis that he had and the results were more successful than anything else that I can think of in a similar vein."

Leigh Kamman had by now moved to New York with his wife,
singer Patty McGovern, and had a radio program on Station WOV.

LEIGH KAMMAN: When I knew Tom in New York in the early 1950s,
he was, as I remember, concentrating hard on developing his own
writing, very much influenced by the classical composers that he
loved—Debussy, Ravel, Stravinsky—and he was doing a lot of networking too. At this time the networking was rather magical—there
was even a Minnesota contingent that included journalists, broadcast-
ers, and musicians, and everyone helped each other make connections.
    Around this time I interviewed Charlie Parker, by phone, for the ra-

dio program. I asked him what he'd like our listeners to hear and explore, and he said, "Well, I like symphony music. Bartok is one of my favorites." And he went on to mention Stravinsky and Petrushka and *Rites of Spring* and *History of a Soldier, Orpheus* and *Card Party* and *Dumbarton Oaks.* He was exploring, in his way, with that marvelous ear of his; and that's what Tom was doing too. But Tom couldn't express it in a solo, the way Parker could, or write it in maybe the way Parker was thinking of. But Tom was processing it and it came out in his writing. I see them both as musical adventurers and travelers. Absorbing and processing the music in their own ways, influenced by the giants of European classical music.

To George Koutzen, Tom remained a talented enigma.

GEORGE KOUTZEN: He's one of a kind, and you wonder where did he get it from?

NOTES

1. *Metronome,* August 1951.
2. *New York Times,* April 24, 1953.
3. *New York Herald Tribune,* April 24, 1953.
4. *Down Beat,* June 3, 1953.
5. *New York Times,* n.d.
6. *Herald Tribune,* February 14, 1955.
7. *Metronome,* July 1953.

9

Wednesday's Child

As Danny Bank observed, this was the time when the LP was king and revolutionizing the record industry. Tom's first LP was a very unusual vocal album featuring Patty McGovern, an all but unknown singer.

TOM TALBERT: I had a close friend named Boris Derujinsky. He was a top fashion photographer, on a par with Richard Avedon, and he introduced me to a fellow named Bobby Said who lived up in Greenwich, whose parents had recently died and left him a million dollars, which he managed to go through in about a year. He wanted to be a race car driver and wasn't that good at it. We used to go up to his place at the weekend. One time I took along Patty McGovern, who had been with a singing group called the Honey Dreamers, and she played and sang some songs she'd written. Everyone just flipped.

PATTY McGOVERN: By the time of the meeting with Bobby Said, I'd known Tom for some time. Even though we both came from the same place, we first met in New York. We'd been working on ideas for an album for quite a while and we became totally consumed by it.

PATTY McGOVERN

I was born in St. Paul. I was a teenager during World War II and I used to go to the Orpheum Theater in Minneapolis and catch every band that I could. My brother Tom, who was about twelve years older than me, was a good pianist and he was my ideal—I listened to him and he'd bring musicians to the house. He liked Art Tatum and Teddy Wilson and he wrote a lot of arrangements—the book, in fact, for Charlie Spivak, just before the war. In fact he was a bit like Tom Talbert—very bright and self-taught. He had a lot going for him until the war came along. He became a pilot and came back with his spirit pretty much broken. On his return, he did, however, organize a band and I started to sing with it. I was at the University of Minnesota and I'd been experimenting with harmonies—I'd always had a good ear and I was crazy about Sarah Vaughan, Mel Torme, and the vocal group the Mel-Tones. When I heard that group, something lit up in me and I thought, "That's what I want—that harmony—I want to sing like that."

The Honey Dreamers was a vocal group that first got together at St. Olaf's College in Northfield, Minnesota. Their manager, Art Ward, was there too. They went to Chicago and had a great success and then went on to New York. At some point Sylvia and Keith Texter, who were original members, left to go with Fred Waring and they needed two new singers. I went along to an audition and they told me they had auditioned 350 singers— that's what they told me. I guess they wanted a particular look and sound—a whole Midwestern thing. Eventually they called me and told me, "You're it!" I was with them for at least five years and they were very busy—commercials and lots of TV. They were doing *Broadway Open House* twice a week and *The Van Camp's Pork and Beans Show*, and things like that.

On one occasion we were working on a CBS show called *Summertime USA*, which featured Mel Torme and Teresa Brewer. I got a call one morning from the director asking me to come in early. He said, "Teresa's sick and we'd like you to take her place." So Torme and I sang together and it went well and out of it I got two offers from men who wanted to be my agent. One of them was mostly interested in my songwriting—the other one got me on the Eddie Fisher TV show as Eddie's singing partner. The combination of singing songs waist deep in a swimming pool and listening to Eddie gradually lose the beat on live TV made me quickly lose my interest in this direction. At that time there were other interesting things coming up and I really wanted to do things that were more jazz oriented.

That was a good time to live in New York. There were all kinds of good things going on—Count Basie was on the road and playing in Birdland. And Birdland is where Chris Connor sang my song "Your Laughter" that I'm so mad at Tom for not recording. Quincy Jones worked on his first arrangement on my piano in our apartment on 106th Street. He was an unknown at that time. Because of my husband, Leigh Kamman, and his radio program, we had all kinds of people coming through our apartment and Quincy, who had no piano, asked if he could come over and use our old upright. And I'm out in the kitchen and hear him playing the same phrase over and over and over. I think, "What's the matter with him, why can't he get past that?"

When we lived there, Billy Strayhorn lived next door; Gerry Mulligan was just around the corner. I remember going to a great party at Gerry's . . . I walked in with Billy Wallington, George Wallington's wife, Gerry was quoting Winnie the Pooh in his whimsical manner and Johnny Mercer was having a furious argument with Thelonious Monk—about music. Johnny was saying, "This music is crap—I don't like the way you play."

TOM TALBERT: I didn't actually hear Patty performing with the Honey Dreamers. Although she occasionally went for solo auditions she was very undriven; in fact, compared to her I must have appeared totally obsessed. She was easy to work with, though. She was a good reader and could learn a part in just a few minutes.

To get the project started, I wrote some simple arrangements of songs like "Will You Still Be Mine," "You Don't Know What Love Is," and a couple of others, just for flute and guitar and bass and we made some acetate recordings of them. We took them to Nesuhi Ertegun at Atlantic and he liked them very much. Of course he also liked the fact that Bobby Said was going to pay the recording costs, so not surprisingly we got the green light to proceed. I got my good friend Bill Hughes to design the cover, and Budd Schulberg agreed to write the notes. I also wrote something about each of the songs. We spent a lot of time picking the material, then the writing really went fast and we started recording in February 1956. I didn't like the way most arrangers wrote for singers—I didn't like the usual backings. So I did what I call lean arrangements using principally flute, guitar, and string bass with French horn added on some and Joe Wilder on trumpet on a couple more. Barry Galbraith was featured on guitar throughout and he held the whole thing together

PATTY McGOVERN: The sessions were very exciting. On the morning of the second session I woke up with a terrible cold and I phoned Tom.

He was very unsympathetic and just said, "Can't you gargle or something?" I think you can hear the cold, particularly on "Crazy He Calls Me." I was in love with Tom's music, even though it was not at all supportive of the vocalist. In many ways he was treating the voice like an instrument. There were some very difficult intervals and sometimes little clue as to where you were going next. I remember the French horn player saying, "Jeez these arrangements are the kind where you could go home and work on them for hours and come back and you still can't play them."

Leigh Kamman also remembers the *Wednesday's Child* sessions.

LEIGH KAMMAN: Patty met the challenge but, in spite of her great skill at sight reading and wide experience in solo and group singing, it had to have been a nightmare for her. To make an album of that standard, live to two track, with such magical instrumental solos in just four sessions would be unthinkable today, without the need to cope with Tom's imaginative way with rhythm, time, and dissonance. When she came home from the sessions she was just exhausted and withdrawn. This was demanding music that was in a state of evolution and Patty and Joe Wilder helped to complete that evolution.

Interestingly, in order to market it in Japan, Atlantic had an artist touch up the cover picture to make Patty's eyes look more Eurasian.

PATTY McGOVERN: Joe Wilder, Osie Johnson, Joe Soldo just knocked me out. They were so marvelous to work with. I assumed Tom knew all the musicians well and had worked with them before.

Joe Soldo is a woodwind player and contractor, now living in Los Angeles, who began his career playing alto sax in bands led by Tommy Reynolds and Elliot Lawrence. By 1956 he was settled in New York and much in demand, especially for his brilliant flute playing. Until *Wednesday's Child*, Joe had only played Talbert's classical music. This was his first acquaintance with Tom's jazz side.

JOE SOLDO: I didn't know anything about the album in advance . . . I didn't know Patty McGovern, the singer, but I was just blown away by the way she sang and the feeling that she had. I remember the interesting lines that Tom wrote for the flute—it was such a thrill to play them and listen to the way that he'd altered the harmonies of the songs. That's something I've always been interested in and Tom really excels at it.

One of the other great things about *Wednesday's Child*—the instruments never get in the way of the lyrics. So many arrangers are only interested in their music and not the words of the songs.

Tom really knew how to orchestrate. I work with a lot of fellows who don't know how to write for the instruments, they just haven't studied—or learned. But Tom learned at a very early age, exactly what each instrument should sound like.

The chamber music ventures of the previous two years had given Tom valuable experience, as well as the confidence to write in an original and uncompromising fashion. On *Wednesday's Child* he took the lessons learned writing for the "legit" chamber groups one step further and demonstrated an ability to synthesize jazz and classical music in a way that is emotionally affecting and completely convincing.

The striking quality of the album is the way in which Tom Talbert really does seem to think of the voice as one of the instruments. Naturally, given the period, the voice is very prominent in the mix, but time and again the result is much more than voice with accompaniment. "You Don't Know What Love Is" becomes a true duet for the voice and Joe Soldo's flute. On "Lonely Town" Patty phrases with great breath control and a big sound, just like a good saxophonist, blending with Tom's delightfully tart-textured woodwind ensemble. "Get Out of Town" places the voice against soaring solo flute lines, while "Winter Song," perhaps the most perfect track on the album, is like a through-composed art song with a jazz edge to it.

Tom's social connections in the nonmusic world provided a bonus for *Wednesday's Child* buyers.

TOM TALBERT: Budd Schulberg, who had become a good friend, generously came through with some notes for the album. This was a real gift from him because at the time he was up to his neck in the film *A Face in the Crowd*, and they were on location in Arkansas taking pictures of school bands. He wrote it there in longhand and mailed it to me. I was flattered and pleased.

THOMAS TALBERT

BUDD SCHULBERG: Listen to Tom Talbert. He makes an interesting sound, whether he is an avant-garde traditionalist or vice versa, I am not sure. He is both exploratory and soundly disciplined. He seems to leap ahead of the modern or progressive jazz vocabulary and his leap often carries him over dangerous crevices. Where he is going to land is never quite sure—smack in the middle of bop trombones or medieval flutes.

All of it, of course, is New York '56 because Tom Talbert lives in Greenwich Village in our dissonant age of anxiety. At 31 he's a child of that age, a Wednesday's Child perhaps. Unlike some jazzmen, he's a reader of books. He's flipped for Celine and Kafka and Wallace Stevens. He's a broodingly thoughtful young man of Manhattan out of Minneapolis. Some think he looks like another Minneapolis boy, F. Scott Fitzgerald.

The net of comparison embraces more than profile and geography. Talbert is a romantic who shuns the cliché. He is a technician who trusts the heart. Even when he's being clever, his notes are warm and tender.

He has written all kinds of music, from arrangements for Kai Winding and Oscar Pettiford to what the long-hair critics like to call "serious music." Both *Down Beat* and the *New York Times* have approved. Said the latter ". . . he writes from the instrument out, his scoring always clean and his colors warm and imaginative . . . the most natural adjustment between jazz and serious music this reviewer has heard to date . . ."

In this album Talbert has fun. He takes old songs and freshly rephrases them. He tells us a different, more haunting story of "New York, New York—it's a Lonely Town." He bounces and laughs us through "I Like Snow" and "Hooray for Love." He winds us back into the fluted past where "You Don't Know What Love Is."

So, listen to young Tom Talbert: a jazz classicist, schooled in the past with a yen for the future.

The year 1956 was a good one for vocal albums that broke the prosaic mold. Just a few months later, in June, Helen Merrill recorded her Gil Evans-arranged album *Dream of You*. Like *Wednesday's Child*, it has remained something of a little-known collector's item to this day. Both collections show their arrangers taking very inventive and bold approaches and both are, in the author's opinion, very moving listening experiences. They share the presence of guitarist Barry Galbraith and woodwind player Danny Bank, and Evans uses Tom's friend Oscar Pettiford and trombonist Jimmy Cleveland, who were important members of the ensemble on Tom's next album.

The January 1957 edition of *Metronome* carried reviews of both albums and—*quelle richesse*—new LPs by Teddi King and Morgana King too. The reviewer, singing editor O. Sargent Mason, said, "An excellent album, from the clever, musical Tommy Talbert arrangements through the excellent performances by a score of New York's best jazz musicians (including such as Joe Wilder, Barry Galbraith, Arnold Fishkin, Don Lamond and Osie Johnson), and the superbly voiced Miss McGovern who sings the excellently chosen, mostly unusual songs as if they came perfectly naturally. What that means of course is that her voice is perfectly controlled and her ear nearly that good. Tracks on the second side are my particular favorites, but the entire album is a wonderful example of what musicians can do, jazz or not and the warm-voiced Miss McGovern is close enough to jazz to make further discussion almost impolite. I'd recommend this without reservations."[1]

Of the Merrill/Evans album he said, "Gil Evans wrote the arrangements which feature such musicians as Jimmy Cleveland, Barry Galbraith, Art Farmer, John LaPorta, Hank Jones and Oscar Pettiford. Again the tunes are mostly unusual ones, several almost exotic, which Gil takes creative advantage of (though I've heard better scoring from him lately) and Helen sings with her usual emotional content. On such as "He Was Too Good to Me," "I'm a Fool to Want You" and "Dream" she is at her best; in that kind of lament where her vocal qualities and problems combine to best advantage. It's a handsomely different album."[2]

Both Talbert and Evans included "By Myself" on their albums, and it's intriguing to compare the respective treatments. Evans's arrangement for Helen Merrill is a dark, brooding affair that begins with, and I think takes its cue from, the rarely heard verse of the song, particularly the line "The dreams I dreamed went up in smoke." A harsh and brilliantly voiced ensemble phrase played by quite a large band introduces the chorus, and that phrase is repeated and utilized later in the arrangement. The tempo is medium and the rhythm solid and relentless. Evans, Merrill, and soloist Art Farmer succeed wonderfully in conveying a mood that is tinged with bitterness and pessimism.

In contrast, Talbert and McGovern may have taken their message from the line in the chorus "I'll go my way by myself, like a bird on the wing." The mood is brighter and more optimistic and the tempo is faster, the accompaniment fairly dancing to a small flute-led ensemble. Joe Wilder takes a solo that is notable both for its harmonic sophistication and melodic sense.

The two versions of the song are a fine example of what can happen when truly original arrangers have total freedom to write for talented, committed singers, and there is enough money in the budget to employ a decent number of the best possible musicians.

A month later *Down Beat* reviewed *Wednesday's Child* and the reviewer was equally enthusiastic: "'Wednesday's Child' . . . has been prepared with unusual intelligence and taste. Tommy Talbert, a gifted arranger for jazz groups and big bands and also a skilled classical composer, made the records himself and then sold them to Atlantic. His arrangements are lean and sensitive, sometimes witty and never banal. The choice of tunes is excellent, with such superior but underdone standards as 'Alone Together,' 'Hooray for Love,' 'All in Fun,' 'Lonely Town,' and 'By Myself.' There are also two songs by Patty; the poignant title tune written by Talbert and Bill Wolfe; and the probing sensitive 'Winter Song' is also by Talbert and Wolfe.

"Miss McGovern, former lead singer with the Honey Dreamers, is careful to set each set of lyrics in its best lighting, and her clear, cool voice is pleasant. She lacks, however, a degree of vigor. Her projection could have been more assured and somewhat more supple. Among the fine accompanists are the superlative Joe Wilder, Barry Galbraith, Jack Lesberg, Osie Johnson, Jim Buffington, Don Lamond, Arnold Fishkind, etc. A fresh approach to vocal packaging. Very good notes by Talbert."[3]

Tom was, naturally, pleased with the results.

> TOM TALBERT: The album proved to be the kind that people come up and say, "Gee, I really loved that album." It's not the sort of thing that's going to sell a million copies but everyone who bought it really loved it and still say they do.

The year 1956 was golden for jazz recordings of all kinds in New York. The city was crammed with excellent jazz musicians and independent record labels like Prestige, Blue Note, Bethlehem, Atlantic, Riverside, and Verve thrived. Even major record companies such as RCA, Capitol, and CBS had significant jazz output. The former had hired Shorty Rogers as a producer and also created a special label—VIK—to record the likes of Bob Brookmeyer and Al Cohn. At CBS George Avakian was producing albums with Eddie Condon, Louis Armstrong, Miles Davis, and Charles Mingus.

The Ertegun brothers at Atlantic were quite happy to consider another Talbert project that would once again come with no production costs to them.

NOTES

1. *Metronome,* January 1957.
2. *Metronome,* January 1957.
3. *Down Beat,* February 20, 1957.

10

Bix Duke Fats

TOM TALBERT: Our next project was *Bix Duke Fats*. Originally I had intended to just do Bix and Fats. But Duke Ellington's name had come back in a big way at this time, so for commercial and artistic reasons I decided to make it a threesome. Ahmet and Nesuhi Ertegun liked the idea, but once again as Bobby Said was funding it, their risk was minimal. A plus for me was that we got Atlantic's top engineer, Tom Dowd, who was wonderful to work with and a really good studio, Coast, right by the public library.

I purposely limited the band to eight on the Beiderbecke and Waller things and I had eleven pieces on the Ellington. I used a different instrumentation with each composer to create the sound that I thought came from their melodies. I had also put a lot of thought into the musicians I wanted to hire, and they meshed as though they'd been playing together for a long time. We ran through the music the day before each recording session. We did the Waller date first and pianist George Wallington got us off with a real good sparkle. Then we did the Beiderbecke tunes with Joe Wilder. They were very tricky—three woodwinds with French horn, guitar, bass, drums, and trumpet. Everyone very exposed meant that every part had to be played very precisely. On the last date, when we recorded the Ellington tunes, I included a composition of my own, "Green Night and Orange Bright," which was a tribute to Fats Waller and Bix Beiderbecke. I said in the notes that on "Green Night" the blues were for Bix and on "Orange Bright" the bright lights were for Fats.

In the world of modern jazz in 1956 the emphasis, where material was concerned, was on new originals and a comparatively small range of standard popular songs and show tunes. It was quite unusual to do what Tom Talbert was doing, going back and reworking jazz tunes from past eras. This was something that Gil Evans would become known for, particularly in his albums *Plus Ten* and *New*

Bottles, Old Wine. It's worth making the point that Talbert recorded his *Bix Duke Fats* album more than a year before Evans's foray into this territory.

Tom struck gold with *Bix Duke Fats.* The reviews were ecstatic, none more so than Dom Cerulli's in *Down Beat* magazine. Cerulli never forgot it and looked back on it in 1999.

DOM CERULLI: This album was actually a breath of fresh air. I had been reviewing records and at that time all you had was a kind of Basie sound and small groups. The Basie stuff was very predictable and the small groups were fiery, uptempo, contrapuntal bop and at the end of the first chorus you were exhausted, as a listener. Suddenly this thing lands on my turntable. I had only been at *Down Beat* for a short while and I thought, "My god I haven't heard anything like this yet." So I said, "Do I dare to give it five stars?" Before I even reached the end of side one I knew it was a five-star album. The playing was so good—the writing and the concepts were fantastic. But the playing! Johnny Richards once told me, "If you want to really hear music you have to listen into it. Isolate the chords, listen to what's going on." And there was so much going on. It's absolutely breathtaking.

I was never aware of Thomas Talbert before then. I didn't know where he'd come from or where he was headed. In the review I said something like "Talbert's [liner] notes are literate and illuminating, a fine argument for having musicians and leaders write the words about their music." That led me right into what he was trying to do and I thought to myself, "Boy do we need him now."

The Beiderbecke pieces, along with Ellington's "Prelude to a Kiss," are extraordinary achievements, and for the author, the high points on the album. Tom thinks he "might once have heard the piano recording of Beiderbecke playing 'In a Mist'" but isn't sure. Reissues were much less comprehensive in 1956 and the versions of "Candle Lights" and "In the Dark" recorded by pianist Jess Stacy in 1933 and the small band Bunny Berigan versions from 1939 were neither readily available nor known to Tom. All of his arrangements and assumptions were based solely on the sheet music. After the album's release, trumpeter Jimmy McPartland, who had known Bix and replaced him in the Wolverines asked Tom why he had given "In a Mist" a markedly slower tempo than Beiderbecke played it. The same question could have been asked of the other two titles too. In fact, Tom rejected the original, rather stilted 1920s-style tempi and "piano novelty" moods, and instead turned the impressionistic themes into beautiful, haunting ballads. To complete the spell, he had the benefit, once again, of one of the most original, sublimely inventive, and consistently underrated trumpeters of the post–World War II era.

TOM TALBERT: Joe Wilder did an absolutely terrific job on the Beiderbecke pieces . . . they were originally piano solos so the intervals are not typical trumpet intervals and, as I said, so exposed with these lean backgrounds. And he played it just beautifully.

Almost fifty years later, Joe Wilder and trombonist Eddie Bert listened to *Bix Duke Fats* again.

Joe Wilder was characteristically modest about his own inspired contribution to the album.

JOE WILDER: When I listen to it, I feel awfully flattered that I was there playing some of that music. It's fascinating—it really is. At this stage of my life I don't think I could come close. It was always a challenge and at that time you couldn't help but be proud to realize that you had done it and played what Tom had written, to his satisfaction, which was quite a compliment.

EDDIE BERT: I think the first time I met Tom was on the date. There was a lot of recording going on in those days; you were recording with many different people and all of a sudden, out of the blue he showed up and it was different. He had his own thing going. He has great control of what every instrument can do. You have to know that and he does. He knows how to write for each instrument so you're not scufflin'. He knows exactly what he wants and how to get it out of you and he writes compositionally—every piece is a complete entity.

Eddie and Joe pointed out the significant difference in the recording process in those days.

EDDIE BERT: We did these dates with everybody in the studio, and that doesn't go on now. Nowadays you come into the studio and overdub . . . you can record with a rhythm section and not even know who's in it. These were done with the entire instrumentation. That's very important in jazz—I mean you can't play jazz with headphones on.

JOE WILDER: That's what contributed to its success. We were all there and we all listened to each other and we matched each others' playing and intonation and style.

Joe Soldo played on this album too.

JOE SOLDO: Tom's music was so refreshing. At the time we made *Bix Duke Fats* I also played on Bobby Darin's hit recording of "Mack the Knife," which was so square. Then to go and play Tom's music—that was so much more thrilling.

"Prelude to a Kiss" is a small, perfect gem that, to the author's ears, has its genesis in "Sabina's Serenade." The weaving contrapuntal lines and surprising textures in the piece scored for the Stan Kenton sax section in the late 1940s are like a matrix for this very un-Ellingtonian treatment. Small, because it is just a little more than one chorus and perfect because it is the finest example of Talbert's ability to edit and reshape a tune, removing repetition and substituting something much more interesting. One can't help but feel that Ellington would have smiled, perhaps wryly, at the way Tom remade the middle eight into a middle twelve.

TOM TALBERT: Alto sax plays the lovely first two bars of the bridge. On the unbelievably dull and mundane bars 3 and 4, which contain the lyrics "nothing fancy, nothing much," I let the alto drift around the theme. Then I insert four bars, a pretty sequence that leads to the ensemble playing the strong (original) bars 5 and 6 and the alto plays the last two bars leading back into the main theme.

Contemporary composer and bandleader Maria Schneider listened to it in 1999.

MARIA SCHNEIDER: That is another extraordinary arrangement. To me what's amazing about that, what Tom has in common with Duke Ellington, Billy Strayhorn, and Gil Evans, is that the harmony is driven by the line. Hearing this reminds me of the Ellington recording of "Variations on Mood Indigo." That interweaving of lines that brings you to harmonic places that you would never come up with if you were thinking of reharmonization in a passing-from-chord-to-chord kind of way, thinking of vertical chords. It's truly a weaving of the horizontal that creates very interesting vertical structures. Structures that aren't just beautiful in themselves—if you were to slice out one point it might not be beautiful—but there's this gravitation that you feel when you feel the whole thing moving over time.

A lot of people nowadays learn to write in such a vertical way and the art of writing those kinds of lines that move the harmony seems to be lost. Tom is clearly a master of that, and "Prelude to a Kiss" is an incredible example of that. I'd love to see a transcription of it.

Joe Soldo played in the saxophone section on "Prelude to a Kiss" and cherishes the experience almost half a century later.

JOE SOLDO: That kind of writing with those lines, at that time I'd never played anything like that. Only four saxophones and everyone having a moving line. That was such an exciting way to write for the saxophones. In fact, listening to it forty years later I still haven't played anything with that kind of feeling. It was wonderful.

Bix Duke Fats also benefited from the playing of another of the most neglected musicians in jazz, clarinetist and tenor saxophonist Aaron Sachs.

TOM TALBERT: I love Aaron Sachs's playing—Eddie Bert says that as a teenager Aaron was playing with Red Norvo on 52nd Street. And Eddie says he still sounds the same way, he still sounds like 52nd Street.

AARON SACHS

The first band I went on the road with was a society band—Michael Loring. I was about eighteen or nineteen. We did a season at the Mocambo in Chicago. At that time they had speakeasies where you could hear the music from outside, to entice the people to come in. I remember passing one and hearing a clarinetist—Mezz Mezzrow—and saying "he had such an awful sound I wouldn't consider going in there." I was so locked into the Benny Goodman sound I figured that's not the way to play the clarinet. I was with Red Norvo, which was a pretty good start. Eddie Bert and Shorty Rogers were in the band and we got to play on 52nd Street, which was big deal at that time and as all the jazz greats were appearing there, I got a chance to hear them in person. And record with them—I won an award for the best clarinetist of 1945 and because of that I got on a lot of recordings—with Don Byas, Eddie Heywood, John Lewis, Dizzy, Bird, Sarah Vaughan. I did some recording with my own group too. In 1957 I recorded for Bethlehem—I had

Terry Gibbs, Tiny Kahn on drums, and Gene di Novi on piano. They reissued it and I guess Terry had a bigger name because on the reissue they made him the leader, which pissed me off. I think I met Tom just through being in the business—maybe socially. At the time, I was doing freelance work—this was before I got into the theaters. I was doing club dates, recording dates, whatever came around. In those days no one wanted to do a Broadway show. It was kind of looked down on, but now it's a big deal because of the benefits you get—you get a pension.

I used to take a band into Birdland on Monday nights. I'd have Billy Byers on trombone and Phil Sunkel on trumpet. It was a throwaway night, but for me it was a chance to play jazz and a chance to be a leader—not that being a leader is always such a big deal. Sometimes it has its bad aspects but at least you get a chance to call the tunes that you like.

Milt Bernhart, Tom's old friend from the Los Angeles days, thought that this album was a significant and reassuring event in Tom's life.

MILT BERNHART: After the incident at the Kenton rehearsal in Philadelphia I worried about Tom for some time—was he a lost cause? But he quickly demonstrated that there was nothing to worry about. The only thing was, could he keep his head above water to the extent that he could get anybody's interest, in order to make albums and find places to play. But he did that, he managed. *Bix Duke Fats* surprised me. I didn't know that he'd ever taken any interest in the likes of Fats Waller. I'd figured that he was going down his own road and wouldn't really want to do an entire album of other people's songs. It was a smart idea.

The excellence and durability of the *Bix Duke Fats* album can be gauged by Ken Poston's thoughts from many years and a couple of generations later.

KEN POSTON: It was the first thing I heard of Tom's—I was in college and I was very, very excited when I heard it. I was studying composition and arranging and it was something that was really so completely different from anything else I'd heard. I thought *Bix Duke Fats* was really kind of a landmark album for the time period when it was recorded. It had so many different influences, not only jazz but also a modern classical approach as well. That was something that just intrigued me a lot.

Dom Cerulli waited for a sequel—which never came.

DOM CERULLI: It was incredible that nothing major happened to Thomas Talbert as a result of hitting a home run his first time out. *Down Beat* had just achieved its highest readership ever, 65,000 and there was no question that *Bix Duke Fats* was a five-star album, but to follow that? An album like that comes along once or twice, if you're lucky, in your lifetime. It's like all the people who were alive when Louis Armstrong was playing and said, "Boy isn't it great to be here while he's here."

Tom Talbert looks back at the absence of a sequel.

TOM TALBERT: I was so pleased with the reviews . . . I thought that someone would be interested in going along a similar way or a tangent away from it. But nothing was ever offered to me as the result of it. When you do something like *Bix Duke Fats* and there's no follow-up, you kind of feel that it fell off the end of the earth. But I know it didn't because for years and years every DJ I talked to said, "I remember, you did *Bix Duke Fats*. It's one of my favorite albums."

Great reviews do not automatically turn into huge sales, especially when there is an absence of marketing by the record company. Tom Talbert's whole focus was on writing music, and the opinion of some of those who knew him then was that the prospect of him beating the Atlantic management about the head with a sheaf of fine reviews, demanding a follow-up album, was extremely unlikely.

PATTY McGOVERN: I'm sure Tom didn't press Atlantic to do the next album—I think it's more likely that he waited for them to make a move. There were two sides to Tom—there was the professional side—getting things done the proper way . . . there was also another side that just said, "Ah, the hell with it."

TOM TALBERT: The fact that *Bix Duke Fats* had such excellent reviews did not lead to a rush of calls from record companies wanting me to record two albums a year from then on. I continued doing the odd arranging jobs.

And some of them were very odd—Tom got work via a song-writer called Sid Shaw who specialized in packaging singers and creating special show material for their acts.

TOM TALBERT: Sid would come up with the lyrics and I would compose the tune. An example would be a song we wrote called "There Ought to Be a Paris, France, in Texas." This was for Adrienne Molnar, a gorgeous blond Hungarian singer from Paris. Sometimes Sid needed a band arrangement to go with the song, but it would have to be like a stock arrangement, and I didn't want to do that. That kind of arrangement is a thankless task; there's nothing creative about it. Sid used to hire Gil Evans to do those. I guess Gil needed the money even more than I did. None of this was very lucrative, but with bits and pieces here and there I managed to survive.

Tom also found time to spend with his friends outside the music world, with Budd Schulberg in New York and also at his new home in Sarasota, Florida, where Earl Mohn was working for him and the local paper.

TOM TALBERT: There were a lot of writers living around there and every Thursday, they'd get together at a good restaurant and have a "writers lunch." Earl and Budd used to take me along and I remember meeting McKinlay Kantor and John D. McDonald.

In junior high school Tom had been "mainly interested in drawing, reading, and writing stories" and "thought I'd like to be a writer or a pilot." Music had become the main part of his life but his tastes and interests remained diffuse and varied.

GEORGE KOUTZEN: I think you could sum up Tom Talbert in New York in those days by saying "He was searching but not pushing." Tom was too laid back for New York.

11

Full Stop

Historians of the twentieth century tell us that the prewar golden summers of 1914 and 1939 were moments in worlds that were to disappear and never return In a more modest sense, the jazz scene in New York City in 1956–1957 was a golden age that would never come back. Bill Haley and His Comets and Elvis Presley were the advance guard of the barbarians and they were inside the gates. Tom was one of the casualties.

> TOM TALBERT: Well now there's thunder on the right—it's the sound of rock 'n' roll and rhythm and blues stomping their feet.

The Ertegun brothers' interest in jazz recording at Atlantic was waning as the success of R&B singers like Ray Charles and James Brown made their fortune for them.

> TOM TALBERT: Amazingly, within a year around 1959 the whole of the jazz recording business really just came to a halt, and many more famous names than mine didn't record again for fifteen years. This changed everybody's life one way or another, and at this time my writing life, in particular, was not working out. I'd been working on a revue for the DeLys Theater, and that folded. Budd Schulberg wanted me to write the score for the movie *A Face in the Crowd*, and I met with Elia Kazan, who was directing. But I didn't get the job because Kazan wanted to use a folk singer, who did it all for no pay. Budd tried to get me another movie that he was writing but Warner Bros. had composers on contract that they wanted to use. As things turned out, there was then a musicians' strike in Hollywood and the studio wound up using library music from discs. In my experience they are probably never happier than when they are doing that.

> GEORGE KOUTZEN: I don't remember him leaving New York—one day he was just gone.

12

You *Can* Go Home Again

By 1960 Tom Talbert had devoted his life to music. He'd experienced the highs of hearing his own work played by some of the greatest musicians in jazz, and the sweetness of critical acclaim. He'd also experienced apathy, rejection, and the disappointment of projects failing to materialize. On a personal level he'd earned the respect of his peers and led what could be described as a "swinging" life in two of the most exciting cities in the world, Los Angeles and New York.

What must his thoughts have been as he returned home to Minneapolis, metaphorical tail between his legs, to live with his parents? And why did he go back?

TOM TALBERT: I spent eighteen years writing, arranging, and playing, and had some successes along the way. But overall, things had come to naught. My father, who was very gregarious and popular, owned a wholesale coal business back in Minneapolis and had begun to develop a barge company with contracts to supply coal to the Dairyland Power Company in Wisconsin, and to transport grain for the Cargill Company. He had a partner in the barge company who lived in Miami and had a great sailboat—a forty-foot sloop that also had an engine. On one occasion, when my father was going down there on vacation, he asked me if I'd like to come along. They were going to take the boat and sail over to Bimini and fish for a few days. I went down and had a great time and that's when my father asked me to get involved in the business so that if anything happened to him I'd know enough about the contracts to not get screwed out of everything. The idea wasn't very attractive, but, on the other hand, the thought of a regular salary for the first time in my life was appealing. Actually when I started, the salary was disappointingly small and it took a few years to amount to anything. Apart from which, I had always hated Minneapolis, so I went back with a bit of a chip on my shoulder. What made matters worse was that initially I had nowhere to live. So, at the age of thirty-five, I went back to live with my parents, which, after I had been out in the world for fifteen years, was terrible—I couldn't stand it. I had to get used to working in an office, albeit a small one— just me, my dad, and an assistant. He started out small with just a few barges, but we were never totally of a mind. His ambition was to get more and have a big fleet; my ambition was to just have enough to have a comfortable life.

My thoughts about music were very jumbled by this time.

Some time would elapse before Tom "unjumbled" his thoughts about music.

TOM TALBERT: After I'd been in Minneapolis for about two years, some people asked me to organize a band for a union-sponsored event in Omaha. There were to be bands from various different cities. They hadn't left enough time to do it properly and I declined the invitation, but it did get me thinking about getting my own band together again. In fact I even settled on an instrumentation, based on some of the things I'd done for the *Bix Duke Fats* album: two trumpets, two trombones, French horn, four woodwind, and rhythm. I found out who the best players in the right age-group in town were, and I got some guys who were very enthusiastic, and exceptional players. I had Irv Williams on tenor sax, who'd played with me right after the war; a trombone player named George Myers, who had been with Woody Herman; and a wonderful drummer named Russ Moore who was one of those guys who could have made it with the big bands but chose to stay at home. We started doing a few gigs around town, including the Walker Arts Center. Although it was musically satisfying, it was lot of work for not much return. By this time I was married—at the age of thirty-five I decided it was about time—and I'd taught my wife to copy the music parts. She was an excellent singer who had worked solo at Leon and Eddie's in New York before moving back to Minneapolis. I met her when I organized a vocal group. It was my idea to get commercial jingle-type work from the advertising agencies in town. It was a really fine group of three women—my wife Bette, her sister Rosita, Patty McGovern who had returned to Minneapolis with her husband—and two men, good musicians who also sang. In my naïveté I thought that the ad agencies would jump at the opportunity to record locally, rather than in their customary Chicago, not realizing that the guys in the agencies would do anything rather than give up their expenses-paid trips to the Windy City. It was a great group—but we never got a single job. I did get a wife out of it, though! Looking back,

I wish I'd overcome my basic anti-girl singer prejudice and featured Bette with both the orchestra and the septet. I now think both groups could have been hits with her singing. She could have made a big difference.

Bette and I bought a really nice house close to the center of town and I had a studio added, built to my own design, so the band had a place to rehearse, which we did. Although we continued to get a small amount of work at a little theater out at Excelsior, by Lake Minnetonka, and some union jobs, there was not really much of an audience for a band like this.

IRV WILLIAMS: He bought this house and added a really nice rehearsal room and we used to go out there and play almost weekly. Sometimes twice a week. We had a few dates, but we rehearsed more than we worked.

IRV WILLIAMS

I was born in Cincinnati, Ohio, August 18, 1919. My mother was a university music teacher and a choir director in Little Rock, Arkansas, where my father was a doctor. She started me out on the piano when I was five. She died and I went back to Cincinnati with my grandmother, who got me playing the violin when I was seven. My sister and I used to go from church to church, giving concerts. She played the piano and we did spirituals, and all kinds of simple tunes. They liked me because I was a little fellow. But when I started growing up, it seemed the uglier I got, the uglier the violin sounded. So I started playing the clarinet. I suffered from asthma and my dad thought that playing a wind instrument would strengthen my lungs, so he bought me a clarinet when I was twelve. I took a few lessons from a guy who was the local mail carrier and I always took the lessons on Saturdays, which also happened to be the day that he was always drunk. And the F on the clarinet was always in two or three different places. I quit him right quick. I used to play along with the radio; I particularly liked Barney Bigard and I tried to get his sound. It was a golden age for hearing jazz on the radio—I remember hearing live broadcasts of Roy Eldridge's group out of Chicago. I thought that was a terrific group. The first song I improvised on was "In a Sentimental Mood." I started playing professionally when I was fifteen, back in Little Rock. I got a C melody sax from a pawnshop for ten dollars and I started fooling around with it when I was fourteen. Then a year later I got a tenor. From then on I played on a steady basis throughout my life. Some of the bands I heard in Little Rock include Chester Lane and the Yellow Jackets, and the Alabama Collegians. Of course all the name black bands came to Little Rock—it was one of the major venues. Bands from Texas like Don Albert's and the Blue Devils from Oklahoma. Right across the street from my dad's office was a ballroom, where Count Basie was leading what had been the Benny Moten band. My dad was a great jazz lover and used to take me over with him. Hot Lips Page was on the band then, I think it was before Jo Jones joined, and Eddie Durham, Lester Young, Walter Page, and Buster Smith on alto. It was terrific—just fantastic. That was a good growing-up experience.

There was a dance hall in Little Rock called the Dreamland Ballroom. It was an old rickety building and we used to get Erskine Hawkins, Andy Kirk, Earl Hines, Duke, Claude Hopkins, Basie, Harlan Leonard, Jimmie Lunceford. They let white people into the Dreamland, but they were supposed to stay up in the balcony. But they would sneak down and start dancing and so the owner, Sweets Baker, would come over and tell them, "Look, you're violating the law but I'm not going to stop you enjoying yourselves so long as you behave and don't start switching partners and stuff." And there was never any trouble.

In high school our music teacher would often talk visiting bandleaders into coming and playing at assembly. So we had Duke Ellington come to assembly and play with a small contingent from his band. That's where I first heard Barney Bigard in person.

I went on to college at Pine Bluff, Arkansas, and I was in the jazz band there, with a music scholarship. There was terrific competition among the college bands at that time and they used to give out music scholarships like they do with sports nowadays. I was at Arkansas A&M for a year then I went to Tennessee State in Nashville and finally to St. Louis. The music in Nashville in the late 1930s—there was a lot of jazz there—

wasn't Dixieland, it wasn't traditional, and it wasn't swing—it was something that was evolving. Then I got a call from the Jeter-Pilars Orchestra in St. Louis and I was with them for six or seven months till 1941. I then took a job with Dewey Jackson's band on a riverboat. We went from Paducah, Kentucky, to Pittsburgh and then played trips out of Pittsburgh. It took about a month to get up there, stopping at towns along the way. Then we spent two months making trips out of Pittsburgh, down to Aliquippa or up to the Monongahela and the Susquehanna. It was a lot of fun and I met Errol Garner on the boat. He used to come on board and play with us. Dewey Jackson had a really good jazz band—we had to play for dancing too, but we had a lot of special arrangements that made us sound a bit like the Basie band. Eddie Batchman was the lead alto; the other tenor was Edgar Hayes, Gene Porter was the second alto, John Orange was on trombone, George Hudson was one of the trumpets, Wendell Black, who resembled Ray Nance, was another. The drummer was Earl Martin—a fantastic drummer who didn't want to leave St. Louis. Singleton Palmer—his nickname was Cocky—was on bass. He later played with Basie and then came back home and organized a Dixieland band.

At that time, I was torn between Lester Young and Coleman Hawkins—I didn't know which way to lean. So that's the reason why my playing reflects both those influences. I was also influenced by Budd Johnson who was in the Lester tradition but had a thing going of his own. I loved his playing and his arranging. And I loved Don Byas. In St. Louis Jimmy Forrest and I were very close—Jimmy was a very underrated tenor player.

When war started, I joined the navy because they were organizing bands for all the naval air stations. That's how I came to Minneapolis. I was supposed to go to St. Mary's preflight school but the guy who was the chief petty officer heard me play and he said to me, "I need a tenor player and a clarinet player and you're it." I said, "No I'm not. I'm going to California." He said, "Oh no you're not." And I wasn't.

I wound up at the Great Lakes Naval Training Station and I met a whole bunch of guys there—Willie Smith, Julius Watkins, George Matthews, and Freddie Skerritt, an alto player who'd been with Machito. He was a helluva player and gave me his card; he told me that when I left the service he wanted me to come on to Machito's band. I said, "Man, I don't play that Latin stuff." But after the war, when I was in New York, I dropped by the Copacabana, where they were playing, and I said, "What am I talking about?" Those cats were just fantastic. I was in the navy band for three years, three months, and fourteen days. Most of the guys in the band I was in were from Louisville mostly unknown but good players. A guy named Dave Goodlow was the chief arranger; he played trumpet and was just wonderful. The charts were a mixed bag. Goodlow wrote in a kind of Tadd Dameron style. It was a twenty-three-piece group and we played all the ceremonial functions, parades, and dances too. Eventually we got shipped out—a couple of the guys got into trouble and the brass decided we should be sent someplace but they didn't know where. First we went to Pier 92 in New York City, which was great because we could just walk down 52nd Street, where everything was happening.

I heard Stuff Smith, Billie Holiday, Errol Garner, Don Byas, Lucky Thompson, Wardell Gray who was just a youngster then—he was so good.

I guess we were having too much fun because they sent us to Norfolk, Virginia, for a few weeks. Finally they sent us to Curacao in the Netherlands West Indies.

After I got out of the navy I went on the road with Horace Henderson's band and also spent several weeks with the later edition of the Billy Eckstine band. I recorded in Chicago with Dinah Washington. Her arranger on those sessions was a school chum of mine, R. C. "Riley" Hampton. I enjoyed playing in big bands but I always wanted to have my own group. I enjoyed being a soloist so that's what I wound up doing.

I married a local girl and we had four kids. We were divorced after nineteen years—she just couldn't stand me being on the road all the time. A year later I married another Minnesota girl and we had five kids. Now I have fifteen grandchildren.

A lot of the guys came back to Minneapolis after the war and I organized an eight-piece band with some of them. Percy Hughes took that band over when I went to New York with George Hudson. When I came back I played with Percy for about two years, mainly at a club called the Flame.

In the late 1950s I was in the house band at Freddie's, which was a highfalutin nightclub here in Minneapolis. They booked

Broadcast of Cello Rhapsody, WNYC, 1955. Talbert conducting; George Koutzen, cello.

Broadcast of Cello Rhapsody, WNYC, 1955. Left to right: Kai Winding, trombone; Harold Wegbrite, trumpet; unknown, French horn.

Wednesday's Child recording, February–March, 1956. Left to right: Joe Wilder, trumpet; Tom Talbert; Patty McGovern.

Osceola, 1967. The house that Tom designed.

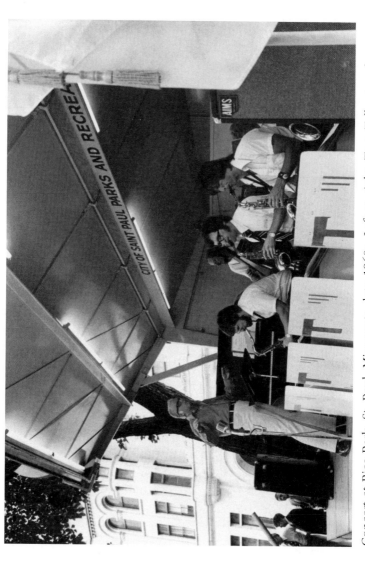

Concert at Rice Park, St. Paul, Minnesota, late 1960s. Left to right: Tom Talbert; unknown, tenor saxophone; unknown, bass; Ed Boike, alto saxophone; Dick Oatts, alto saxophone.

The septet at Tom Talbert's house in Laguna. Left to right: Bruce Paulson, trombone; Bob Summers, trumpet; Dick Mitchell, alto saxophone; Bob Efford, baritone saxophone; Jeff Hamilton, drums; John Leitham, bass; Tom Talbert, piano.

Laguna, 1988. Tom Talbert, Betty Talbert, Ken Borgers (then program director, KLON).

The Trianon Ballroom, April 1948. Left to right: Billy Shuart; Tom Talbert; Warne Marsh, tenor saxophone; Bob Stone, bass; Benny (?), alto saxophone; El Koeling, alto saxophone; Roy Harte, drums; Steve White, tenor saxophone; Harry Brainerd, trombone; Don Davidson's argyle sock and shoe.

Concert, Long Beach, February 28, 2001. Left to right: Tom Talbert; Barry Zweig, guitar; Jim Hughart, bass; Bob Efford, tenor saxophone; John Leys, trombone; Don Shelton, flute; Bob McChesney, trombone; Sal Lozano, alto saophone; Bob Summers, trumpet.

Concert at Long Beach, February, 28, 2001. Left to right: Bob Efford, tenor saxophone; Don Shelton, alto saxophone; Sal Lozano, alto saxophone.

Concert, Long Beach, February, 28, 2001. Left to right: Bob McChesney, trombone; Sal Lozano, alto saxophone; Bob Summers, trumpet; Bob Payne, trombone; Frank Szabo, trumpet; Jennifer Hall, baritone saxophone.

all the big acts—Sarah Vaughan, Ella Fitzgerald, Brook Benton, George Shearing, Billy Eckstine, Lenny Bruce. Johnny Hodges and Harold Baker were very good friends of mine and they both tried to get me into Duke's band. Duke was willing to listen to me but I was scared and just wouldn't do it. Count Basie also tried to get me out of here. He phoned me up and said, "I'm playing here at Freddie's—come down and bring your horn." I said, "I don't think so. You'd have to pay me at least $300 a week for me to give up what I've got here." Basie laughed and said, "Well come down anyway, and don't bring your horn."

My own playing has evolved a long way from what I was doing twenty years ago. I was listening to an LP I made in the 1970s; while my sound was better then, harmonically I've gone a long way from that stuff . . . I don't hear what I was doing then, any more. I'm still evolving.

At home I'd be most likely to listen to Joe Henderson. I still listen to Prez and Hawk a lot. I also like Derek Alexander.

Tom Talbert had built his reputation in Los Angeles and New York City. Minneapolis was like starting all over again.

IRV WILLIAMS: Tom wasn't really known when he came back. It's a strange town; they forget you pretty quick. I played a job with Tom at a ballroom in Austin, Minnesota, around 1946 or 1947. Just a one-nighter. I played with him again when he came back in the 1960s. That was a really good band. He always says it was one of the best bands he ever had. He had some great local talent.

One of the young Twin Cities musicians who benefited from his experience playing with Tom Talbert was trombonist Bruce Paulson.

BRUCE PAULSON: I first heard Tom's band at one of the series at the Walker Playhouse. I grew up in Minneapolis and started playing trombone at the age of eleven in the school band. When I was in the ninth grade, I went to a summer band session at Roosevelt High School and that was where I first heard a jazz band playing. I was impressed and really got absorbed in the music. I took lessons from the band director at Roosevelt High, which incidentally turned out a lot of fine professional players, guys who went on to play in Woody Herman's band, for instance. My class produced two of us who wound up in the *Tonight Show* band, and a couple in the Buddy Rich band. The band at

Roosevelt was actually called a dance band, as there wasn't a jazz program as such. But we went along on Tuesday nights as an extracurricular activity and in my senior year I became its leader. There were lots of opportunities to play in the Minneapolis area during my high school years. We had rehearsal bands and the older musicians would frequently drop by and help us out. Although rock was really the music of my generation, I never really gravitated to it. When I graduated from high school in 1963, the Beatles were hitting but I was already listening to Horace Silver and John Coltrane. In fact the first band I had of my own, while I was still in high school, was a Dixieland band, which I think is a great way of learning to play independently, melodically, and rhythmically. Thanks to musicians like Doc Evans and Harry Blons there was a strong Dixieland tradition in the area; the first professional bands I was exposed to were Dixieland bands. Later I used to sit in at some of the black clubs in the Twin Cities like Beedie's Ebony Lounge, usually organ rooms where you'd be the only white guy in the club, and that was a great honor. But those audiences in those places back in the 1960s—there was still a mature, well-informed, well-dressed black audience that knew and appreciated their own music.

Tom was one of the bandleaders who had a name and recognition on the Minneapolis scene. His band was professional and interesting, but his music didn't have much impact on me until I played it. I remember going up to his farm in Wisconsin to rehearse. It was a very mature band and I was the youngest member and I was very thrilled to be part of it. Tom and I got along well from the start because we are both "no vibrato" men. As I was classically trained, I had no trouble reading his music. But you had to have your ears together because he writes lines that are intervalic—there are big skips and unusual intervals. There's a classical or chamber element to Tom's jazz writing and I've always wanted to have a chance to play his classical music. I don't know how well I interpreted his music. I've heard some people play improvised solos on his pieces that sound so great—tenor saxist Bob Hardaway and alto saxist Dick Oatts, for instance, and other guys who just didn't make much sense out of it. I may be one of those guys for all I know, but I always enjoyed it and felt at home in it. As Tom had two trombones and a French horn rather than a regular trombone section there was always an extra need to blend carefully. I hear a lot of French chamber music in his work. He always seemed to want to stay away from that shouting big band kind of approach.

I'm a member of the last generation of self-taught jazz musicians, and ironically now a professor of jazz studies at the University of Nevada at Las Vegas. Teaching jazz at universities has ensured that everyone now sounds the same. But Tom always wanted you to sound like you.

TOM TALBERT: In 1964, some friends bought a restaurant on 7th Street, right across from the Radisson Hotel, called the Running Fox. They were desperate to build up the business and I suggested putting a seven-piece band in for the cocktail hour, when people were getting off work. You could bring them in for a drink and a chance to listen to the band and hope that some of them would stay for dinner. We came in on the two worst nights, Tuesday and Wednesday, and I started at 5:00, playing solo piano, then at 5:30 the band came in. We played in the basement, which filled up quickly and soon people were standing on the stairs too. We did very well there and lasted thirteen weeks, until it was time for Bette and me to take our annual vacation. We put a trio in for the interim, but unfortunately by the time we came back and the septet began again, the momentum was lost and it just didn't seem to work anymore.

The seasonal nature of the barge business forced Tom to take his time off during the winter when the river was frozen. He and Bette needed a break, and they headed for Mexico. A more single-minded and committed leader might not have gone on vacation at a time when the gig was working so well but, as Kent Hazen observes, the engagement may already have run its natural course.

KENT HAZEN: Jazz in the Minneapolis/St. Paul area has been a peek-a-boo or hide-and-go-seek kind of situation across all the eras. You'd get a club or a venue that would spring up and last for a few months or years then it would be gone, or you'd have a band with couple of jazz soloists in it and you'd go and see them on their commercial jobs and wait for the odd solo.

Tom's next move would have caused gasps of amazement in Charlie's Tavern, had anyone known of it. He added "rancher" to his résumé.

TOM TALBERT: Around this time I got the idea I wanted to get out in the country, so Bette and I bought an abandoned forty-acre farm over in Wisconsin on some high hills overlooking the St. Croix valley. It was about forty miles from Minneapolis and about seven miles from Osceola and Somerset. There was an old farmhouse with no heat. It did have water and that was about all, but we were out in the country and we liked that. We'd been using it as a summer place and I got the idea that I should get some yearling cattle to crop the grass, about thirty-two acres of sandy rolling pasture. The day the cattle arrived the truck driver let them get away and they went running over the hills—there was a tired old fence and one of the animals went through it into a neighbor's place. It took me about a week to get it back, which alienated those neighbors forever.

It was a sad time in the fall when the cattle were taken away to the stockyard, so the next year I got some more. At the end of the year when they were going to the feedlot, I bought a few cows that could have calves. That meant we had to be there in the winter so we had a house built up on top of the hill with a wonderful view. It was a modest house but I liked it because I designed it. The cattle were loose in the forty acres and the neighbors thought we were a little nuts because we didn't have them cooped up somewhere. Then I really started getting foolish. I decided we needed a bigger place so we found a wonderful farm down near River Falls, Wisconsin. We had about four hundred acres on the Rush River, which was lovely with woods, but it was a lot of terribly hard work. I put up miles of fences and built pens and loading chutes and the cattle kept multiplying. I got really interested in genetics and cross-breeding, and guys from the university would come out and see what I was doing. And when I think back on it now, I think, "What on earth *was* I doing?"

BRUCE PAULSON: The cattle ranch—I found it fascinating. I saw Tom as a kind of renaissance guy with very wide interests. Everybody thought, Well, Talbot's got a farm and we go out there to rehearse. He always had great food for us when we finished and it was all very high class. He always treated his musicians well. It was very, very civilized.

Perhaps Tom Talbert's Irish genes were coming to the fore. (He was a Murphy on his mother's side.) Having demonstrated a great gift for making music, he now became a successful farmer, running the Troubadour Ranch at Spring Valley, Wisconsin. An advertisement for the ranch in *Shorthorn World* carries a photo of a bull named Lox and a caption: "FOR SALE: Yearling bulls by 'Lox.' They are big and good. You'll have to see them to believe them. Also a limited number of select heifers." Another full-page advertisement has photos of not only Lox but also Laddie, Skol, and Harvey.

TOM TALBERT: We had a terrific boy working for us, who was back from Vietnam. He'd been raised on a farm and he was big and strong and a good worker but he was looking to graduate from school and didn't stay any longer after that. So eventually I started looking at selling the place. During this time I was still doing the occasional job with the band.

In 1968 I got a three-week job at Diamond Lil's in Minneapolis that was running a Spirit of the Forties event. They got Helen Forrest and Ray Eberle and Helen O'Connell—a week each—with a big band that I conducted. It was a good-sized club and the project had already begun with another conductor before the management called me to take it over. I agreed but insisted on replacing some of the musicians with people who had played with my band so that I could feature some of my own music. My regular first trombone, Jim Ten Bensel, wasn't available so I hired Bruce Paulson, who was just graduating from the university. The featured singers had their own arrangements and I wrote some new things for the band to play for dancing in a kind of updated '40s style, probably subverting the intentions of Spirit of the Forties to some extent. We had to play some stock arrangements too, including a Tommy Dorsey set, a Glenn Miller set, and so on.

BRUCE PAULSON: He had that gig at Diamond Lil's, which he took on primarily to play his own music. But of course we had to play all the 1940s Glenn Miller-type stuff because that's what the gig was all about.

It was the grand opening of the club with the music of the big bands of the 1940s. They were going to have a whole hour of Tommy Dorsey, and DJ Leigh Kamman was in the announcing booth. I had to be Dorsey, even though I'm not a high note player nor a vibrato player! I had another gig so didn't make the first set. My sub, Bob Jenkins, who was one of my teachers, played lead on that. I arrived in time for the set that was the Tommy Dorsey set and I pleaded with Bob to stay and play it as he was a good high note player who did vibrato. But like a good teacher he said, "No, you've got to do it." So we opened with "Getting Sentimental over You" and I stepped all over the solo, clams everywhere, and finished up by missing the high note at the end. It was truly one of the worst experiences of my life, but there was still a whole hour of Tommy Dorsey solos to go. What would have been the second trombone was a French horn, hired to fit Tom's own arrangements, so I had to play lead and all the trombone solos. After that evening I found out that the owner of the club told Tom to fire "that trombonist" and Tom said, "No. He works for me. You can fire me but you can't fire one of my musicians."

I look back at that as a very important event for me. Had I been fired I might have given up on music and the trombone. I look on Tom as someone who looked after me and had the integrity to stick up for me. So I owe him a lot.

TOM TALBERT: The first week we had Helen Forrest and she was delightful—easy to work with and still a good singer. Then the middle week we had Ray Eberle and that was a disaster—he drank a lot and he'd get lost in the middle of songs. On Sunday night, he'd been out on Lake Minnetonka on somebody's boat and had too much to drink. He got completely lost in the middle of one number so I had to go out and say, "Thank you Ray, thank you everybody" and walk him off the stand. Then we had Helen O'Connell and she was fine.

Perhaps it was the long, hard winters, perhaps the isolation of the farm and the burden of the work there but Tom's marriage to Bette was failing. They separated and put the ranch and the cattle up for sale. Tom spent a last winter at Troubadour, alone except for 110 bovines, two poodles, and a hired man in another house. In spring with the cattle gone, he moved into an apartment in St. Paul and took stock. There were a few opportunities for the septet but little else. Finally Tom started to look west again.

13

Welcome (Back) to LA

TOM TALBERT: Friends were writing me, saying things were changing and getting better in the music world there. In particular I had a close friend in Terry Keegan, who'd had a good job at NBC and had moved over to Paramount Pictures, developing new shows. He encouraged me to come out because he felt he was in a position to see that I was considered for work at Paramount. So in 1975 I put my dog, Maigret, in the car and set off for California.

BRUCE PAULSON: I left the area about the same time as Tom. I went on the road in 1970 with the Buddy de Franco–Glenn Miller band and then with Buddy Rich. And then I got an offer to join the Johnny Carson *Tonight Show* band. I was actually having a great time with Buddy Rich, playing solos and getting into *Down Beat* polls, when I got a call from Doc Severinson asking me if I wanted to join. I thought, "Gee, you haven't even heard me play." I wasn't sure I wanted to join a studio band, but everyone insisted that it was a step up for me and of course it was an all-star band—Snooky Young, Conte Candoli, great musicians like that—and we got to record with people like Frank Sinatra. I was very lucky.

TOM TALBERT: Naturally after more than twenty years my old friends in Los Angeles had moved on in many different ways, and for a while it was difficult to renew contacts. Some of the people I was in touch with were urging me to form another rehearsal band and I tried it, using the charts I had written for the twelve-piece band in Minneapolis. These arrangements just didn't have the charge and the power that the LA guys liked, so I put it on hold and started writing some new material for a band that would have four trumpets.

In 1977 I recorded an album called *Louisiana Suite*, which consisted of new, enlarged versions of arrangements that I'd written for the twelve-piece band in Minneapolis back in 1962–1963. Back in the fall of 1962 I'd had a boat that I owned lifted out of the water and put on the prow of one of our barges in St. Paul and taken down to Baton Rouge. Once the boat was there my wife and I and our poodle, Charra, drove down and we sailed the boat to Lake Ponchartrain. We spent a month there and that inspired me to write *Louisiana Suite,* which I was originally going to call *New Orleans Suite* if Duke Ellington hadn't got in first.

Tom actually confessed that part three of the suite, "Watermelon Days," had already been written in Minneapolis before he went to New Orleans.

TOM TALBERT: Edgar Rice Burroughs didn't go to the jungle to write his Tarzan books, most of them were written in Tarzana, California. On the other hand, "Royal Street" was very much inspired by the facades of the eponymous street, the buildings, the balconies. "Too Wet to Walk" was something someone said while we were avoiding a tropical downpour one night in the French Quarter, and I wrote "Grieve Softly" after exploring the old cemeteries.

When we came to record, I didn't want to play so I replaced the piano with Joe Di Orio on guitar and we recorded it at Jim Mooney's Sage and Sound Studio. The room was small, but Joe did a very good job.

Louisiana Suite is, to the author, very much a transitional album, bridging the music Tom wrote in New York and the full maturity of his coming work in Los Angeles. It benefits from some superb alto sax playing by an expatriate from England, Andy Mackintosh, who returned there soon after and also affords a glimpse of some of Tom's TV writing, with an extended version of a theme he wrote for the *Serpico* series. The title "suite" is made up of five pieces notable for engaging melodies and some intricate and interesting woodwind writing. The album was a gorgeous musical indulgence, but Tom Talbert was now getting involved in a very specialized and demanding area of composing. In spite of protestations to the contrary, it is the experience of the author, and many others who have worked in the TV and film medium, that concern for the music sound track comes low on the scale of priorities. Budgets are squeezed and music is written and recorded late in the production, often in a great hurry. In recent years the use of the videocassette and very sophisticated electronic film and music editing systems have simplified the process. But Tom was working at a time when sound track music would be composed in line with mathematical calculations provided by the film editor, and the music would be recorded while film of the relevant scene was run in the studio on a screen in front of the conductor. He would control the progress of the music and its function of "illustrating" or "underlining" events onscreen, while conducting to a kind of electronic metronome called a "click track." The successful film conductor would contrive to conduct the performance of the orchestra so that the important musical "comments" would coincide with the events in the film that the director wanted reinforced by music.

Until this time, Tom's music had been notable for its taste and originality, as well as his demonstrable refusal to compromise artistically. These are not the qualities most required in the ruthlessly competitive world of TV and movies. For the first time in his career, Tom was called on to write music that was dictated by nonmusical values.

TOM TALBERT: It took a while for something to come along that Terry Keegan thought was right for me. Then they developed a TV series based on the film *Serpico* and I was hired, along with some others, to write music for it. I was very nervous at the first session. I'd never worked in this medium before, I'd had no experience of recording to film or working to a click track. So I got a very experienced friend Lyn Murray to conduct the music I'd written, and I learned from what he did.

By this time my friend Joe Soldo had come out from New York with the *Carol Burnett Show* and was doing some music contracting. Joe knew all the best musicians, so rather than having the studio contractor pick them for me, Joe and I would make up a list of the people we wanted and we had really terrific bands, right from the beginning.

Tom and Joe booked the best studio players, with a sprinkling of great jazz musicians like Art Pepper, pianist Pete Jolly, drummer Jack Sperling, and Larry Bunker on percussion.

TOM TALBERT: I was also getting work on comedies. Even though I never used an orchestrator, I enjoyed the work except for the fact that you're always rushed.

JOE SOLDO: He had a friend at Universal who produced the show *Emergency.* I think we did thirteen weeks and Tom wrote a lot of the music. That was very interesting because that was the first time I heard music that Tom was scoring for a film. It was jazz music—there were classical instruments but it was jazz. The shows that I saw, I thought the music worked very well. Unfortunately the show didn't stay on the air.

Woodwind player Bobby Tricarico had known Tom in New York and worked for him in the LA studios.

BOBBY TRICARICO: I remember seeing Tom in Jim and Andy's. Then he disappeared and I didn't see him again until I came out to LA. I'd been on staff at NBC in New York and when that started to sink, all the guys I was with—David Shire, Don Costa, Marvin Hamlisch (who was rehearsal pianist on *Funny Girl*)—came out to the coast. I came out on the strength of the *Carol Burnett Show* in 1972. There was a long time before I let anybody out here know that I was a tenor saxist—they thought I was just a bassoon player. If they knew I was a "doubler," then they'd pigeonhole you as a doubler and wouldn't take your bassoon playing seriously. So I started doing things like the Hanna Barbera cartoon shows. Joe Soldo was contracting and Tom came in and did a couple of things and that's where I met him again. In addition to the TV work he wanted me to play with his big band but I just couldn't work it out, time-wise. I went to hear his band in one of the clubs on Ventura Boulevard. And it was marvelous—the arrangements were something else.

Unlike some of his contemporaries, Tom seems to have adapted easily to the particular demands of TV and film work. Bobby Tricarico was there.

BOBBY TRICARICO: The music business is very tough; the arranging business is very tough. A good example of that is Gil Evans. I worked a lot with Gil in New York. Gil came out here to do a TV show at Universal and he called me to book the guys. One of the people he wanted was Jimmy Cleveland. And he told me to get the guys and he would let me know when the dates were. A couple of days later he phoned me up and told me, "Forget about the whole thing!" I asked why and he said, "I went down to the studio and brought down what I was going to do and they wanted me to make all these changes. And I said I'm not going to make any changes." JJ Johnson, on the other hand, was willing to do whatever was wanted but he had trouble with film timings and using the click track and we were wasting time in the studio. No matter how brilliant a writer might be, a major part of the job is dodging the bullets. In this world Tom was marvelous. He had no problems with the timings; he was relaxed and calm. He never appeared nervous. I don't know what was going on inside but from the outside he was cool. He was very strong in his opinions about the music that he'd written, but he was willing to change it if it would help the show.

Tom looks back with mixed feelings.

TOM TALBERT: To a lot of people, writing for a television show is just a commercial thing, but I put a lot of myself into it and I didn't have anything that I wished I hadn't written. I realize now that in a lot of places I overwrote—it may have come off well but I could have achieved the same effect with a fourth of the effort. There's nothing that I'm ashamed of and quite a bit that I think was really very good. We always had really top musicians and I think they were glad to be paid for playing my music. But ultimately it was really kind of disillusioning because you'd do a wonderful score and record all day with the best musicians in the world and none of the top executives at the studio even knew you'd been there. It was as if the gate had never opened.

BOBBY TRICARICO: There's a lot of politics involved too. Tom would come and have a drink with us after a session, but he wasn't going to the Hollywood parties, he wasn't socializing. A lot of guys who wouldn't make a pimple on his butt were making all the parties, hobnobbing and socializing—the Hollywood routine and these people kind of got a foot in. Your face has to fit. And also very noticeably Tom couldn't stand the phonies. He'd choke on the bullshit.

TOM TALBERT: I lost out on writing the score for an Irwin Shaw movie—actually a two-part made-for-TV movie called *Top of the Hill* with Elke Sommer, Adrienne Barbeau, Wayne Rogers, Mel Ferrer, and Sonny Bono. I was all set to do it but the producer said, "I want someone who has won an Academy Award—I don't care who it is, as long as he has an award." For a TV movie! In fact I supervised the recording of some location music—scenes in a ski lodge with Don Abney playing piano, but I gradually dropped out. They'd call me and I'd do one or two episodes of a comedy but for three years I just sort of withdrew.

By 1980–1981 the arrival of the synthesizer and the drum machine was about to change the way sound tracks were written and recorded, destroying the livelihood of many studio musicians.

TOM TALBERT: All the talk at the studios was how they were going to be able to slash their budgets—which later became the sad fact of the film being scored by the producer's daughter-in-law on a synthesizer in her garage.

14

One, Then Seven, Then Fourteen

Once again Tom experienced a musical hiatus and, after a time, an unlikely return to music. Indirectly, this came about through his friendship with the brilliant cartoonist Virgil Partch, who had also been at Fort Ord in 1944.

TOM TALBERT: I'd go down to Laguna Beach and have riotous, boozy lunches with Virgil and his friends. I'd been thinking of living at the beach and had checked out Santa Barbara and La Jolla, but finally settled on Laguna and in 1980 wound up in a fabulous architect-designed house overlooking the town. About 1981 I had a strong urge to get back into music and I really don't believe what I did next. The music scene was bleak and there was little I could do as a writer. Although I had never cared for my own piano playing—I'd had no schooling and I'd never played very much—other people seemed to like it. I asked the owner of a restaurant in Laguna Beach called Gauguin, "How would you like to have piano for cocktail hour two nights a week? What kind of a deal could I make with you?" The guy was a cheapskate and said, "Well, how much will it cost?" "I said it won't cost you anything; just give me a bar tab." I did a couple of nights a week, which got me thinking. Then there was a restaurant called the Ivy House, which was the main place in Laguna. It had just changed hands and had been renamed the Cedar Creek Inn. The woman who bought it said, "Oh, I'd love to have you come here." So then I went there for the Friday and Saturday cocktail hours and Sunday afternoons. I was getting a little cash and drinks, and even enjoying playing piano, probably for the first time in my life. I was there a while, then I moved to an even nicer place at Corona Del Mar and started to think about the septet that I'd had in Minneapolis. Thinking that it would be wonderful for Sunday afternoons, we worked out a budget and I got a group together, including Bob Summers on trumpet, Bruce Paulson on trombone, Dick Mitchell on alto sax, and Chuck Flores on drums. The profits were going up the owner's nose pretty fast, and the place disintegrated, but at least it had gotten me started again and I actively began looking round for opportunities.

BRUCE PAULSON: When Tom came out to LA he called me when he began his TV work. I helped him with suggestions of guys he should hire and I played on some of his sessions. When he was putting a septet together, I helped him again with some players that I thought would be sympathetic to his music.

Was a bar in Newport Beach the right venue for the Tom Talbert Septet?

BRUCE PAULSON: I think Tom was bit unfulfilled by it, but he had a very laconic approach. A core of people would come into the club who were interested, but it was a bar and you'd hear applause and think, "Oh, they liked my solo." But it would turn out that they were watching the football game on TV. Tom's music is too sophisticated for that kind of venue. It's not for dancing, it's not for partying—unless you're going to sit down and listen to it. It's art music and certainly there were people who came to listen but ultimately it was a bit unsatisfying. The band was good, and Tom had good players and you got a chance to blow.

At this time an even more important event occurred in Tom's life.

TOM TALBERT: In 1985, living as a bachelor, I got really tired of doing all the work when I had guests. A friend recommended someone who worked with a caterer in Newport Beach, and that turned out to be Betty. She came and fixed a wonderful dinner for eight of us. Later, when she showed me how easily I could assemble the endive salad I'd liked so much, I blurted out, "But now that I've found you . . ."

The salad was far from her only attraction—she is beautiful, warm, and caring and we became involved quite quickly. At that time she was very active in the Orange County Hospice group and came up with a great idea. We put on five annual jazz concerts featuring the septet in my house nine hundred feet above Laguna and the Pacific Ocean. Each year we had more and more people in the house and on the three-tiered deck. The septet often included star subs like Jeff Hamilton or Jake Hanna on drums. The warm, enthusiastic crowd, the view, good food, and drink made these memorable occasions.

Betty and I got married in 1991, and in August the following year we moved to our present Beverly Hills home, a large, warm Spanish-Italian house about halfway up Coldwater Canyon.

MILT BERNHART: When he moved down to Laguna, he met Betty, and that was very good for him. He'd previously had a misfire of a marriage, I believe, but he and Betty are a great match. They are very compatible—she's all for him—and I'm very pleased for them both.

Meanwhile, the Newport Beach location had its limitations and Tom felt that a gig in town might be better.

TOM TALBERT: There was a restaurant in Los Angeles on Melrose Avenue called Linda's. Linda was Terry Keegan's ex-wife and a friend. I started playing piano there on Monday nights and talked her into having the septet on Saturday afternoons. We did that for thirteen weeks, by this time with Andy Martin on trombone, Lee Callett on baritone, and John Leitham on bass.

Kent Hazen, on vacation from Minneapolis, heard the band at Linda's.

KENT HAZEN: It was quite a memorable experience for me. As we pulled up, the doors and windows were open on this beautiful sunny Southern California day and as we walked up we could hear this contrapuntal West Coast music coming out. I felt like I'd been transported back to 1954. The musicians were outstanding, the audience was attentive. It was a nice casual scene.

TOM TALBERT: In 1987 I recorded the septet and then I started writing for a big band again. In 1991 I started doing concerts with a fourteen-piece group.

The music and the musicians had changed, but essentially Tom had arrived back where he'd been in 1947—running a very high quality rehearsal band that occasionally did gigs. Bruce Paulson echoes the thoughts of Don Davidson and Jack Montrose.

BRUCE PAULSON: When Tom started his big band again, I played with it for a while but eventually I drifted away, due to other commitments. I helped Tom find guys of my age to play in the band and people kept coming to play in it—it gave them a chance to play music that was subtle and not brassy. He loves to have one trumpet play, instead of all three, for instance, or maybe two trumpets, French horn, and baritone—and guys enjoyed it and they came to rehearse with him. In a town like LA that's so competitive, rehearsal bands fill a necessary function. If you don't make them you lose your visibility, but Tom always paid guys to rehearse too, so that was an added incentive.

Bruce underlines a change from the 1940s days.

BRUCE PAULSON: He's known for forming the band for a while, then stopping, and starting up again later—unlike, say, Bob Florence or Bill Holman who rehearse week in, week out, year in, year out and the guys fix their own subs if they can't make it. I don't think it has hurt Tom's cause but it means that when he does start, he has to start all over from scratch, calling people. It probably wouldn't work very well if he had to deal with a lot of subs—you have to play his music over and over. He doesn't tell you how he wants things played. I can't remember a single time he's sung a phrase and said, "I want it this way." He had a core group of people here who stuck with him for years and years.

Why, after all of his previous experiences, did Tom take on the headaches involved in running a big band?

TOM TALBERT: Well, I'm more valuable as a writer if I have more horns. The septet was great fun and, again, if I were more of a pianist I probably could have done more with it too—some featured things for the leader to throw his hair around and pound away. If all things are equal financially, what I really love is a medium-sized band of twelve or thirteen pieces. That's really wonderful because first of all it shows who can write and who can't. It can stay so light and swing, yet you've got enough horns for color.

This is the size band I had in Minneapolis. In Los Angeles I added two pieces to make fourteen.

For a time in the early 1990s, the band performed constantly, and this was probably Tom Talbert's most concentrated period of activity.

TOM TALBERT: We started to play eleven or twelve concerts a year . . . colleges and schools, Ken Poston's Back to Balboa festival, and occasional clubs. When I formed the band I picked everyone very carefully, and right away I started to think about recording the band. We played lots of colleges in the area, from Long Beach to UCLA to Northridge. Most of these concerts were funded by my foundation, which is, alas, just me! I learned a lot doing this.

Altruism and good works aside, there were pitfalls and frustrations too.

TOM TALBERT: Apparently I wasn't dealing with the right people at the right administrative level and there were many problems. You couldn't get parking for the musicians! On several occasions we'd turn up and I'd say, "Where are all the music students?" only to be told, "Oh, they're in class—they can't spend time listening to music." This was ultimately all very disheartening.

Don Shelton, who plays alto saxophone and clarinet with Tom, remembers those times too.

DON SHELTON: For a year or two, it was just one venue after another. We played for a lot of young children—it may have been their first exposure to jazz, improvisation, or a big band. One of the things Tom likes and one that he was very good at was talking about the era that the particular piece of music represented. Talking about the music and people of the time, then tying it all together with his own version.

In 1991 Tom recorded some of the pieces the band was currently playing and released them on a CD called *The Warm Café*. This album contains some of his finest writing and some of the most sensitive interpretations of his work by his soloists. Don Shelton's clarinet work on Django Reinhardt's "Manoir de mes rêves" and alto sax playing on "Tell Summer No" is inspired, as are the improvisations of trumpeters Bob Summers and Steve Huffsteter. Don's alto playing is also exquisite on the title track—a reworking of a theme Tom had originally composed for a TV movie. Also revisited was "La Bayadera"—a piece he'd offered Stan Kenton forty years earlier in Philadelphia. Rewritten for the smaller Talbert orchestra, it's a moody mix of Latin and straight-ahead sections, with a particularly effective tenor solo from Bob Efford. "La Bayadera" never became part of the Kenton repertoire, and one can't help feeling that Stan made the wrong decision—the effect of the powerful Innovations Orchestra performing it must have been spectacular. "Someone's Rocking My Blues" demonstrates how well Tom had absorbed and digested the Basie tradition of the "shouting" blues band, even though it's the kind of thing he hardly ever recorded.

Like all of Tom's previous works, *Warm Café* received excellent reviews, for example, "a low-key masterpiece"[1] and "this is a wonderful album."[2]

TOM TALBERT: *Warm Café* took quite a time to get finished. We were recording straight to two track and there were a couple of sessions where I was unhappy about the sound. So I had to swallow them financially, but I didn't want to release something I thought was below par. There are some real high points on the album like "Manoir de mes rêves" by Django Reinhardt. People loved that at concerts and I would talk about Reinhardt as I did about Fats Waller when we played "Ain't Misbehavin'." I'd talk about those days, who Andy Razaf was . . . the audience loved that, and I enjoyed doing it.

The *Warm Café* sessions were the genesis of Talbert's next album.

TOM TALBERT: Originally I was going to include a couple of Duke Ellington pieces on the album. Then I thought, "I've got arrangements of so many Ellington and Billy Strayhorn tunes that I should do an album of their music." This was well before the "religious" fervor of the years around 1999–2000.

There's a lot of speculation and there have even been lawsuits about who wrote many of the Ellington tunes. So I decided that I would only record bona fide Ellington and Strayhorn compositions. I didn't, for instance, do tunes associated with Duke like "Caravan," much as I like and respect the composer Juan Tizol, and I tried to pick Strayhorn things that were acknowledged as being solely Strayhorn's.

The resulting music on Tom Talbert's Ellington/Strayhorn album, *Duke's Domain,* is quite different from most Ellington tributes.

KEN POSTON: Tom's arrangements of other people's compositions become almost like Tom Talbert originals. He reworks them with his own approach to the extent that he sheds a whole new light on them. I think one of the great things about the *Duke's Domain* album is that while everyone has done their own tribute to Ellington and many of the great writers have used Ellington and Strayhorn material, Tom's really stands out. He's done it in such a different way from everyone else. He doesn't try to capture the spirit of Duke Ellington. He uses the material to make it his own with fascinating results. It's a brave thing to do too. I think a lot of arrangers, when dealing with Ellington material, are afraid to take that kind of approach. Tom really showed what could be done and how modern jazz writing today could be approached from an original standpoint rather than reworking the same old formulas over and over.

And he'd already mapped out the path he'd take with his highly personal treatment of "Prelude to a Kiss" on the *Bix Duke Fats* album back in 1956. One of the most appealing features of *Duke's Domain* is

Tom's use of some of the beautiful compositions that Duke mostly ignored in later years. Tunes like "Someone," "After All," "All Too Soon," and "In a Sentimental Mood." Once again he had the benefit of superlative solo work from his "LA regulars" with Don Shelton and Bob Efford particularly moving on the aforementioned "Someone" and fine contributions throughout from Steve Huffsteter, Bob Summers, and Andy Martin. An extra treat is the presence of alto saxist Gary Foster on "After All" and the triptych that gives the album its title. The original compositions pleased Bob Efford, a longtime member of Talbert's sax section who has a slightly different perception of Tom Talbert as arranger compared to composer.

> BOB EFFORD: His own pieces are definitely the outstanding part of his writing I think. When he writes other people's material you have a preconceived idea of what you might hear and you might not always agree with his interpretation because it's different from what you were accustomed to hearing, but his own pieces are so fresh and so unique and that's what to me he seems to do best.

Tom Talbert's approach as described by Ken Poston meant that a good deal of his own original composition became an essential ingredient in his Ellington tribute, particularly in the "detail"—the accompanying phrases and lines that he wrote behind Ellington's and Strayhorn's themes—and the often very "un-Dukeish" voicings and textures he conjures up. The first chorus of "Chelsea Bridge" is a notable example with its French horn lead, backed by poignant woodwinds, leading into Steve Huffsteter's austere trumpet bridge. This is an example, in the author's opinion, of all that's best in Talbert's writing. The touching mood of "Lotus Blossom" reflects his interest in Chamber music, and he remakes "I Got It Bad" and "In a Sentimental Mood" with deceptive simplicity. The reactions were very rewarding.

Mark Holston in *Jazziz* wrote, "Tom Talbert is the kind of perfectionist today's big band movement could use more of. On 'Duke's Domain' Talbert and his 14 piece band . . . go beyond the typically reverential approach . . . in favor of an approach that favors genuine appreciation over imitation . . . Duke's Domain . . . is a triumph of the arranger's art—a masterful accomplishment in every regard."[3]

Robert Tate concluded his review for *Jazz Now:* "this is genuinely beautiful music without a trace of artificial sentiment."[4]

TOM TALBERT: I was so pleased with the reviews because I fully expected that a lot of reviewers would say the kind of thing one reviewer in New York complained of—that "the alto player doesn't sound anything like Johnny Hodges," which was never my intention of course. The album was meant as an appreciation of Duke and not a replication of him. In fact I wrote the three-part piece as an appreciation and reworked one of the art songs I'd written back in the 1950s as the slow piece "Autumnal." Another original—a salute to Billy Strayhorn called "A Backward Glance"—got its title before I realized that there was an Edith Wharton novel with the same name. I'm very pleased with this piece. I started it at home in Beverly Hills and finished it while on vacation in Mexico."

Thanks to the writing and the fine solo work, *Duke's Domain* is almost Tom Talbert's finest album, only let down by a lack of cohesion in the rhythm section. John Leitham and Jack Sperling fail to find the common groove that pieces like "Snibor" and "Take the A Train" need, and Sperling, a very experienced big band drummer, did not fare well in the final sound mix, often seeming to be tapping away in the next room. That criticism aside, the *Duke's Domain* album is an extraordinarily moving piece of work and one that can be listened to, over and over again.

TOM TALBERT: Then after I finished *Duke's Domain* I spent a small fortune in remastering old acetate discs of my 1940s band and releasing the results on CD.

Anyone remotely interested in the evolution of the jazz orchestra in the 1940s can feel grateful that he did so, and marvel that the fragile surfaces of the acetate and shellac discs actually survived four decades of handling and frequent playing on the primitive and damaging equipment of the time. Experts at saving old recordings—Jack Towers, Steven Lasker, and Doug Schwartz—worked wonders on sources of varying quality and have given us the opportunity to hear what the youthful Talbert was writing in Los Angeles in the 1940s.

NOTES

1. *Jazziz*, December 1994.
2. *Jazz Times*, December 1994.
3. *Jazziz*, March 1995.
4. *Jazz Now*, February 1995.

15

Autumn in New York, and Spring Too

TOM TALBERT: In 1995 my wife and I bought an apartment in Manhattan and decided to try to split our lives into "Autumn in New York" and spring too, and summer and winter in Beverly Hills. Coming back to New York gave me a strong desire to record there. Four of the musicians who had played on *Bix Duke Fats* were still playing and still friendly and taking my calls. So they were the nucleus of a band that I put together in the summer of 1997.

Tom decided to record with Joe Wilder, Eddie Bert, Danny Bank, and Aaron Sachs again and to also use the talents of some of New York's fine younger musicians like alto saxist Dick Oatts, trumpeter Glenn Drewes, tenor saxist Loren Schoenberg, and guitarist Howard Alden.

Eddie Bert was delighted.

EDDIE BERT: The thing is, I had seen Tom in California at the Kenton fiftieth anniversary, so I renewed acquaintances again. I figured he was living on the coast. I didn't think I'd see him in New York, then all of a sudden I got the call in New York and it was great. He's got a band out there also, so I guess we're the New York contingent.

A first album, *This Is Living*, was released in 1998 to great acclaim. The material included Talbert originals old and new, interpretations of other jazz composers' classics, such as John Lewis's "Django," Tadd Dameron's "Our Delight," and Willie "The Lion" Smith's "Echo of Spring," and some rarely played ballads like Gordon Jenkins's "This Is All I Ask." Some who have heard the album think that the New York group gave the music an edge that had been lacking on Tom's West Coast albums. That is not the author's opinion, even though there is quite a different feeling to the interpretations. Tom would not be drawn on this matter, except for the following observation.

171

TOM TALBERT: There's an energy level in New York that's not just in the music, it's in the shoe business, the restaurants, or anything else that you can think of—it's still the capital of the world, after all. I have a lot of feelings about this but they're very ephemeral and very vague.

What is not in doubt is the inspired performances Tom's writing evokes from some of his soloists irrespective of geography. He loves to feature the clarinet and he is particularly well served by both Don Shelton and his East Coast counterpart, Aaron Sachs, whose playing on "This Is All I Ask" is particularly moving.

TOM TALBERT: I liked the album, but I lost the studio I'd originally booked and had to record in a smaller room, which made for a less spacious sound than I wanted. I wasn't entirely successful in getting all of the musicians I'd wanted, in spite of spending a lot of time and effort. I did have everyone I wanted on the next album, though.

Talbert returned to the studio two years later with a similar lineup and recorded *To a Lady*. This album contains some of the most brilliant, witty, and tender writing of his entire career, and includes an extended work inspired by Ernest Dowson's poem "To a Lady Asking Foolish Questions," definitive readings of "Round Midnight" and "Little Girl Blue," and a sensitive jazz treatment of Ravel's "Pavane de la belle au bois dormant." And several very hard-swinging Talbert originals too. This time he had the room and the band he wanted. For most of the musicians this was a second outing with the Talbert mode of writing, and Tom agrees that by now they were more attuned to it.

TOM TALBERT: My music "takes paying attention" by the people who play it.

16

The View from the Stand

What is it like to play Tom Talbert's music and what is he like as a leader?

DON PRELL: I'll tell you, Tom was the best bandleader I ever worked with. It's too bad he isn't more recognized. The atmosphere at rehearsal was very relaxed and cordial and the music was terrific, but so was his attitude—he was so fair where his players were concerned.

Bob Stanton remembers his brother's opinion.

BOB STANTON: Dick thought that Tom was the most progressive, most advanced arranger around and he had enough musical knowledge and schooling to appreciate Tom's writing.

AARON SACHS: Tommy loves to write and he loves to hear his music. I love his writing—it's very astute—his orchestration. He gets an idea and he gets it through. It's not easy to play Tommy's music—cause it's not going where you think it's going. I've spoken to the alto player Dick Oatts and he concurs that improvisation doesn't come all that easy with Tom's chords . . . it's challenging.

IRV WILLIAMS: I think Tom's main reason for having a band is to hear his music played. He's not after the accolades or looking to have a commercial band. His music is actually fairly simple but the way he writes is hard. It's hard because sometimes he wants a certain way of phrasing that might not be the way you feel it. But once you hear it, then you understand what he's doing. Once I had a clarinet part with a low B-flat, which might have sounded okay if there were more than just one clarinet. I flinched when I played it, but later when I heard the playback, it sounded really good. Sometimes your ears can be just too good, but—Tom's a great writer. Playing his music has been a marvelous experience.

His ability to write music that gets the best out of his musicians is striking. Top New York alto saxist Dick Oatts was succinct.

DICK OATTS: Tom always gets something extra out of me.

Like Duke Ellington and Charles Mingus, Tom Talbert writes with particular musicians in mind, and the success of his music requires a great degree of empathy from his players.

DON SHELTON: Tom is a very gentle, soft-spoken man. In terms of discipline he's very relaxed and he makes a nice environment to produce music. His rehearsal technique is very loose. First of all, he puts a lot of responsibility on the players. He hires players who are very competent, whom he believes in and whose capabilities he knows. From then on it's pretty much up to us. Sometimes, where dynamics are concerned, if they're not adhered to he'll point out that he really wants triple piano here and double f here. Exaggerating the dynamics might be something he's looking for, but mostly he leaves it to the band to interpret his music. If something isn't quite right he'll say so, but in that very gentle way. But Tom always knows exactly how he wants a piece played.

Bob Efford, one of the busiest saxophone players in the Los Angeles area, not only plays in Tom Talbert's band but has the perspective of playing in the bands of Bob Florence, Bill Holman, and Frank Capp.

BOB EFFORD: A leader, I would think, is perhaps the last thing he really is. Because he's so undictatorial and so undemanding in that sense, and that's why I think it's necessary for him to surround himself with musicians who have some empathy with what he's doing. If he doesn't get what he wants, I guess, he just shrugs and walks away and hopes to get it next time. In rehearsal he tends to sit back and waits to see what he gets. Some other leaders may make some suggestions as to perhaps even style or almost tell you how to play. He would never do that. He might subtly suggest that it's too loud or too soft but that's about as far as he would ever go. I think he would probably prefer, not to read his mind, but I think he would probably prefer to change the person sitting in the chair rather than tell the person sitting in the chair how to play.

And what is it like if you are the right person "sitting in the chair"? Joe Wilder has been one of Tom's most empathetic soloists.

JOE WILDER: His writing is very challenging and it's sort of surprising. When you're playing it, you're not always aware of the different things that are going on within the arrangement itself. But when you back off and hear the finished composition, you think my god he's got the mind of a genius because of all the different things he's added and all of them can stand alone. But when they're put together it's amazing to hear how well they work together. I think sometimes of a person who wrote and could do things like Tom—Johnny Richards who would write and as you were playing you were saying, "This doesn't seem to be connected to the other thing" or whatever. But when it was done and you're listening to the playback, you think my goodness all these different things that were going on and the excitement that it created, and Tommy does that same thing.

"Can I check the second quarter note in bar 46?"

BOB EFFORD: Tom's music requires listening to—it doesn't hit you between the eyes. It needs delving into and requires some attention. Compared to other writers and bandleaders I play with in the LA area, Tom's music is a little more difficult to understand. We all have a built-in "wrong note detection system," and one has to learn to curb that with Tom. More often than not, a note that you feel is wrong is what he wants to be hearing and perhaps it's a matter of where you are sitting and what you are surrounded with at the time. But eventually you learn not to have egg on your face and tend not to say anything at all, even though you may question what you have in front of you. That's unfortunate, perhaps, in some ways because there must be times when the note actually is wrong, but one's pride does not permit one to keep on asking questions only to be told "No! That's right." If anything is more unusual about his writing and his rehearsals compared to anybody else's that's the point that I would make.

AARON SACHS: I know what he means—in fact I used to have the same feeling when I used to play Sy Oliver's arrangements you think it's not going to resolve and then it resolves. You have to get used to that kind of orchestration.

It has been said that director Alfred Hitchcock envisioned the entire completed film in his mind before a single scene was shot. Tom Talbert could be a musical equivalent. Joe Soldo has spent many years working with Tom.

JOE SOLDO: At the rehearsal he'd hardly change anything. With other bands, a lot of times you'd go in and do a session and you'd play something down once and the leader would say, "Okay leave out the second four bars of the bridge"—he'd decided it didn't work, or got in the way. But Tom hardly ever changed anything.

No doubt having a resident band to write for everyday at Fort Ord gave Tom an almost laboratory-like opportunity to hone his writing skills. He would also have absorbed a great deal of knowledge from Johnny Richards and his unrivaled experience working in Hollywood with Victor Young during the 1930s. Don Shelton compares Talbert's music to that of his peers.

DON SHELTON: I think it's highly sophisticated, which is a reason why the mass public fails to identify with it. He generally does not have the band roar in the way that you might think of a big band roaring. There's a lot of competition out there and many people like to get hit over the head with pomposity—the sound of a band roaring. And Tom is more subtle than that. That sophistication is there and, once again, that's a reflection of personality.

BOB EFFORD: There are in fact times when I forget I'm playing with a big band when I'm playing with Tom. Sometimes you look around and think "my goodness, are there this many people here." His music has almost a small band feel from time to time.

DON SHELTON: Sometimes it's chamber music-like.

17

Influences

Along with his surviving contemporaries, Tom has seen jazz evolve beyond anything imaginable in 1939. I asked him to describe his major influences.

TOM TALBERT: When I say I might be influenced by someone, I don't know how great a degree that would be. I would admire something—for instance, I could look back and think of Jimmy Mundy's arrangement for Count Basie of "Fiesta in Blue." It was a rich, very well written piece. I loved it and thought, boy, that's really great but I don't know if it ever propelled anything out of my system. I never sat down and tried to analyze what the voicings were.

I admired Eddie Durham, who really wrote what I would refer to as the first "swing" arrangements. He was a wonderful writer, as were the other guys who wrote for Basie—Buck Clayton and Buster Harding. I don't know if Jimmy Mundy had more training or schooling, but I always thought that his arrangements for Basie and Benny Goodman had a little extra elegance to them.

And Jimmie Lunceford—I guess you could say I was influenced by everyone who wrote for him except that I never wrote anything that sounded like a Jimmie Lunceford arrangement. I sure listened to them and studied them, to the little I could. When you saw them in person, their attitude was the same as the way they sounded. The class and confidence that they exuded when you saw them seemed to be reflected in the polished, disciplined way they played. It took a little while to assimilate to Ellington—I was not bowled over and I was put off by the drum style and some different things. The more I listened the more I liked it. I was growing up when the band was going into the so-called Blanton Webster period, so when the new records started coming out it was wonderful. It was what I considered the peak of the band, in both writing and execution.

By the time I was with the army band I had records with me and I remember particularly for a while I had a little cottage in Carmel and the guys would come over at night and we'd play Billie Holiday records and we'd sit around and ooh and aah. Then when the 1942 record ban started to lift, I heard the Woody Herman band which was really something. Even though they were only slightly older than me, I liked Neal Hefti's and Ralph Burns's arrangements very much. I still like the same arrangements. I don't know how influential they were on me but there were probably little things that I picked up. But without the schooling that I really wish I'd had, if I heard something, I couldn't always tell what it was. I could tell the overall sound but I couldn't break it down into each little quiver and quaver.

Ken Poston feels that the limited opportunities for musical education available to Tom in Minneapolis in the 1930s may have been a blessing in disguise.

KEN POSTON: I think that one of the things about his writing is that not having anything in the way of formal music education played a role in developing this great individual voice. That's something we find in many of the great individual figures, whether they're instrumentalists or writers. Not having been told formally what voicings are not appropriate or correct allowed him to develop this incredible writing style that provokes all kinds of emotions, from the beautiful cerebral-type things to the hard-swinging things that come from his big band experiences.

Composer-arranger and bandleader Maria Schneider has worked with important writers like Gil Evans and Bob Brookmeyer and puts Talbert at the same level of excellence and, in particular, individuality. She has some useful thoughts on "influence" and "learning to write."

MARIA SCHNEIDER: To listen to Tom's music and know a little bit about him is to show that music is a deeply personal thing; ultimately it's something you cannot be taught. You can be taught certain things, but if you're going to write music that has your own statement you have to search and find what's unique to you. When I used to work for Gil Evans, people used to ask me what did you learn from him. After a time I realized that what I learned from him was that I needed to learn things for myself. What's incredible about the music of Tom Talbert or Gil Evans or Bob Brookmeyer is that their music is uniquely them: they found their own way. I always think of it as a manifestation of a personality: Tom's music is a manifestation of Tom in sound. I believe that's what each of us has to find—that's the impulse to create.

To learn to write music that way I think really brings out someone's personality. Tom writes melodies in all the parts. Everybody has a beautiful line and those fit together in such a unique way. You can only learn to do that kind of a thing by listening—and practicing. It doesn't come easily. Now so much of music is taught in the universities and people are trying to find tools to help them to learn to write, and I think that that can be really dangerous. The writers I love best mostly weren't taught to write, but they found their own way. And I think that's why Tom's music has Tom's own sound because Tom found his own way. He didn't have somebody else tell what you can and can't do. I'm sure in fact I know that in the arrangement of "Prelude to a Kiss" on the *Bix Duke Fats* album there are all sorts of things that break the rules. For instance, many arranging teachers will tell you never write an interval of a minor ninth—that's one half step more than an octave—because it's too dissonant. But if you look in Ellington's music, Gil Evans's music, Tom Talbert's music, it exists all over the place. The thing that's incredible about that interval is the tension it creates if you're dealing with it in a vertical kind of way with lines converging and lines expanding.

Ken Borgers knows Tom Talbert's recorded output well.

KEN BORGERS: There's a continuity to everything he's done from the time he started. And like all the great bandleaders, he's written for soloists, and some of the soloists he's writing for, he was writing for forty years ago. Men like Eddie Bert, Aaron Sachs, and Joe Wilder. He has not been affected, it seems to me, by modern developments at all— the Beatles never fazed him. But he never sounds dated: whether it's the 1990s or the 1950s his music sounds current. His swinging stuff has a lightness to it, an airiness that is missing from most other bandleaders and writers. His arrangement of Duke Ellington's "Koko" is once removed from the swinging of Ellington. It swings very well in its own right but there's also so much texture and subtlety to what he's doing.

How much influence did Tom absorb from Johnny Richards?

TOM TALBERT: Although I was impressed by Johnny's command of the orchestra and his total knowledge of what the instruments could do, I felt that his approach to writing was very busy and it wasn't exactly what I wanted to do. Ironically, in spite of his knowledge of the instruments' capabilities and limitations, he never seemed to take the players into account very much. His belief always was, "If you own an instrument, play it." He wrote correct but difficult music. I remember

Frank Beach bitching about some of the things Frank Comstock had written in the Les Brown book . . . he said, "They wear you out, but to what avail? Nothing great is happening—I'm just hitting high C twice a bar for thirty bars—and what for? Nothing comes of it."

My personal approach is to write as though we are on the road—I look out for the trumpet players, I pace their playing as if we were playing all night. This doesn't seem to worry a lot of my contemporaries. Pat Williams, for instance, will instead hire a fifth trumpet player because he's already worn out the other four.

Tom seems to have developed his writing style through a combination of experimentation, responding to "his own drummer"—the one he "heard in his head"—and just sheer hard work. Continual writing. He puts it down to "my nature, and the lack of formal training." There were frustrations though.

In the early days of his band he was frequently criticized.

TOM TALBERT: Some guys would say, "Why do you have to write all these notes . . . why can't you write something simple like Count Basie plays?"

Later, Tom's confidence in his direction was reinforced as his band attracted more adventurous musicians.

Perhaps inevitably, due to factors such as the use of instruments like French horn, tuba, bass clarinet, and bassoon, an interest in reworking an earlier jazz repertoire, and a sensitive and soulful approach to ballads, Tom Talbert has often mistakenly been thought of as a follower of Gil Evans. A couple of hours listening would dispose of this notion. While both writers use often startling voicings and textures in their ensembles, there is a lyrical melodic dimension to Talbert's writing that is rarely found in Evans's work. Compositions like "Green Night," "Tell Summer No," "No Time to Be Blue," and "Too Soon" have a melting (but never cloying) sweetness that is Talbert's alone. His ensemble writing behind his soloists is notable for the beauty of the accompanying phrases and there is exquisite attention to detail too.

Danny Bank has played for both Tom Talbert and Gil Evans.

DANNY BANK: To be continually compared to Gil Evans must be a pain in the neck. Tom is a top writer—who are you going to compare him with? Gil Evans was different. Tom was different, very different. It's a pleasure to play his music, particularly for woodwind players.

There's a natural dynamic with wind instruments, where you don't overblow and you don't play too soft. Benny Goodman had a way of describing the word "sostenuto." He represented that sostenuto was a sound that went parallel to the earth forever so the thing to avoid was "going into the toilet," Benny's term for going flat. He says, "You go into the toilet you're fired." And that's the kind of thing I think Tom likes to hear when we play—natural dynamics.

Joe Soldo was equally forthright.

JOE SOLDO: I can't see how they say he's like Gil Evans because that's a different kind of feeling. Gil Evans had his own stamp of sound, you could tell, but for me Tom has his own sound, his own stamp. In the car, listening to the jazz station without hearing who it was, if one of Tom's records came on I'd really know it was Tom. He has his own sound, Gil had his own sound, Duke Ellington had his own sound, Tom's got his own sound. Absolutely.

PATTY McGOVERN: His sound is so individual—when you hear it you just know that "that's Talbert." His textures are so much just him. There isn't anybody else who writes that way. I don't think he writes at all like Gil Evans.

BOBBY TRICARICO: How would you describe his music? Very exciting, very deep a lot of thought went into it. And the harmonies were marvelous. I heard a lot of Duke's stuff in his writing and a lot of original Talbert stuff as well. You could hear classical influences when he wrote a ballad—I think he wore many hats. But he was like Gil Evans in that he didn't need money so badly that he would prostitute his music.

Milt Bernhart hears another Gil Evans connection.

MILT BERNHART: I heard Tom with his band at Catalina's and there wasn't much of a turnout that night. The band sounded lovely, especially on the quiet numbers. As far as uptempo jazz things were concerned, Tom didn't look as interested nor did the band get into them as much as they did the pretty things, which sort of goes for Gil Evans too. Gil didn't write anything that was shouting or swinging, a bring-the-roof-down Basie kind of thing. We got so we didn't expect it from Gil and I tend to think of Tom as going down that road too. And that's not an insult by any means—it's a compliment.

Earlier Ken Poston remarked on Tom's ability to truly synthesize jazz and classical influences in his writing.

TOM TALBERT: I don't have two separate compartments—one labeled my classical vogue and one labeled my jazz vogue. A lot of things in classical music just don't work in a jazz sense, but there are a few things that do, particularly harmonically. The classical composers that I listened to, like most people of my generation, were Debussy, Stravinsky, Ravel, and Bartok, who became one of my favorite composers. I always had a particularly soft spot for Ravel—he was such a magnificent orchestrator as well as composer. In Minneapolis, before I went into the army, I had a friend named Bob Allen, a pianist who introduced me to Rachmaninov, whom I also listened to a lot. He was a marvelous pianist as well as a moody romantic composer. I loved listening to Chopin too. Bob Allen also led me to the American composer Charles Griffes, whom I liked very much.

18

The Enigma

Over a sixty-year career Tom Talbert showed that he could write successfully in several genres of music, excel at arranging and composing in a very original manner for the jazz orchestra, and attract the services and respect of some of the most talented, creative, and discerning musicians in jazz. He conceived and produced albums to great critical acclaim and his band has played at many venues, particularly in Southern California. Why isn't he better known? Where, if at all, did he go wrong?

The critical success of *Wednesday's Child* and *Bix Duke Fats* did not win him the attention of the people with influence in the jazz/recording world. Joe Soldo went from playing saxophone and flute with Tom Talbert in the 1950s to become one of the top music contractors in Hollywood. There isn't much he doesn't know about the industry.

JOE SOLDO: The music business is so odd . . . it's a roll of the dice. Someone will make one record and everyone will listen to it and doors will open and this guy will be on his way. For Tom, that never really happened. He got the recognition from the players but those are not the guys who are going to get him the top work.

But he was not known as an effective self-promoter, as Don Davidson recalls.

DON DAVIDSON: He never really searched out too much publicity, at least to my knowledge. There were a few little brochures and things from the early days when he was with Paramount records. But just about the time that he got things recorded was the time when the band business went into a very steep decline. So many bands gave up the ghost around 1946–1947; I don't think there was much opportunity to get publicity. Unfortunately that was about the time I got involved in the big band business and it was on the downslope from that time on.

Don makes an important point: Tom was trying to make his way as a writer, someone who "fell in love with swing bands playing their own special arrangements" at the same time that bands were breaking up and the music world was changing. Back in the days when such things were still possible, could Tom have been a successful bandleader in the accepted sense—entertaining the crowd, going to all the radio stations and sitting down with the disc jockeys, and plugging the latest record, and then driving to the next gig.

PATTY McGOVERN: No, gosh no, never. He's one of a kind—there never has been, never will be another Tom Talbert. No way was Tom going to be another Stan Kenton or Woody Herman—that wasn't his calling.

DON DAVIDSON: I don't know if Tom had the personality to make it as a successful bandleader. I don't know if he would have been amenable to all the things that a successful bandleader has to do. He had his own idea of how things should be done, what things should be done. His early records made a bow toward commercialism—I think, to get his foot in the door, so he could expand his horizons. Whether he would continue along in a commercial manner, I doubt it. I think he was too caught up in what he wanted to do and how he wanted to do it, to bend too much toward commercialism.

Leigh Kamman attests to Tom's originality—and tenacity.

LEIGH KAMMAN: I first met Tom Talbert around 1946–1947. He was living in California and came back home on a visit and gave me the first discs that he made out there. I played them on my program and got a similar reaction from the trad audience as I did when I played Stan Kenton. I think it took incredible intestinal fortitude for Tom to constantly generate this music and try to establish an audience for it. When you hear it now, he was fifty years ahead of his time. There were just a few writers who were generating this kind of music—Johnny Richards, Pete Rugolo, Bill Russo—and Tom was another. And what Tom was doing was quite original and different from these contemporaries.

PATTY McGOVERN: I am amazed at what Tom has followed through with, over the years. He has kept himself going, he really has achieved a lot.

There is probably no one alive today who has experienced more of the jazz scene, played with, employed, or associated with more musicians than Howard Rumsey. From playing bass with Gus Arnheim, Johnny "Scat" Davis, and Vido Musso in the 1930s, Stan Kenton and LA clubs in the 1940s, playing at and running the Light House All-Stars in the 1950s, and subsequently Concerts by the Sea, Howard has an unrivaled perspective

HOWARD RUMSEY: Tom is a hero—a straight-out hero. He's only interested in the music. But it seems to me that he's never been in the music business, as most people know it. And I can't think of a niche that you can put him in. Because he has no degrees under his name and had no formal training as such, in his own mind he doesn't understand his position. He doesn't know what he's up against, and because of the success of that first album, he's totally at a loss to understand why he wasn't accepted further and why he hasn't done more. And it will never change because in his own mind he feels that he's not really qualified. The reason I'm telling you that is because you're looking at a guy (me) who did well in the music business, but I never had any of those qualifications either.

HARRY BETTS: Maybe Tom is the Jimmie Lunceford of his day—everyone else does the *Chesterfield Show* but Lunceford does one-nighters. To sum up—not only a nice person but a really nice writer. If you sat down to play something of his you'd never be disappointed. I take his records out from time to time and listen to them . . . but somebody as good as he is needs to hear his music performed live, once in a while.

DANNY BANK: I wish he had played piano more—he didn't want to. He might have done better if he'd played a little more piano, you know.

Since joining the Lionel Hampton band in 1942, Joe Wilder has played with the most illustrious names in the business and has great insight into its workings—and Tom's status.

JOE WILDER: I just wonder—sometimes it's a matter of envy. I don't mean to put anybody down but sometimes there are people who are so established in their own way that they consider anybody from the outside, especially anybody with that kind of talent, as being a little too competitive—as being a threat and I think that might be one of the things that contributed to his not being as well-known as he should be.

Trombonist Milt Bernhart remembers hearing Tom's septet in Laguna and takes a longer, more philosophic view.

MILT BERNHART: They were playing in one of the very posh galleries with some pretty expensive paintings on the walls. There was a large turnout of luminaries and there is Tom on the landing of one of the staircases with his group. I listened to the group. He was very proud of it—young players like Andy Martin, the very fine young trombone player who was just getting started. The only thing wrong was—it was pretty noisy in there. They got paid and they were there for atmosphere. I felt sorry for him because he had a look on his face of having been let down. Disappointment. Anyone who wanted to hear could get closer but sadly people were on the move and went by. Here was an orchestra playing very, very fine music. Listenable—you could listen to it and not have to know exactly what they were doing—it's reachable. His music is usually accessible to the unknowing, and he's not doing that on purpose. It's the way he writes, and this should have turned him into a much more successful composer from the standpoint of numbers. But he's a well-kept secret, and that has applied through the centuries to a number of composers. In Mozart's time and Beethoven's there were some who were just run over by the big stars of the period. Someone like Salieri—he could write, but we wouldn't know he was there if they hadn't made *Amadeus*. Tommy falls into that category—steamrollered by others who become more important. That doesn't seem right but as time passes, since he has records and there are people to play them, some people who wouldn't know will find them and be grateful.

Tenor saxist Steve White was the most upbeat.

STEVE WHITE: Everybody liked Tom—he was like a young Duke Ellington. One thing's for sure: Tom isn't through with the music business yet, so you never know what will happen with him. Hopefully it will be something good.

For Jack Montrose, Tom still seems an enigma.

JACK MONTROSE: Everyone in the LA area lost track of Tom after he went to New York in 1950. I didn't get to see him again until recently.

I was on a panel with him at one of Ken Poston's jazz events and when I told him how much I enjoyed playing in his band in the '40s and how much everyone else did and how important an event his band was to all of us at the time, he seemed genuinely surprised.

Finally, there's the matter of luck, chance, fate, hazard, accident.

BOBBY TRICARICO: I think that if Tom had been in a certain place at the right time with a vocalist that became a real smash hit he would have been made, like so many others have.

19

Coda

What drives Tom Talbert to persevere with something as difficult, expensive, and in many ways unrewarding as writing, rehearsing, and recording albums of music by a large modern jazz orchestra?

TOM TALBERT: I continue to write and record because—for one thing I enjoy the writing, especially when it really gets going. I used to do an arrangement a night when I worked for people like Buddy Rich, and it's just a wonderful feeling when it gets flowing. I enjoy the rehearsal if everyone's on time, and I love to record. I love the recording process. I'm sure I'm putting down a slice of my life, I'm putting down a tablet, you might say . . . and much of my pleasure comes from how the musicians are. If the musicians are enjoying it, I feel we're doing it right and I have double pleasure then.

Maria Schneider puts herself through the same process.

MARIA SCHNEIDER: I think the thing that makes somebody compose is an impulse that you either have or you don't. My reason for composing and I'm sure Tom's is the same—is not because it's something that you want to do but you feel like you have no choice—that your life is incomplete unless you are creating. Of course it's a nice thing if people recognize what you do and support you but it also shows how deep he is as a musician that, even though at many points in his life he hasn't been recognized to the extent he should be, he keeps going and doing what he needs to do—he's an artist, that's what artists do.

Ken Borgers expands on that.

KEN BORGERS: There is a feeling among some people that Tom isn't in touch with the realities of the music world. I'm not sure that that is true. I think Tom is in touch but he chooses to march, as he would put it, to his own drummer. He refuses to compromise what he thinks is important and he shuns self-promotion. That's not a good combination and unfortunately the major reason why more people don't know about him.

Tom's priority has always been making wonderful music, and he hopes that the world will catch on to him.

BRUCE PAULSON: This is the crux of it. He still, even to this day, he still wants a record company to come to him and say, "Would you do these recordings?" Whereas he has the means to have his own record company—and that's the nature of the business today—you have to put it out. Whether it's on a vanity label or your own company. Also, his great beauty—and limitation—is that he has always only wanted to write what he wanted to write. He's always looking for something different too. And that's not popular—you do need to sit down in front of the speakers and concentrate. It takes listening and that's not always quite what's required. Certainly these days.

After fifty years of significant musical output, Tom Talbert could scarcely be said to have achieved fame in the accepted sense. I asked Maria Schneider her thoughts about that.

MARIA SCHNEIDER: Does fame matter? When it happens it's a bonus. But I think that to produce the music that Tom has produced all these years and not to have found recognition in a really big way must be frustrating. Mostly because as a writer it's fun to share your music. You want people to hear what you've done. You make all these creations and you want to share them. To have people know your music is a really nice thing and I think it's something that Tom deserves.

I asked Tom what advice he would give to another young Tom Talbert just starting out on a musical career today.

TOM TALBERT: Follow your heart. That's poetic perhaps, but it's true . . . If you do what you really want to do and you have any talent, you should be able to come out of the pack. Some people have good luck, some people have bad luck. But at least if they follow their own vision they aren't so sorry if things don't work out. If they do have good luck and they get the right breaks and get through the right doors, then maybe they'll wind up rich and famous—and fulfilled too.

BOBBY TRICARICO: Even when we used to hang, he was "priestly." Everybody loved him.

Thus Tom Talbert. His friends from the 1940s still call him "Tommy," and there was a time in New York City when concert programs and Atlantic Records carried the more formal "Thomas." Apart from his qualities as a composer, arranger, jazz musician, and bandleader, which have been revealed, I hope, in this book, Tom is a very kind, extremely civilized man with myriad interests beyond music. He has a great love of poetry in particular and literature in general and is an excellent writer and a perceptive critic. Two pieces that he wrote for the *Minneapolis Tribune* in 1963 and 1965 are included in the appendixes. He is a great gourmet and excellent judge of wine, a connoisseur of fine cars—owning at different times a V12 Jaguar and a Studebaker Avanti. Beautiful women have always been part of his life. He appears to have succeeded in living in and contributing to the jazz world, while living a very full life in a wider community.

Some of those who achieve great success in artistic endeavors seem to make a kind of Faustian contract whereby fame and recognition are achieved only with the sacrifice of taste, decency, sensitivity, and humor. Fortunately for jazz—and us—Tom Talbert did not need a Mephistopheles as he negotiated the obstacle course that is the music industry for the past half century. Tom Talbert is not, as Zoot Sims said of one of his contemporaries, "a strange bunch of guys." He has been true to the music he has heard in his head and amassed a rich collection of recorded work and an even bigger store of unrecorded scores. He is uncompromising where musical standards are concerned but loyal to the musicians he respects, and his musical foundation has underwritten aspiring jazz youngsters.

Tom is currently writing new music and planning to make studio recordings of his classical compositions.

SPECIAL THANKS FROM TOM TALBERT: I want to thank the friends who did the music copying for me in the days when there was no money to pay them. Ronnie Rochat, "Umpsie," and Don Davidson took on this thankless task for several years back in the 1940s. Later my first wife, Bette, learned the art, particularly to help me, which she did all through the 1960s. Above and beyond the call of duty.

APPENDIX A

Discography

JUNE 25, 1946, RADIO RECORDERS, LOS ANGELES

Tommy Talbert and His Orchestra
I've Got You under My Skin (vocal Billy Shuart)
Stop Your Knockin'
Released as Paramount 112
Down in Chihuahua
Deep in a Dream
Released as Paramount 113
All reissued on Seabreeze CD The Tom Talbert Jazz Orchestra
1946–49 SBCD 2069
Personnel: Leighton Johnson, Bill Cherones (as); Babe Russin,
Tony diMiscio (ts); Hy Mandell (bar); Lou Obergh, Ronnie Rochat,
Frank Beach (tp); Lionel Sesma, Ollie Wilson (tb); Tom Talbert (pno);
Ernie Hood (gtr); Jim Stutz (bass); Billy Shuart (drums)

NOVEMBER 4, 1946, LOS ANGELES

Lyle Griffin Orchestra
Flight of the Vout Bug
Released as Atomic A 270
Reissued on Seabreeze CD The Tom Talbert Jazz Orchestra
1946–49 SBCD 2069
Love Eyes (rejected)
Personnel: Tom Talbert, direction, arrangement, and composition;
Hal McKusick, Ethmer Roten (as); Lucky Thompson, Ralph Lee (ts);
Larry Patton (bar); Al Killian, Ronnie Rochat, Ray Linn (tp); Ray
Sims, Ollie Wilson, Gene Roland (tb); Dodo Marmarosa (pno); Mike
Bryan (gtr); Paul Morsey (bass); Lou Fromm (drums)

DECEMBER 31, 1947, LOS ANGELES

Tommy Talbert and His Orchestra
 Please Be Brief (unreleased)
 Don't Call It Love (unreleased)
 Love Is a Pleasure (unreleased until issued on Seabreeze CD The Tom Talbert Jazz Orchestra 1946–49 SBCD 2069)
 Personnel: Elmer Koeling (as); Dave Madden (ts); Lou Obergh (tp); Harry Brainerd (tb); Tom Talbert (pno); Bob Stone (bass); Dick Stanton (drums)

AUGUST 1949, LOS ANGELES

Tommy Talbert and His Orchestra
 'S Wonderful
 Between Loves
 Four Camellias
 Over the Rainbow
 All unreleased until issued on Seabreeze CD The Tom Talbert Jazz Orchestra 1946–49 SBCD 2069
 Personnel: Talbert (dir); Elmer Koeling, Art Pepper (as, clt); Steve White, Johnny Barbera (ts); Don Davidson (bar); Wes Hensel, Johnny Anderson, Johnny McComb (tp); John Halliburton, Harry Betts (tb); Claude Williamson (pno); Don Prell (bass); Jimmy Pratt (drums)

NOVEMBER 1949, RADIO RECORDERS, LOS ANGELES

Tommy Talbert and His Orchestra
 I Cover the Waterfront
 Love Is Just around the Corner
 I Get a Kick Out of You (vocal Jean Louise)
 April in Paris (vocal Jean Louise)
 Is Is Not Is
 'S Wonderful
 Personnel: As for August 1949, but Jack Montrose replaces Steve White.
 Recorded as audition records and unreleased until issued on Seabreeze CD The Tom Talbert Jazz Orchestra 1946–49 SBCD 2069

MARCH 15, 1951, NEW YORK

Marian McPartland Quintet
It's Delovely
Four Brothers
Liebestraum
Flamingo
Released as Federal 12029 and 12034; reissued on King LP 540 and
Swing (F) SW 371
Personnel: Marian McPartland (pno); Reinhart Elster (harp);
Bernard Greenhouse (cello); Bob Carter (bass); Don Lamond
(drums); Tom Talbert arrangements and direction

MARCH 15, 1951, NEW YORK

Gene Williams and His Orchestra
Pretty-Eyed Baby
Now I Lay Me Down to Dream
Released as King 15107 and 15108. Pretty Eyed Baby reissued on
Quality (Can) 4029.
Personnel: Gene Williams (vocal); Sam Marowitz, Ernie Mauro
(as); Mickey Folus (ts); Danny Bank (bar); Jimmy Blake, Tony Faso,
Dick Hoffman (tp); Harry diVito, Kai Winding (tb); Billy Taylor
(pno); Barry Galbraith (gtr); Eddie Safranski (bass); Jimmy Crawford
(drums); Tom Talbert arrangements

APRIL 27, 1951, NEW YORK

Kai Winding's Band
Deep Purple*
I'm Shooting High
You're Blasé*
The Moonshower
The first two titles released as Cosmopolitan 300 and reissued on
IAJRC 15. All reissued on Xanadu 172, and Cool & Blue (SW) CD 110.
Personnel: Kai Winding (tb); Warne Marsh (ts); Billy Taylor (pno);
Jack Lesberg (bass); Charlie Perry (drums) Melvin Moore (vocal)*;
Tom Talbert arrangements and direction

MARCH 4, 1952, NEW YORK

Kai Winding All-Stars
    I Could Write a Book
    Speak Low
    The Carioca
    The Boy Next Door
    Released as Savoy 840 and 969, reissued on Savoy LPs MG 12020,
15048 and Japanese SVCD 1063 ("Speak Low" not on CD)
    Personnel: Kai Winding (tb); Lou Stein (pno); Eddie Safranski
(bass); Tiny Kahn (drums); Al Young (bongos, timbales); Tom Talbert arrangements

NOVEMBER 17, 1952 NEW YORK

The Don Elliott Septet
    Mighty Like a Rose
    Darn That Dream
    Oh Look at Me Now
    Jeepers Creepers
    Released as Savoy LP 883, XP 8093, MG 9033 and MG 12054
    Personnel: Don Elliott (tp, vib, mellophone, bongos); Kai Winding
(tb); Phil Urso (ts); Danny Bank (bar); Jimmy Lyon (pno); Arnold
Fishkin (bass); Sid Bulkin (drums); Tom Talbert arrangements

AUGUST 1953, NEW YORK

Johnny Smith Group
    Cavu
    I'll Be Around
    Yesterdays
    Cherokee
    First two titles released as Roost 581, all as Roost R413, 1,3 & 4 on
LP 2211. All on Fresh Sound FS 892 and Roulette CD 300016.
    Personnel: Paul Quinichette (ts); Johnny Smith (gtr); Sanford Gold
(pno); Arnold Fishkin (bass); Don Lamond (drums); Tom Talbert
arrangements

AUGUST 12, 1955, NEW YORK

Oscar Pettiford
  Titoro
  Part of Bethlehem LP BCP33 *Oscar Pettiford*; also Bethlehem CD
BET6017–2
  Personnel: Gigi Gryce (as); Jerome Richardson (fl, ts); Donald Byrd,
Ernie Royal (tp); Bob Brookmeyer (v-tb); Don Abney (pno); Oscar
Pettiford (bass); Osie Johnson (drums); Tom Talbert arrangement

FEBRUARY–MARCH 1956, FINE SOUND STUDIO, NEW YORK

Wednesday's Child: Patty McGovern Sings Tom Talbert Arrangements
  Wednesday's Child
  I Like Snow
  Patty McGovern vocals on all titles
  Personnel: Al Block (fl); Jim Buffington (fhr); Barry Galbraith (gtr);
Arnold Fishkin (bass); Don Lamond (drums); Tom Talbert arrange-
ments and direction
  All in Fun
  By Myself
  As above plus Joe Wilder (tp)
  You Don't Know What Love Is
  Personnel: Joe Soldo (fl) Barry Galbraith (bass); Arnold Fishkin
(bass)
  Hooray for Love
  Get Out of Town
  Personnel: As above plus Ernie Bright (clt); Sey Schwartzenberg
(bassoon); Jim Buffington (fhr); Don Lamond (drums)
  Crazy She Calls Me
  Love Isn't Everything
  Alone Together
  Personnel: Jerry Sanfino (fl); Barry Galbraith (gtr); Jack Lesberg
(bass); Osie Johnson (drums)
  Lonely Town
  Winter Song
  Personnel: Joe Soldo (fl); Danny Bank (clt); Sey Schwartzenberg
(bassoon); Jim Buffington (fhr); Joe Wilder (tp); Jack Lesberg (bass);
Osie Johnson (drums)

Will You Still Be Mine
Summer Rain
Personnel: Joe Soldo (fl); unknown guitar and bass.
Originally released as Atlantic LP 1245; reissued privately on CD
by Tom Talbert

AUGUST 24, 1956, NEW YORK

Thomas Talbert
Bix Duke Fats
Originally released as Atlantic LP 1250, reissued as Seabreeze
CDB 3013 and Discover Jazz CD EMG 1100
Clothes Line Ballet
Bond Street
Black & Blue
Keepin' Out of Mischief Now
Personnel: Aaron Sachs (clt, ts); Joe Wilder, Nick Travis (tp); Eddie
Bert, Jimmy Cleveland (tb); George Wallington (pno); Oscar Pettiford
(bass); Osie Johnson (drums); Tom Talbert arrangements and direction

SEPTEMBER 7, 1956

In a Mist
Candlelights
In the Dark
Personnel: Joe Soldo (fl); Danny Bank (clt, bs. clt); Harold Goltzer
(bassoon); Jim Buffington (fhr); Joe Wilder (tp); Barry Galbraith
(gtr); Oscar Pettiford (bass); Osie Johnson (drums)

SEPTEMBER 14, 1956

Prelude to a Kiss
Do Nothing Till You Hear from Me
Ko-Ko
Personnel: Herb Geller (as); Joe Soldo (as, fl); Aaron Sachs (clt, ts);
Danny Bank (bar, bs.clt); Jim Buffington (fhr); Joe Wilder (tp); Eddie

Bert (tb); Barry Galbraith (gtr); Oscar Pettiford (bass); Osie Johnson (drums)
  Green Night and Orange Bright
  Personnel: As above plus Claude Williamson (pno)

OCTOBER 3–5, 1977, HOLLYWOOD

Thomas Talbert Jazz Orchestra
  Louisiana Suite
  Released as Sandcastle LP SCR 1041; reissued as Seabreeze CDSB 107–2
  Louisiana Suite: Royal Street; Too Wet to Walk; Watermelon Days; Grieve Softly; Shipping Out
  It's the Style
  No Time to be Blue
  Don't Delay
  Strolling Home
  Is It Time to Let You Go?
  Hard Dollar
  Personnel: Joe Soldo (fl, sop, as); Andy Mackintosh (clt, as); Bob Hardaway (ob, clt, ts); Lee Callet (bar, bs.clt); Brian O'Connor (fhr); Frank Szabo, John Harner, Bob Summers, Steve Huffsteter (tp, flhrn); Bruce Paulson (tb) John Leys (btb); Joe Diorio (gtr); Harvey Newmark (bass); Harold Jones (drums); Jerry Steinholz (perc); Howard Fallman replaces Joe Soldo on "Hard Dollar"

AUGUST 11–12, 1987, SAGE AND SOUND STUDIO, HOLLYWOOD

Tom Talbert Septet
  Things As They Are released as Seabreeze LP SB 2038 and CDSB 2038
  Dangraddy Blue
  Wednesday's Child
  Hello Dolly
  No Time to Be Blue
  Don't Get Around Much Anymore
  A Month of Sundays
  Every Girl Is My Valentine
  Lulu's Back in Town

Between Loves
Cute
Strolling Home
Things As They Are
Personnel: Dick Mitchell (as); Lee Callet (bar); Bob Summers (tp); Andy Martin (tb); Tom Talbert (pno & direction); John Leitham (bass); Jeff Hamilton (drums)

OCTOBER 10, 1991, GROUP IV AUDIO, HOLLYWOOD

Tom Talbert Jazz Orchestra: *The Warm Café* released as Seabreeze CDSB 2052 and Discover Jazz CD EMG 1200
La Bayadera
Flirtation
Personnel: Don Shelton, Lee Callet (fl, clt, as); Bob Efford (clt, ts); Bob Carr (bar); Suzette Moriarty (fhr); Frank Szabo, Wayne Bergeron (tp); Bob Summers, Steve Huffsteter (tp, flhrn); Andy Martin (tb); Bob Enevoldsen (vtb); John Leys (b-tb); Tom Talbert (pno); John Leitham (bass); Roy McCurdy (drums); Tom Talbert arrangements and direction on all numbers

MAY 18, 1992

Someone's Rocking My Blues
Tell Summer No
What Is This Thing Called Love
Dangraddy Blue
The Warm Café
Ain't Misbehavin'
Swing Will Be On Time
Personnel: As above but Jennifer Hall replaces Bob Carr; Jack Sperling replaces Roy McCurdy; Alan Steinberger replaces Tom Talbert; omit Bob Enevoldsen

JUNE 2, 1992

Manoir de mes rêves
Too Soon
Personnel: As above but Tom Ranier replaces Alan Steinberger

OCTOBER 10, 1991, GROUP IV AUDIO, HOLLYWOOD

Tom Talbert Orchestra: *Duke's Domain* (released as Seabreeze CDSB 2058)
Talbert arrangements and direction on all numbers
Bojangles
Personnel: As October 10, 1991 above

JUNE 1992, GROUP IV AUDIO, HOLLYWOOD

Ko-Ko
Ellington Group: The Brown Skin Gal in the Calico Gown; All Too Soon; I Got it Bad; In a Sentimental Mood
Take the A Train
Personnel: Don Shelton, Lee Callet (fl, clt, as); Bob Efford (clt, ts); Jennifer Hall (bar); Suzette Moriarty (fhr); Frank Szabo, Wayne Bergeron (tp); Bob Summers, Steve Huffsteter (tp, flhrn); Andy Martin (tb); John Leys (btb, tuba); Tom Ranier (pno); John Leitham (bass); Jack Sperling (drums)

MAY 18–19, 1993, MARTINSOUND STUDIO, ALHAMBRA, CALIFORNIA

Duke's Domain: Night Moods; Autumnal; Down Stage Strut
Lotus Blossom
After All
Personnel: As above plus Gary Foster (fl, as); Bob Hardaway replaces Bob Efford; Alex Iles (tb) added for Duke's Domain; Tom Garvin replaces Tom Ranier
Someone
A Backward Glance
Personnel: As June 1992 but Tom Garvin replaces Tom Ranier; Alex Iles added
Snibor
Personnel: As June 1992 but Tom Garvin replaces Tom Ranier
Chelsea Bridge
Personnel: As June 1992 but omit piano

APRIL 9, 1993, WOODLAND HILLS, CALIFORNIA

Vic Lewis West Coast All Stars Featuring Andy Martin (released on Candid CCD 79711)
 A Backward Glance
 Personnel: Bill Perkins, Don Shelton (fl, clt, as); Bob Cooper (clt, ts); Bob Efford (bar); Andy Martin (tb); Frank Strazzeri (pno); Tom Warrington (bass); Bob Leatherbarrow (drums); Tom Talbert arrangement and direction

JULY 1, 7–8, 1997, CLINTON STUDIOS, NEW YORK CITY

Tom Talbert Orchestra: *This Is Living* released as Chartmaker CD PDP14480
 The Brio Trio
 Django
 A Little Tempo Please
 Blame It on My Youth
 That Harlem Express
 Echo of Spring
 A Fool and His Honey
 This Is All I Ask
 Personnel: Dick Oatts (fl, as); Aaron Sachs (fl, clt, as); Loren Schoenberg (clt, ts); Danny Bank (clt, bsclt, bar); Janet Lantz, Chris Costanzi (fhr); Joe Mosello, Danny Cahn, Glenn Drewes, Joe Wilder (tp); Scott Whitfield, Eddie Bert (tb); Dave Taylor (b-tb); Howard Alden (gtr); Chip Jackson (bass); Jim Saporito (drums); Tom Talbert arrangements and direction on all numbers
 Love Is A Pleasure
 Of Thee I Sing
 Our Delight
 Personnel: As above but Joe Beck replaces Howard Alden

DECEMBER 9–10, 14, 1999, CLINTON STUDIOS,
NEW YORK CITY

Tom Talbert Orchestra: *To a Lady* (released on Discover Jazz CD EMG 1000)

To a Lady Asking Foolish Questions
Tune for Two
'Round Midnight
Pavane de la belle au bois dormant
Divertissement
Personnel: Dick Oatts (as); Roger Rosenberg (fl, clt, as); Aaron Sachs (clt, ts); Danny Bank (bsclt, bar); Joe Mosello, Danny Cahn, Brian O'Flaherty (tp); Joe Wilder (tp, flhrn); Janet Lantz, Chris Costanzi (fhr); Jim Pugh, Eddie Bert (tb); Dave Taylor (btb, tuba); Howard Alden (gtr); Dick Sarpola (bass); Jim Saporito (drums); Tom Talbert arrangements and direction on all numbers
  Chiripa
  Love's Melody
  Green Night
  Personnel: As above but Glenn Drewes replaces Brian Flaherty; add Joe Passaro (conga drums) on Chiripa
  Dance Delively
  Little Girl Blue
  A Month of Sundays
  Personnel: As original personnel but Lawrence Feldman replaces Roger Rosenberg

APPENDIX B

Talbert on Jazz

"REFLECTIONS ON JAZZ" (*MINNEAPOLIS TRIBUNE*, NOVEMBER 1963)

The reader of any collection of thoughts, in an essay or a story, is most comfortable if he assumes that the writer knows more than the reader about the particular subject. At least the writer is expected to know *what* the subject is. While I think I know what jazz *isn't*, I confess I cannot define what it is. Musicians constantly hear, "I don't know much about music, I just know what I like." That's about what any of us know about this most abstract of the arts. Technical aspects aside, it is hard enough to know what is jazz, and in this age of electronic whistles, tapes playing backwards, altered pianos and minutes of silence . . . What is Music?

The Twin Cities musical climate proportionately reflected the national interests prior to the end of World War II. There were many clubs with good and bad combos. The name bands played one-nighters at the ballrooms and the old Happy Hour booked such fine bands as Fletcher Henderson's and Fats Waller's for several weeks at a time. Jazz pianists such as Bob Zurke and Joe Sullivan worked for extended periods in local clubs. I remember a short leave from the army in the winter of 1944 and the smaller joints truly roaring with jazz. Art Van Damme's fine young combo was one above average—one of many projecting a fierce zest for life. And for music.

By the beginning of 1946, six months after the end of the war, there was tremendous decline of interest in music, across the country as well as in the Twin Cities. Some leather-bound sociologist may tie this together one day, but the fact remains that a business had been made out of an art form and the expressor was no longer in control of what he was expressing. People don't need music, as compared to bread, and thereby hangs the axe of the jazz musician. He had to make the public *want* it, want to be moved . . . and he didn't do it.

There grew up during this period a vast smog enveloping the cliché terms of good and bad. Why is the latter successful? Why is the good thing doomed? There is still today a feeling that if something is good, no one will like it; if it's as mediocre as possible, no one will be offended, and therefore everyone will be pleased. I have never been convinced that not offending anyone necessarily equates pleasing everyone . . . but that has been the climate of our times. Understandably, this has led to a great deal of confusion on the part of club-owners and committee chairmen hiring musicians, and with the musicians themselves.

Herb Klein's place, now gone in the interests of Lower Loop development, had a steady policy of both local groups and names. The latter was usually a name soloist brought in to play with a local rhythm section and while this made a session, rather than a presentation out of the evening, it went well with Herb's unpretentious and moderately priced establishment. Freddie's, now closed, mixed the better jazz groups with comedians and Nelson Eddy. Due to the current costs of engaging top talent, the tabs often ran a bit higher than the customers expected. Several places on Lake Street's 3.2 Row, principally the Padded Cell, have attempted various jazz approaches and have met with varying degrees of success for a time. I believe Hootenany has not yet replaced Rock-and-Roll in most of them.

Depending on night-clubs as a base, musicians have often had to work in plain bad conditions to encourage delivering their best. Some of this is, of course their own doing. Many work in a casual and unprepared frame of mind that quite naturally alienates an employer and even worse, proves to an audience that there is no reason to give the music any particular attention. All too often the night-club operator finds mediocrity good enough indeed . . . if it's for flat scale.

There is not, as of this writing, a great deal of jazz in the Minneapolis and St. Paul clubs. In fact, outside of the White House and the Downtowner, very little more than a couple of trios spotted about. I have often felt that jazz soloists and groups should expand their areas of material as a means of creating wider interest. It is very safe to say that so-called society groups play a far superior choice of compositions as compared with the run-of-the-hip combo. They may not do much with the latent possibilities, but they are covering a vastly wider range of musical exposure. After all of these years, how much can anyone do on "Indiana"?

I do feel, that on the individual dance jobs and social events, there is a definite swell of interest in better music. An urge to upgrade the level of jazz (or whatever) that people are willing to hire and pleased to enjoy.

"AND ALL THAT JAZZ" (*MINNEAPOLIS TRIBUNE*, MAY 1965)

Duke Ellington and his Famous Orchestra recently played the first big band concert given in the Guthrie Theatre. It seems to me that "famous orchestra" was how Ellington was billed in my long ago youth and perhaps this is a clue to the curious and restless feeling I had during the program. There was a constant awareness of Duke's prestige and position in American music and the audience was virtually push-button in its reaction to this awesome reputation. If it was disappointing to me it is partly because the orchestra, and Ellington fell short of high expectations.

Edward Kennedy Ellington has led his own orchestra since the early 20s. It has been almost as constantly excellent in its performance as his writing has been creative. The orchestra has been a tool for Ellington more than any other leader or composer and this has made both his composing and the orchestral version a unique and telling combination that is without parallel in a highly businessed business. He has always been an envied composer from the standpoint of writing for a set personnel. This personnel was held together by great sacrifice on the part of Ellington, and it is to his credit that he has plowed so much of the so-called net back into the orchestral conception.

To discuss the Ellington orchestra is to discuss the individual soloists and the individual chunks of material. Many of the pieces were written for specific members, not only as solo vehicles, but a sort of concerto-grosso slice of writing. More than any other orchestra this nucleus is on review as a group when you discuss the individuals. You cannot discuss the ensemble without singling out the highly personalized voices of the featured instrumentalists. The overall performance was very sloppy and perhaps by commenting on the soloists we can bring more of their contributions to the fore.

Harry Carney was easily the star of the saxophone section and he has only one thing to worry about. Because he has been with Ellington since 1926 he does not have too many references in the unlikely case of finding himself out of a job. His concertmaster leading of the band gives it one of the distinctive sounds that has made the Ellington ensemble so identifiable. Paul Gonsalves played a lovely solo on Billy Strayhorn's "Chelsea Bridge" but his uptempo solos were relatively undistinguished, although the crowd applauded madly at every grimace. Johnny Hodges appeared to consider the audience as locked in and treated his solos with little care. He and Jimmy Hamilton missed a number of entrances while presumably arranging their music for the next evening's concert. It's fine to be prepared for the future but not at the expense of the immediate ticket buyer.

Lawrence Brown was the only other soloist that performed with any distinction. Brown was a trombone star of the band 25 years ago, but is practically unknown in new musical circles. None of his old featured vehicles were played and so he did not stand out. His gorgeous tone did cut through a few mood numbers and parts of "Black Brown and Beige." The latter was, by the way, one of the few pieces of meat on a soufflé menu. Carney, Brown and the entire orchestra achieved some magnificent sounds reflecting the originality in writing and execution perfected by the band. These pieces are selected short works tied together with various bridges but Duke and his adoring fans are kidding a little when they are referred to as symphonic works. Nonetheless they are vibrant and fun to hear.

The low point of the evening was the standard Ellington medley played at the end—although the audience apparently thought that "Satin Doll" was the most applause-worthy number of the evening. Duke suffers, in a sense from a gratifying embarrassment. He is top heavy in superb material and a little editing would be flattering to his end result.

The next night, Count Basie and his orchestra played the Prom ballroom in St. Paul. There are interesting differences between the two bands, and hearing them on consecutive nights clarified more than a few of these points. The Basie band was purely magnificent. As an ensemble effort, the group effort was breathtaking. The discipline and respect for the job was evident. They were loaded with class.

Bill Basie at 61 is five years younger than Ellington and came up quite a different route.

He was playing second piano with the old Bennie Moten Band in

1935. When Basie took over he accepted the style that has remained relatively unchanged to this day. A light teasing rhythm section, plus a solid emphatic ensemble brass section makes a total sound that is without comparison in the current music marketplace. That early band out of Kansas City was smaller, made up of three trumpets, three saxes and the fabulous four rhythm with Freddie Green on guitar, but it established the basic Basie sound of today.

The Count is not a composer and therefore he bears a slightly different relation to his orchestra than the Duke. Basie is particularly unwilling to comment on his role as an organizer and leader, although this has to be the element wherein he wields a big influence.

There is just plain nothing in the sound world that compares to a piece opening with Basie soloing, then the rest of the rhythm section filling in and finally the whole ensemble entering with their excruciating sense of time. WOW.

The audience at the Prom seemed a little more knowledgeable, but this may be from the plain looseness generated in a ballroom when compared to a concert atmosphere. The people were extremely attuned but less automatic than the Guthrie crowd. Both of these legendary orchestras are propelled by a sense of individualism shading the ensemble, but the big push in both kingdoms is the group. Basie's band is much more geared to the main stream of music with out being in any way avant-garde. Ellington's band long ago ceased doing any trailblazing, but no doubt at all, if you loved it once, it will stir you still. The Good Count keeps putting down that effortless rhythm and when you hear him "plink," you're plinked for good.

INDEX

About the Author

Bruce Talbot was born in Wellington, New Zealand. As a young radio producer in the late 1950s, he first heard and was impressed by Tom Talbert's music. Moving to London, England, in 1963, he worked for the BBC in radio, television, and record production. In 1991 he came to the United States as executive producer of the Smithsonian Collection of Recordings record label. He managed to survive Washington politics until 1998 and now concentrates on writing.

Talbot lives in Oakton, Virginia, with his wife, his dog, and a tenor saxophone that is now rarely touched.

Tom Talbert Recordings
1949–1999

The CD contains recordings of fourteen Tom Talbert compositions, chosen to offer a sampling of his writing and a hint of its scope. For copyright reasons the selection was limited to Talbert's originals and a song by Patty McGovern. Tom's arrangements of other composers' music is, of course, a significant part of his work and can be found on all of his albums—the discography in appendix A has full details of all Tom Talbert recordings.

RECORDING DETAILS AND SOLOISTS

1. "Is Is Not Is" (3:08) from *Tom Talbert Jazz Orchestra 1946–49*. Los Angeles, November 1949. Claude Williamson, piano; Jack Montrose, tenor sax; Harry Betts, trombone; John McComb, trumpet; Johnny Barbera, tenor sax.

2. "Four Camellias" (3:19) from *Tom Talbert Jazz Orchestra 1946–49*. Los Angeles, August 1949. Elmer Koeling, clarinet; Art Pepper, clarinet; John Halliburton, trombone.

3. "Winter Song" (2:10) from *Wednesday's Child*. New York City, February–March 1956. Joe Wilder, trumpet; Patty McGovern, vocals.

4. "I Like Snow" (2:48) from *Wednesday's Child*. New York City, February–March 1956. Jim Buffington, French horn; Patty McGovern, vocals; Barry Galbraith, guitar.

5. "Orange Bright" (4:30) from *Bix Duke Fats*. New York City, September 14, 1956. Barry Galbraith, guitar; Joe Wilder, trumpet; Eddie Bert, trombone; Aaron Sachs, tenor sax; Herb Geller, alto sax; Claude Williamson, piano.

6. "Dangraddy Blue" (4:21) from *Tom Talbert Septet—Things As They Are*. Hollywood, California, August 1987. John Leitham,

227

bass; Dick Mitchell, alto sax; Andy Martin, trombone; Bob Summers, trumpet.

7. "No Time to Be Blue" (5:08) from *Louisiana Suite*. Hollywood, California, October, 1977. Joe Soldo, flute; Andy Mackintosh, alto sax.

8. "Someone's Rocking My Blues" (6:04) from *The Warm Café*. Hollywood, California, May 18, 1992. Jennifer Hall, baritone sax; Steve Huffsteter, trumpet; Lee Callett, alto sax; Don Shelton, alto sax; Andy Martin, trombone; Bob Efford, tenor sax.

9. "Tell Summer No" (6:40) from *The Warm Café*. Hollywood, California, May 18, 1992. Bob Summers, trumpet; Don Shelton, alto sax.

10. "La Bayadera" (6:17) from *The Warm Café*. Hollywood, California, October 10, 1991. Andy Martin, trombone; Steve Huffsteter, trumpet; Bob Summers, trumpet; Bob Efford, tenor sax; Don Shelton, alto sax.

11. "Duke's Domain—My Appreciation" (10:01) from *Duke's Domain—Interpretations of Ellington & Strayhorn*. Alhambra, California, May 1993. (1) Night Moods: John Leitham, bass; Tom Garvin, piano; Wayne Bergeron, trumpet; Gary Foster, alto sax; Andy Martin, trombone. (2) Autumnal: Gary Foster, alto sax. (3) Down Stage Strut: Bob Summers, trumpet.

12. "To a Lady Asking Foolish Questions" (5:10) from *To a Lady*. New York City, December, 1999. Jim Pugh, trombone; Aaron Sachs, clarinet; Joe Wilder, trumpet; Howard Alden, guitar.

13. "Green Night" (3:18) from *To a Lady*. New York City, December 1999. Howard Alden, guitar; Dick Oatts, alto sax.

14. "Chiripa" (5:46) from *To a Lady*. New York City, December 1999. Glenn Drewes, trumpet; Aaron Sachs, tenor sax; Eddie Bert, trombone; Dick Oatts, alto sax.